HISTO
IN HIS H

HISTORY
IN HIS HANDS

A CHRISTIAN NARRATIVE OF
THE WEST
BY

BRENNAN PURSELL

A Crossroad Book
The Crossroad Publishing Company
New York

The Crossroad Publishing Company
www.CrossroadPublishing.com

Printed in the United States of America.
The text of this book is set in Sabon
The display face is Sabon

Project Management by
The Crossroad Publishing Company
John Jones

For this edition numerous people have shared their talents and ideas, and we gratefully acknowledge Brennan Pursell, who has been most gracious during the course of our cooperation.

We thank especially:
Cover design: Stefan Killen Design   Text design: Web Fusion
Development: Sylke Jackson and John Jones   Printing: Versa Press

Message development, text development, package, and market positioning by
The Crossroad Publishing Company

Cataloging-in-Publication Data is available from the Library of Congress

Books published by The Crossroad Publishing Company may be purchased at special quantity discount rates for classes and institutional use. For information, please e-mail info@ CrossroadPublishing.com
ISBN 13: 978-0-8245-26726

14 13 12 11

Contents

Dedication

For my history students.
You are the present that looks toward the unknown. You are
immediate and new and surprising without trying. Thank you for your
listening, your patience, and every challenge you offer. I learn more
from you than you know. Perhaps the better part.

Acknowledgements

An author can do nothing without those who support him.

Profound thanks go to DeSales University for the sabbatical leave to write the first draft of this book, and to my faculty colleagues especially to all those who offered frank, unsparing critique of the approach and central argument. More thanks to Gwendolin Herder for agreeing to bring the work to press, and to John Jones, Sylke Jackson, and Pat Aliazzi, for careful editing from beginning to end. Still more thanks go to Abbot Wolfgang Hagl, OSB, and the Benedictines of Metten, who generously and hospitably provided me with a retreat of prayer and work to complete the book.

And finally my gratitude goes to my wife and children, who give me daily reminders of what history is all about.

Introduction

God Matters

At that time Jesus exclaimed, "I give praise to you, Father, Lord of heaven and earth, for although you have hidden these things from the wise and the learned, you have revealed them to little ones. Yes, Father, such has been your gracious will." (Matt 11:25-6)

God exists. He is really there, always and everywhere. God is Love—true, total, pure, just, and unadulterated in any way.

Out of nothing God creates everything, including humanity and our common history, because he loves us.

God generates the story that is history. Our story is his story. He gives it motion, direction, and meaning. He imbues it with truth, and this truth, like himself, is vast, manifold, mysterious, terrifying, and wonderful.

This book tells the story of humanity's movement in time, with God as the central character. We, all people everywhere, share in the same, common journey, and God, though hidden, is there, ever-present, behind and above us, on all sides, and in our very midst. For the sake of argument, simplicity, and length, this book mainly concerns the lands and peoples of the so-called "West." The narrative is Christian, because it maintains that Jesus of Nazareth was who he said he was, and said and did what witnesses said he said and did. It relies on the New Testament as the best set of textual sources about him. Jesus was, and is, in some mysterious, ultimately inexplicable way, God and Love. This revelation,

God's self-revealing to us, together with history, shows us his will for humanity across all time.

History in His Hands argues that this mysterious way is one of unity in diversity; beginning as separate particles, we head toward oneness. The tale, however, is jagged, confusing, and even tortuous, anything but the Lord's monologue. For God refuses to make history without us; he gives us freedom to live and love as we will. While each person cuts his or her own path, the story of the West stems directly from God's creation and participation and our varying response to it. How we love determines our salvation or destruction.

Such statements can make most professional historians squirm. The overwhelming majority write as if God did not exist, whether out of personal atheism or professional reticence about faith in general. Religion, for most historians, is a set of shared stories, beliefs, and practices, and Christianity is just one among many in the world. That Christianity may be true in itself or at least convey great truths about humanity in history is a possibility that most historians prefer to avoid or dismiss as irrelevant to the academic discipline.

Historians are trained to ask questions about the past and to make arguments, based on material and documentary evidence, to answer those questions. All histories, assuming they are more than just collections of supposed facts, contain interpretive arguments about the significance of events, how and why things happen—and all such arguments at least partly rely on belief or trust that this or that theory, idea, or story is true. Whether overtly or covertly, therefore, historical interpretation always involves philosophy, ideology, or theology. So all historians work to serve a purpose and a goal; if they do not, they indulge in antiquarianism, assembling facts merely out of curiosity. In their teaching and writing, they tend to follow an intellectual leader, or even a master, named or otherwise.

Quite a number of historians for the last century or two have closely followed the teachings of Karl Marx, Niccolò Machiavelli, David Hume, Max Weber, Friedrich Nietzsche, Sigmund Freud, Simone de Beauvoir, Michel Foucault, and other extremely intelligent and compelling thinkers. Despite their diversity, these formidable intellectuals all denied Christianity outright, or wrote as if God did not exist or was too distant to care about his creation and participate in any discernible way. This is not to say that all historians are radical atheists. While many write about the religion of the people they study, they are generally not supposed to say that what might have been true for earlier people is still true for us today, let alone true, period. When it comes to God, the scholarly establishment generally expects the historian to fall silent. Universities, colleges, associations, and other institutions pressure Christian historians to keep their faith to themselves, and especially to keep it out of the classroom and out of their writing.

The Secular Narrative

Most narratives of the West therefore run along secular lines: God plays no role and has no voice. History seems to happen on its own, either by random accident or according to economic, political, social, or gender-based mechanisms. From this perspective, humanity develops biologically, settles in ever higher concentrations, and builds the great civilizations of the ancient world. Then, after the collapse of the Roman Empire, come about a thousand years of the Middle Ages, characterized by a general absence or low level of technological progress and economic growth, and, conversely, a higher incidence of uncivilized behavior. Things become more interesting and relevant in the Italian Renaissance, the Protestant Reformation, and the rise of the nation-states, as in the case of England and France, during the sixteenth and seventeenth centuries—what is dubbed the early modern period. Then, with apparent inevitability, arrives the modern era, successfully replete with industrial production, economic enrichment, materialist philosophy, secular democratic government, society, and culture, and scientific knowledge based exclusively on empirical data.

The direction and point of this story, its teleology, is unmistakable: the West progresses. It begins primitive, immature, and irregular, and improves over time, ending up in the best yet, what we have and live with today. The apparent culmination of history is liberalism, capitalism, high technology, and democracy, and the story's main character is usually "power" in its various forms, such as: social, political, economic, legal, sexual, intellectual.

This story has become the conventional way of viewing history, but in the larger scheme of things it is a fairly recent development. The basic outline for this conventional perspective derives from the work of

Leonardo Bruni, a prosperous scholar in Italy during the early 1400s. Bruni's *History of the Florentine People* begins his story in an ancient period that ends with the toppling of the last Roman Emperor in the Latin West in 476 A.D. Thereafter comes a rather tiresome middle age that drags on until the twelfth century, when increased economic activity brings significant material prosperity, especially to the elite, in certain Italian towns. Then dawns Bruni's own era, the modern, from the thirteenth century on, when northern and central Italian towns such as Florence manage to free themselves from both the Germanic Holy Roman Emperors and the Roman Popes. In the twenty-first century, historians use largely the same outline, but they date the modern a bit later, when nation-states ascend to prominence and power, while the Holy Roman Empire and the papacy recede into political irrelevance. In both accounts, money and violence seem to dominate the course of events.

Bruni's tripartite periodization, the ancient-medieval-modern ordering of history, has become entrenched in our thinking over the past couple of centuries. We hear and read myriad references to "the ancient world," "medieval women," "modern man," and the like so often that these divisions start to seem self-evident. But they are not. They imply that humanity differs according to era, that a chasm of discontinuity divides us from our forebears of ten thousand, a thousand, or even a hundred years ago. Such a false view denies the unity of the human family across time and strongly implies that it is not possible for all people always and everywhere to share a common nature.

Augustine and the Christian Narrative

History in His Hands, on the other hand, argues that St. Augustine of Hippo is right where Leonardo Bruni is wrong.

A thousand years before Bruni's time, St. Augustine's well-documented life exemplifies the error in Bruni's three-part periodization. Neither Augustine nor anyone else in his time thought they lived in "the ancient world" or "late antiquity." The world he lived in was totally up-to-date, with a venerable past behind it. The reigning order of the day was the Roman Empire, at once ancient and yet completely contemporary, embodying all the tremendous changes in her thousand-year history. Numerous other empires around and beyond the Mediterranean Sea – such as the Egyptian, Babylonian, Hittite, Assyrian, Persian, Alexandrine, and Carthaginian empires – had already come and gone. Each in turn had begun in obscurity, subdued nations by wielding money and violence, and eventually given way to other contenders. Rome in the early fifth century A.D. had trodden far along a well-worn path.

Like Leonardo Bruni's work, St. Augustine's monumental text, *The City of God*, puts forth a markedly different philosophy of history. With exceptional brilliance, it details a historical, moral order rooted in the unchanging nature of the human person, as relevant for his day as for our own.

Augustine wrote for all time, about a human nature that is given and does not change, and the enduring accuracy of many of his observations suggests that he was right. More than a few of his observations apply rather well to the situation found in many parts of the twenty-first century West:

> [T]he perverse and unruly hearts of men think human affairs are prosperous when men are concerned about magnificent mansions, and indifferent to the ruin of souls; when mighty theaters are built up, and the foundations of virtue are undermined; when the madness of extravagance is highly esteemed, and works of mercy are scorned; when, out of the wealth and affluence of rich men, luxurious provision is made for actors, and the poor are grudged the necessaries of life; when that God who, by the public declarations of His doctrine, protests against public vice, is blasphemed by impious communities, which demand gods of such character that even those theatrical representations which bring disgrace to both body and soul are fitly performed in honor of them.

Augustine lived in a time when the Roman imperial order faced such financial and military challenges that one could easily conclude that it was in decline, if not in danger of complete collapse. Nonetheless, many people, especially among the elite, vociferously defended the establishment and devoted their energies to upholding it. But the empire did not flourish. No one could do anything to stop the disintegration.

In 410, an army led by Visigoths sacked the city of Rome, sending shockwaves throughout the educated, cosmopolitan circles of the empire. By that time, Rome was no longer very important in terms of military strategy, apart from the abundant plunder. The significance of the event, however, far outweighed the violent act. In Hippo, where Augustine served as bishop, he heard the cries of many who attributed the defeat to Rome's adoption of Christianity as the official state religion. The Christian God, they cried, had failed to protect the empire where her earlier, polytheistic pantheon had made her great, powerful, victorious, and glorious. Christianity, they argued, was a recipe for weakness. Edward Gibbon, the famous eighteenth-century author of *The History of the Decline and Fall of the Roman Empire*, recycled this argument, and even today the growing ranks of those hostile to Christianity repeat it regularly.

St. Augustine wrote *The City of God* in response to these attacks, never hesitating to strike at the critics themselves:

> Why, when afflicted by adversities, do you complain against the Christian era unless because you wish to maintain your luxury untroubled and to abandon yourselves to the most damnable practices with no harsh touch of vexing problems? For your desire for peace and abundant wealth of every sort does not spring from any intention of enjoying these boons in a respectable way, that is, decently, soberly, temperately, devoutly. Rather you would use them to procure an infinite variety in your unwholesome dissipations; you would engender in times of prosperity a moral plague of ills worse than raging enemies.

Again, the challenge pertains to our own day. Rome, Augustine said, was not built by the graces of an unruly mob of gods and a chaos of demonic cults, but, as with every empire, through ruthless ambition, relentless violence, and insatiable greed, undergirded by unassailable human pride at its worst.

For Augustine, Rome, like all earthly kingdoms, states, and empires, differed from the small-time, local robber band only in size, not in nature. Such bands, he said, follow a recognized leader and operate according to certain social norms, even laws, especially when it comes to divvying up the spoils of pillage. If they succeed in their depredations, and more and more people come to join them, they occupy territory and establish a firm base or stronghold. In time, if they manage to take over whole cities, regions, and peoples, the leader or leaders declare their accumulated spoils a principality, kingdom, or state. In giving their regime a public name, they seek legitimacy and impunity for their actions among their neighboring rivals, but they never tame their desire for more wealth and dominance. Thousands of years of human history showed Augustine that large-scale political order was impossible to establish without significant, continual injustice, usually in the form of confiscation, enslavement, and slaughter. Such is the nature of empire.

Human history, however, according to Augustine, is more, and actually rather beautiful; it is a matter of Love. God is the great giver, who out of love creates and sustains all life and all existence. All that he gives is beautiful; he is the source of all true happiness. God creates all human beings, equally gratuitously, and sustains their lives, giving them the freedom to love him in return, or not. He gives each of us an intermediate nature, somewhere between beasts and angels, and he leaves us the choice of which to emulate.

Human nature is of necessity intense. "For there is nothing so discordant when it deteriorates or so sociable in its true nature as the human race." The best way to keep from abusing, oppressing, and murdering each other is to recall that we have a common parent. God created humanity "as a single being for the propagation of a multitude in order that we might thus be reminded to preserve a single-minded unity even when we are many." The point of every human life is to find fulfillment in Love, in other words, to return to God. This truth gives history its trajectory and meaning. History does not meander aimlessly but points toward unity, unity in manifold variation. We are all in this together.

Love is perhaps God's greatest gift to humanity, a wondrous blessing, but at times terrible, if misapplied. Love guides life. People live as their loves guides them to do. Our free application of love produces all actions, orients all thoughts, induces all feelings: our desires and revulsions, our pursuits and our gift-giving, sensuality and intellectualism, sexuality and contemplation, the making of human life and the taking of it, our victories and our downfalls. "My weight is my love," Augustine wrote in his famous spiritual autobiography, *Confessions*. Human love, therefore, drives history and determines the human search for happiness. No other creature loves as we do. God gave us the freedom to love as we will, and as he wills, if we so choose.

In *The City of God* Augustine presents an allegory of two cities, coexistent and intermingled throughout all of human history, each established by and governed according to love: "the earthly city, by a love of self carried even to the point of contempt for God, the heavenly city, by a love of God carried even to the point of contempt for self." His theory of history depends entirely on this definition. By "contempt for self" he did not mean self-hatred or loathing, but rather indifference or light estimation. Relative to God's love, human love of self, even the healthy variety, ought to be rather small.

Adherents of the earthly city glory in themselves and their achievements, some going so far as to deny and insult their creator. Those who do not love God tend to love themselves and their own use and domination of things and people around them. Rarely finding more than a lingering satisfaction in either things or human relationships, they perpetually seek their own advantage as long as they do not seek God's selfless love. In such a situation, people with greater strength automatically, perhaps even without conscious desire, exploit and oppress the weaker. Human society will always be divided against itself, so long as people, individually and collectively, pursue their own goals and pleasures at the expense of others.

Those, however, who glorify the God who is Love, who desire him above all, and who embrace peace, coexistence, and reconciliation— these people grow, increase, and open themselves to God, as he always leads to higher, newer, grander horizons. The mystery of God, his ever-greaterness, is the source and way of true love, peace, prosperity, and happiness. True lovers of God unify the world and give humanity life and hope.

Love leads history. Institutions, constitutions, and practices, social structures, cultural influences, and gender roles in history merely reflect the simple fact of what people love, individually and collectively. A people, a realm or state, Augustine defines as "a large gathering of rational beings united in fellowship by their agreement about the objects of their love; ... surely the better the objects of its united love, the better the people, and the worse the objects of its love, the worse the people."

With regard to government, therefore, form makes little difference. Democracies can be just as horrid as monarchies, and even more so, if their leaders and peoples misdirect their love. Because of human weakness, no republic or democracy can truly be "a people's estate." When the execution of justice errs as it inevitably will, then the so-called "rights", however one may insist that they derive from principles of pure justice, invariably serve "the interest of the strongest." If mere legality becomes the standard of good and evil, then there is no room for God. In the earthly city, the strong say what is legal, right, and wrong, and live by their man-made creed. Such is the nature of democracies, republics, and other states.

Rule of the strong over the weak often takes the form of war. No state or community built on war, Augustine argues, can make people truly happy. No one should glory in war or military victory. These do not save souls and return them to God. Those who look to states and their leaders for salvation misapply their love, and anyone who brags about the size, wealth, and power of his empire automatically reveals a lack of both wisdom and rationality. Misdirected love strengthens the foundation of all sin and error: human pride.

Pride is the problem, not political, social, economic, and cultural "power structures." Pride, an overblown sense of self-importance, tempts us to take creation for granted, to ignore or deny God's love, and to blame him for our unfulfilled wishes and our manifest failings. With pride comes envy, which leads us to resent those who have what we do not, to compete for glory, to war with neighbors. Pride leads people to lie, to commit injustice and try to mask it as its opposite, to turn the given kingdom, state, or empire into a false vehicle for salvation. Pride always makes ready excuses for sin.

Pride, Augustine emphasizes, is our mistake, certainly not God's: not "a defect of Him who gives power or even of power itself, but a defect of the soul that misguidedly loves its own power while it despises the more righteous power of a higher Power." Human pride perverts God's greatness in his greatest creation. People who live according to God, however, love the truth, because Christ said, *I am the truth*. But those who live for themselves and fashion their own individual truths must of necessity lie to themselves and to others. To live following God's design is authentic; to live solely to fulfill one's own pleasures is necessarily erroneous, not to mention anti-social. "For [pride] abhors a society of peers under God, but seeks to impose its own rule, instead of his, on society."

Augustine's interpretation of history cuts through any number of knotty historical obsessions in our own day. The endless debates about Nazi Germany provide a perfect example. In the first place, the proper operation of the German republican constitution allowed Adolf Hitler to become Chancellor; one government system readily replaced another. As to the Holocaust, it makes little difference whether it was a hallmark of or a departure from Germanic culture, whether the Germans served as Hitler's sadistic executioners or the obedient, disciplined, misguided tools of his demonic regime. The truth is that people who loved their pride, their race, their nation, their delusional leader, and even themselves, almost as gods, above God, were the ones who justified mass murder through various means, and so perpetrated, or at least permitted, the horrors of the 1930s and '40s. Evil is a matter of human choice. Loving something that is less than God, instead of God, invites error, sin, and potential disaster.

Similar things have happened before, in and beyond Germany. On December 5, 1349, after a nightmarish year of the Black Death (a pandemic that killed roughly a third of the population of Europe), people in the city of Nürnberg lashed out in anger, despair, and greed; responding to rumors that Jews were behind the tragedy, they destroyed the Jewish neighborhood and slaughtered 562 men, women, and children. Such insane massacres, whether of Jews or others, blemish many and perhaps all parts of the world and its history: the nineteenth and twentieth centuries, an era of reputedly progressing civilization, provide numerous well-documented examples on all continents, perhaps excepting Antarctica. Some slaughters were locally inspired, others planned and ordered by more distant authorities. The truth is that had genuine, self-less love of God prevailed, none of these atrocities would have happened. Needless annihilation occurs in states around the world even today, such as in Darfur, where leaders, fighters, and followers actively endeavor to identify, isolate, and destroy whomever those in power have defined as unworthy.

But this truth should not lead to despair! God's history is not a tragedy but the greatest of all epics. Human suffering has meaning; it need not be in vain. God, St. Augustine reminds us, raises up and hurls down empires for good and bad people alike: "He does this in accordance with an order of things and of times which is hidden from us but very well known to him." All events bear meaning; nothing is truly random, utterly accidental, or empty. The story has a direction and a point, however mysterious. Taking this as a matter of trust or faith may seem too simplistic, a childish way to understand developments that appear wildly, unbearably complicated, especially when one attempts to comprehend and explain them in detail. But Jesus taught that this is precisely the way we should follow him and God. Christianity demands leaps of faith, and such an approach to history is one of them. But we can see its truth in the events themselves, especially in the unsung side of the story, when we look beyond the robbers and conquerors, to the huge majority, the simple people, who merely try to live in peace.

Finding Truth in History

God's will reveals itself in the story of humanity; he writes straight across crooked lines. Love cuts through the paradoxes. God and history show us that humanity's path in time points toward unity in diversity. The success or failure of humanity on earth depends on how we love. God's gift of freedom to humanity makes our common tale endlessly interesting. Western Civilization results from God's creation and revelation, and humanity's free response to it. History, therefore, changes constantly, but humanity and its creator remain the same.

History in His Hands aspires to truth, because truth is bigger and grander than purely physical, empirical measurement. For the sake of clarity, let us delineate three levels to truth in history.

The first is the *exterior aspect* of what actually, physically happened— things that could have been recorded in video or audio, if such devices had been present at the time.

The next level is the *interior human experience*: feelings felt, images seen in the mind's eye, messages and words heard in the soul's dialogue, whether awake or asleep, conscious or unconscious. Take physical pain, for example. No person or machine can see it or measure it. X-rays, MRIs, and such things detect physical damage, deterioration, areas of inflammation, but they have no way to picture aches and pain. Yet pain, however intangible, is still truly part of human experience. The heart's pain, the suffering soul, is even more elusive, but still very real nonetheless.

Finally, the third level of truth is that of *meaning*, the significance of events, experiences, and messages correctly understood. This level is uniquely, exclusively human, discernible by reason in union with the heart; no other animal can explore such matters. In this way, humanity reaches toward divinity.

For source materials, this narrative draws on hundreds of books and articles, written in the past few decades by professional historians, and at least as many primary documents, i.e. the writings from diverse people of bygone centuries or millennia. And in a special way, *History in His Hands* relies on Scripture, the Holy Bible, a unique book in the history of humankind, in the West and the world, arguably the most important of all. More than a compilation of historical documents, Scripture's words live and communicate God's will across all perceived boundaries. Love of God and God's Love inspired and inspires that text. A Christian history makes no sense without it.

And now let us proceed.

1

God and Man

In the beginning was the Word, and the Word was with God, and the Word was God. He was in the beginning with God; all things were made through him, and without him was not anything made that was made. In him was life, and the life was the light of men. The light shines in the darkness, and the darkness has not overcome it. (John 1:1–5)

In the beginning God created the heavens and the earth. The earth was without form and void, and darkness was upon the face of the deep; and the Spirit of God was moving over the face of the waters. And God said, "Let there be light"; and there was light. And God saw that the light was good; and God separated the light from the darkness. (Genesis 1:1–5)

God the Alpha, Love, and Reason

God's history is one of mystery and paradox, and all being belongs to him.

But what is God, really? Who is he?[1] In many of the world's great religions and philosophies, he is the Creator, the first of all causes, ultimate truth, all-powerful, omniscient, indescribable, the source of illumination, a being that transcends our comprehension more than we can possibly imagine. Our words, images, and symbols will never be able to do him adequate justice. No intellectual or religious authority can ever fully sum him up or restrict him to the confines of theoretical construction or semantic definition.

God is a mystery, *the* mystery, not in the sense of a puzzle or a riddle with a definite solution, but as an infinitely complex reality that the human must live and love in order to begin to understand. Scripture tells us that God is being—*I am who am*—or simply *I AM* (Exodus 3:14), reality itself, always and everywhere, one that is exterior to us, fully independent, and yet sharing in our interior lives. Nothing is like God; he is that which is truly, totally Other, our creator, while needing no one himself. We use a personal pronoun and not "it" to refer to God, because God is not a mere thing. He manifests qualities we, in our limited way, associate with persons.

Though ineffable, God allows us to know him, in part, by means of his creation, through his creatures living and inert, and in the miraculous moments where he reveals himself to us. God's truth is that we are not alone, all absolute individuals trapped inside ourselves, each fashioning his own, private universe until death comes to end everything. God, the One, gives us freedom, enables us to open ourselves, to escape the trap of relativism, and approach his absolute standard of truth. Only God encompasses all apparent contradictions in life with truth and righteousness.

---

[1] *History in His Hands* uses masculine pronouns to refer to God out of deference to two thousand years of Christian tradition and practice. While there is much about God that makes us think of "she," such as his self-giving love and his fecundity, it goes without saying that God is in, beyond, and above the two sexes. "It" is inappropriate, because God is not a mere thing or device. "She" denotes the feminine, something more specific and special than the common default "he." To use no pronouns at all, to write only "God" in all instances, contorts the prose and belabors the point. To refer to God as "he" does not impose a gender on him to the disadvantage of the feminine. Jesus Christ unfailingly referred to God as "he."

We can try to understand God as true love and right reason, both of which only we humans, among all creatures, can really appreciate. Let us begin with reason, and rely on an explanation that holds true after more than two millennia. Marcus Tullius Cicero, one of Rome's greatest orators, writes:

> [T]he most marked difference between man and beast is this: the beast, just as far as it is moved by the senses and with very little perception of past or future, adapts itself to that alone which is present at the moment; while man—because he is endowed with reason, by which he comprehends the chain of consequences, perceives the causes of things, understands the relation of cause to effect and effect to cause, draws analogies, and connects and associates the present and the future—easily surveys the whole course of his life and makes the necessary preparations for its conduct.

No creature besides the human has any idea of what reason is. No other creature reflects about the universe, the nature of things, how it all fits together, and how things ought to be.

God is what reason does. He not only creates; he connects—all that is known with all that is unknown. He causes everything in fact, and he imbues the universe with meaning and significance. God bestows on humanity the faculty of reason as a gift. If human reason is the result of random biochemical reactions over billions of years, then reason itself is meaningless. As C.S. Lewis argued, there would be no reason to trust it. But we all know this cannot be. It is no accident that two plus two equals four. Reason helps us to discover God's workings and live in accordance with his will; it shows that we are made in his image.

In the beginning was the Word [logos]... The first sentence of St. John's Gospel offers a disarmingly simple statement about the beginning of all things. *Logos* in Greek (λόγος) refers to "word," "reason," and "meaning" in English, and one really cannot separate the three. Words without meaning are gibberish. Reason cannot be meaningless, and reason and meaning are both conveyed through words. Only those creatures that use words, i.e., human beings, have the faculty of reason and can consider the meaning of things. All that exists can be named; all that exists has meaning; and all that exists can be explained, at least in part, by the use of reason.

Word, reason, and meaning are not spontaneous accidents. They have a source. According to Christianity they emanate from the being even more mysterious and ineffable than the universe itself. This being reveals itself in space and time as *logos*. Christianity and other great religions call this being God. Gratuitously, God creates time, space, matter, and the inexplicable phenomenon called "life," in its innumerable forms, sustaining it in a kind of enduring miracle, now and forever. Why should this great being do such a thing? The answer lies in love.

Love is another, glorious part of God's whole. *God is love, and whoever remains in love remains in God, and God in him* (1 John 4:16). In defining love, the New Testament, originally written in a Greek dialect, used three words denoting its different aspects: *eros*, the yearning, passionate, ecstatic love, the kind that drives us crazy and tends to self-indulgence; *philia*, the love among friends that builds mutual respect and trust; and *agape*, the self-giving love that cares and makes us willing to sacrifice for, and receive love from, the beloved. *Agape* allows people to open, to others and for God; *agape* redeems *eros* and elevates *philia*. All three kinds are equally human, although *agape* is the greatest and most beautiful.[2]

To be able to love is humanity's greatest capacity, an attribute even beyond reason, and both are free gifts of God, to use and abuse as we decide. To love best of all is to love God first. Love of God helps us to reach beyond ourselves for the sake of the common good. Those who love God love truth and beauty, without wanting to possess or dominate either. Loving God allows one to give of oneself freely and completely, without thought of reciprocity. Such love strips away pretense and falsehood and brings peace in an ever-changing, turbulent world. How we love determines the very fabric of human history.

As with reason, God is what true love does. Through conjugal love, people can partake in God's creative power and experience familial love, a fundamental source of meaning and identity in life. Those, however, who limit love and degrade it, who reduce it to biochemical events in the brain that we experience as sensation, distort the human spirit and stunt

---

[2] The Greek New Testament's *eros* and *agape* parallel the Hebrew terms, *dodim* and *ahabà*, in the Old Testament's *Song of Songs*. In both languages, the former searches and struggles, while the latter gives of itself for the sake of the beloved other.

its growth. Those who choose to love finite, frivolous things like money, metals, gems, products, passing sensations, and social recognition, confine their love, misdirect it, and frequently fall into self-seeking and exploitation. They then abuse reason in the vain attempt to justify wrongdoing. All people, in their weakness, imperfection, and freedom, do such things, and it makes the world endlessly interesting, dramatic, and at times terribly painful, to say the least. God, or true love, is the way through and the way out of this painful drama. If his love sounds challenging, it should. *Be perfect*, Jesus said, *just as your heavenly father is perfect* (Matthew 5:48).

Cosmos and Earth

God is the perfect beginning of all beginnings, the originator of being, time, space, and life. Love in heaven and earth creates and opens everything. The cosmos, a gift of *logos*, given by God, is good, even *very good*, according to Genesis (1:31). Nature is good and great and mysterious and limitless because it reflects its creator.

The infinite cosmos is the realm where reason reigns, despite the fact that our finite intellects will never completely grasp its mysterious totality and particularity. The beauty of creation is proof not only of its goodness, but of the nature of the creator who made such gorgeous, abundant diversity, in inexhaustible space, with immeasurable might. Uniqueness is the norm throughout. No heavenly body is a carbon copy, and no living being is exactly like any other, even if they belong to the same species. From God and his works, we learn that truth, love, goodness, and beauty belong together; one makes little sense without the others.

Let us turn to the origins of time, space, and life. The first of all event, in the minds of perhaps most people in the twenty-first century West, is the Big Bang. About fourteen billion years ago, give or take a billion, a single, instantaneous, massive explosion commenced time, space, and existence, laid out the universe, and flung matter across it, all at once. Creation in this story is a bomb blast, a standard metaphor from the twentieth century, but bombs only destroy, and the Big Bang resulted in the glorious cosmos. Most people accept this story as scientifically verifiable truth, and in many respects it certainly appears to be, but the whole question of creation-in-time is actually as metaphysical as it is scientific. Searching for the answer needs rational thought as much as the telescope.

If the Big Bang happened as astrophysicists describe, then we may ask, what were things like before the blast, and what led to it? "Nothing," is a standard answer, but if there *was* nothing, no being or any kind of existence, how could the big bang have come about? How can being come from nothing? Other scientists, however, put forward a "big bounce" theory, where the present universe is merely a recasting of a previous one that contracted, condensed, and collapsed, resulting in the Big Bang, with that previous universe resulting from an earlier one, and so on, infinitely backwards. But if there was a different universe before our universe, what came before that one? Looking at eternity and infinity, we find few conclusive answers of our own making.

The cosmos is a wonder of superhuman, supernatural dimensions; its true nature is far beyond what our technology can establish about it. Scientists can only scratch at the surface of the observable universe, debating the awesome numbers related to it. Their research points to wild sums and varieties of galaxies (about 100 billion of them), stars (about 100 billion in our one galaxy), as well as planets, moons, asteroids, comets, black holes, and God-knows-everything-else. Physicists estimate masses of galactic clusters as great as a quintillion suns, and they measure distances between galaxies in millions and billions of years spent moving at the speed of light, a velocity (ca. 300,000 kilometers per second) that no human being will ever attain. And yet despite the universe's vastness, things in it are immeasurably small, from the atoms to the electrons, neutrinos, color-changing quarks, and so on. The littlest bits get measured in terms of billionths of the width of an atom, and smaller. In all likelihood, there are many more things as yet undiscovered. The full dimensions and aspects of the natural world beyond earth are ultimately immeasurable.

In the universe, reason and paradox reign together. Light, so normal and essential in everyday life, seems to have an indeterminate nature. Neither quite a particle nor a wave of energy, light seems perfectly content to act like both, but its behavior is mathematically predictable. Without light's simplicity, much astronomic research would be vain, numeric musings. We all know about matter and the periodic table of the elements, a beautifully simple, rational system accounting for matter in the universe, but quantum theory blurs the difference between matter and energy, showing that matter's apparent stability is actually a mere likelihood. Matter comes from energy and sometimes goes back to it. String theory is a recent attempt to explain how one can be and become the other, unified in their duality. Gravity is another paradox; a simple mathematical formula calculates its force, but what it really is and why it is there are as yet unanswered questions.

We seem to know so much about the universe—observatories and orbiting telescopes gather more data than anyone knows what to do with—but outer space, the limitless expanse, remains forbidding and impenetrable. Light travels about 10 trillion kilometers in a year, and our "neighboring" galaxy, Andromeda, is two and a half million of those light-years away from us. Local stars in our galaxy, like the bright Sirius, are at ten light-years' distance, and the center of our galaxy around 30,000 light years. Our exploratory satellites have told us much about our solar system, but earth's sibling planets remain remote, barely touchable, and basically inaccessible and useless to humanity. Expensively dressed people occasionally hop about on our one moon, and some day human beings might walk on the surface of Mars, but because neither place is remotely livable, the venture has limited merits. Space travel exposes people to horrific cold (ca. $-271\ C°$ or $2.7\ K°$, nearly absolute zero) and lethal radiation, and even weightlessness is inimical to human life.

The universe seems empty, a dead vacuum; the vast distances between stars and galaxies, even between the nucleus and electrons, make matter itself seem insignificant and incidental. But the cosmos is full! There is actually no truly empty space, no areas devoid of electromagnetic and gravitational forces. Black holes are possible candidates, but just because we cannot see what is going on in them does not mean that nothing is happening in there. And then there is "dark matter," as yet unexplained, which some say is four times more prevalent than the matter we think we know. Known rays, waves, and other forms of energy (X- and gamma-, radio-, micro-, etc.) are in all likelihood only a few of the trees in the wondrous cosmic forest, with plenty of room for "dark energy" and other inexplicable mysteries. The cosmos' forbidding vacuum, then, is a screen, an illusion. The fundamental truth is that no one and nothing is actually ever alone, anywhere.

Despite mind-boggling numbers and daunting complexity, order and structure pervade all aspects of creation, unifying the stupendous diversity in nature. Of all the snowflakes in the world, it is said that no two are exactly alike, but each has six tips and a distinct, symmetrical flair. Without reason and order in the universe, scientists would not be able to make their measurements and put together the arguments that answer the questions they research. While quantum theory claims that no thing in the empirically observable natural world is perfectly stable, it also allows scientists to calculate probabilities about the changes that will most likely occur over time.

Cosmic diversity makes sense in its unity; it is no passing accident amid chaos, and it is stunningly beautiful. The computer-generated and colorized images of vast dust clouds, some engaged in the birth and death of stars, astound us. Satellite photographs of the planets, with their storms, gas clouds, moons, and rings, inspire awe. We have yet to discover an ugly or unimpressive galaxy. The further technology allows us to look into space, the more light we find in the dark. Beauty in nature is unique, individual, and authentic. All forms of natural light are pure; even the powerful light of the blazing sun is never garish or lurid. All kinds of landscape, from the desert to the rain forest, have varying degrees of beauty, no matter how stark and forbidding. As long as they are pristine, they cannot be truly ugly. The same goes for the world under the sea, in the light as in the dark. All nature, all life points to God's superabundant, limitless splendor, his wild imagination, and his sensuousness. Nature on earth can only lose its inherent beauty when mankind disturbs, destroys, and pollutes it. The universe, in short, is the beautiful realm where reason reigns. Those who see it as an arena of chaos, terror, and violence do so of their own volition.

The same is of course true of life, beginning at the cellular level. The most basic unit of life, the cell, is structurally and functionally incapable of being a meaningless, unintelligible, random accident. If it were, it would not function with such impressive regularity and seemingly intelligent ability. The cell is a prime example of coincidence so fortuitous that it justly deserves the term "miracle." Through scientific experiment, using human senses enhanced by technology, we know much of what goes on in a single cell, but certainly not all, let alone how it came to be the way it is. The same goes for any molecule or star.

Time, space, and life are all wonders, simply given—then, now, and always. The extravagant magnitude of the gift, the way life is, the way it works, tells us much about the nature of the giver. The truth of our beginnings we can find in reason, in the free gift of life-giving love, and in the beauty of both. God is the loving giver, the giving lover.

Adam and Eve

The heavens and the earth have existed for a very long time; relative to them humanity is radically new. Still, we are part of the whole. In our being we are made from and for eternity, and God creates us out of love. Each human being is part of the stupendous miracle of life and existence, going back through all human generations, through every unique combination of human egg and sperm to the very first human, back through all other animal life forms, and all cells, to the very first cell, and still further back through all spinning heavenly bodies and dust clouds of the universe to the Big Bang and before. In a certain sense, God's loving creation of the universe had each of us in mind, not as the highest culmination, but as an integral part of the story, however small and fleeting.

The story of Adam and Eve teaches us that humanity has a definite beginning as a spiritual being, and it also unveils a paradox: human nature does not change, no matter which way history seems to turn and twist it. While historians usually tell the story of how the body of *homo sapiens sapiens* evolved from the ape over the millions of years, they usually do not dwell on the human being's spiritual anthropology. Human beings have a common nature; we share an identity that remains the same across recorded time. In brief, we are the only living creature that seeks God. No other animal does. When did we become human, if from ape or any other life form? It was when our earliest ancestors, no matter how unsophisticated, first asked the question, "God, are you there?"

It actually makes no difference when and how the first *homo sapiens sapiens* came into the world—whether, as St. Augustine says, it was 5,000 years before his day or 600 million. Whenever anyone claims a certain date, another can always ask, "Why not before then?" Augustine adds that we will be able to ask this same question after 5,000 years, and will do so after 600 million, "if our mortal condition with its ignorance and weakness were to endure so long through the rise and fall of generations." To say that God creates us in his image means that he gives each and every human being a nature, reason, and freedom, as well as a desire for love. God sets into play the same drama for all people everywhere. There is one age of man, which people live at every moment of human history. It begins again at every birth. Ancient, medieval, early modern, and modern man are one.

Just as God brought life to the primeval waters, he forms each of us in the waters of the womb. He gives each of us a body, imperfect in any number of ways. While the finite genome plays an important role in this process, the potentially infinite combinations of proteins act in ways both known and mysterious, putting the genes in their place in the scheme of things. A human's miraculous act of living, his or her life, owes itself also to a spiritual force, an immaterial, yet essential being, created by God out of nothing. He gives each of us a soul and a mind. There is no divide between mind and body; the brain plays along with our thoughts and feelings. The brain's modest dimensions belie the nearly immeasurable complexity of activity within. No matter how much we learn about what goes on in the brain, we will probably never find out the extent to which it generates thoughts, or perhaps responds to other, outside stimuli. When it comes to inspirations, however, the mind clearly transcends the cerebral organ.

The soul surrounds, suffuses and fuses the human being, connecting the mind to the heart. The human soul is not a thing residing within the physical confines of the body; it is a spirit that gives life, acts, feels, and communicates with all other energies and spirits in the living world. One could say that it gives each human person his or her unique form. The soul enables us never to be alone, even in the depths of apparent solitude. The soul connects us to the creator. The soul is essential to the human being, and while the body has mechanical properties, the soul transcends mechanism. The soul gives a person presence and beauty much deeper than anything cosmetic. Much of what passes for human beauty in our day, the standardized, commercialized face and body templates of the entertainment, fashion, cosmetic, and medical industries, have little to do with the interior illumination of the person. This inner beauty shines out when the soul loves and rejoices.

Of all life forms, humanity possesses the greatest capacity for love, and the only one for reason. Where reason resides in the mind, love dwells in the heart. Love can uplift the human soul on earth from beginning to end, but love often depends on a conscious choice, made over and over again, unlike other human sensory and mental faculties. The universal drama of each human life is the extent to which we say Yes to love. When we do, we draw closer to God. One seeks God with the heart; the eyes, hands and feet and mind should be at its service. One does not get close to God by being noisy and powerful, but by joining nature in her wondrous, meditative silence, by reaching within to the quiet sanctuary of the human heart.

All this sounds rather positive, and it should because it is so, but as we all know, much of human history is a relentless tale of slaughter and woe. Perhaps the greatest challenge to a Christian historical narrative is the problem of suffering: how can God be love, and how can we love, when there is so much evil in the world?

The answer lies in freedom.

Suffering and Death – The Omega

Throughout history God gives with exorbitant generosity, and he takes with a suddenness that can shake us to our foundations.. God grants abundant pleasures and allows for pain. He is the lord of hosts, a warrior god, and the dove of peace and reconciliation. He is ultimate truth and unsullied justice, and yet he allows us to live unjustly, self-blinded by pernicious lies. He gives us freedom: to choose between good and evil, to follow him or to deny him, to live in his light, truth, and love, or cut ourselves off and close down to him. We are free to worship him, or to manufacture and worship idols of the basest taste. And yet God never leaves us in the lurch. For every disaster that we make for ourselves, love and forgiveness, the only reasonable solution, always provide the way to continue. The world will always be difficult and imperfect, but God will never let it, or us, out of his hands.

We all know from experience that humans are imperfect, which means that we often choose to do wrong over right, and every choice we make proves that we are free. We all make mistakes, in varying degrees, which does not detract from the God-given miracle of our existence. While no human being is a purely evil creature, a perfect embodiment of wrong, all are vulnerable to temptations large and small. *Woe to the world,* Jesus said, *because of things that cause sin! Such things must come, but woe to the one through whom they come!* (Matthew 18:7). Why such things must come, Jesus does not say. He faced temptation, as do all people, but he did not sin. Temptation, he says, is part of human life. Men and women and children are neither flawless nor perfect, and, given the chance, will often choose the wrong path for the wrong reason. The history of the West gives ample evidence that any individual or group that claims to have found the way to perfect humankind and purge everyone of their God-given frailty is wrong. Such false ideas are sure signs of an unhealthy spirit, and can promote the worst of evils.

But why do we feel pain? Why is there so much suffering in the world? If life is so good, then why on earth do we have to face death? Does the story of the West, its relentless wars and bloodshed, its perennially falling empires, and terribly dissatisfied, unhappy peoples, in the end make no sense? Is history ultimately meaningless, random, or indecipherable?

Christians say No, because of Love.

The truth of the matter is that suffering is indispensible. Suffering is a response to pain, but not pain itself. If we suffer, then we bear that pain and deal with it in various ways. There is no life without pain; everyone suffers sometime. A core belief in Christianity is that an individual's suffering can actually bring about good, in ways both directly obvious and mysteriously indeterminate, both to the sufferer and to others near and far. The same goes for whole peoples. Wars, famine, plague, and other disasters are misfortunes; there is no denying that they are evil. But at the same time, love, and love alone, can redeem them. All people are called to help reduce pain and violence in this world, while not giving in to the lie that they can be eliminated.

The alignment of the spirit determines our response to suffering. In this very human world of lies, oppression, and abuse, suffering is often the price of truth. It is the only way to attain and achieve true freedom— the freedom from self and from falsehood, the freedom that comes from loving God above all, with all our heart, mind, soul, and being. In this truth we find the source of real hope. Ultimately, however, intellectual analysis of suffering does not help much when pain comes. Suffering is one of those puzzles that must be lived in order to be understood.

We, God's creatures, suffer, because he does. His example shows us that suffering is necessary for life, in this world and beyond. We can suffer *for* others, on behalf of our friends, our loved ones, and our enemies. Jesus showed us this kind of suffering in his death, but his resurrection tells us that suffering is only part of the story, that self-giving love can conquer even death, if we choose it. Christians believe that all members of the human family are called to joy, through love, in spite of pain. This joy is not giddiness or a passing happy feeling in the midst of bad times. Christian joy does not deny the inevitability of pain and suffering; rather it admits them without succumbing to them. Happiness is closeness to God, however rocky the path to him may be. Seeking him is the reason for life; otherwise, mere survival is a meaningless exercise. Those lucky few who through love manage to live their pain as rapture are those who come closest to God.

All who devote their time and energy to avoid suffering at all costs do so in vain, and thereby consign themselves to bitter frustration. A life's journey with no struggle is a purposeless, circular meandering. The person who lives in perfect satisfaction without a trace of suffering attains only perfect selfishness. Whoever bears no sorrow can at least, using an ounce of empathy, share in the woe of millions the world over. Sadness must never be excluded from life. Always searching for ways to attain freedom from sadness is another example of misguided love. This truth is not masochism, but simple reality. To grieve is just as human as to rejoice.

Suffering walks hand in hand with death. All people know, unlike animals, that we will eventually face death. While dying is usually extremely unpleasant, and can be gruesome and horrifying, death gives us the chance to meet Love and Truth face to face. Death is the moment when the game ends, when all the posturing and deception of self and others stops, when our spirit returns to its maker in its true condition, the one we have chosen for it. While humanity lives collectively, each of us goes into death alone, no matter how many come to comfort us as we take our last breaths. Belief in a final judgment after death is wider and older than Christianity, and the urge to pray and sacrifice for departed loved ones is found in nearly all cultures in our own day. Death, one of many great, necessary mysteries in life, marks an absolute limit for empirical science. In Christianity, death is part and parcel of human imperfection, but it need not be the end of the story. This was perhaps Jesus' greatest, most revolutionary message, that we can conquer death through love.

Much of recorded history can come across as a remorseless chronicle of misery and death, but in a Christian understanding, these things can actually draw humanity together. Wherever and whenever we are and have been, we all face the same great trials. This reality underlies the story of unity in diversity.

Human "Prehistory"

All people everywhere are the same, and yet everyone is a little different. It has been this way for many thousands of years. The story of humanity begins a very long time ago, in prehistory, which refers to a period any number of millennia before the appearance of written records, the time when God brought humanity into being. Historians usually avoid prehistory, because it is a very uncertain place. No one knows how the first woman and man appeared on the planet nor how and why they or their descendants first began to leave behind evidence that survives to our present day. Academic anthropologists, however, readily speculate about the tiniest fragments of physical leftovers, but they persuade about as successfully as biblical literalists who argue that nothing existed until whichever year they prefer, B.C. Meave Leakey, an affiliate of the National Museum of Kenya, and one of the more famous anthropologists who research in East Africa, has said, "There are all sorts of hypotheses, and they are all fairy tales really, because you can't prove anything."

Drawing up a family tree for the *homo sapiens sapiens* over the last seven million years is a creative pastime. Scarcely one chart appears before another group of anthropologists tears it to pieces in order to promote its own. Professionals design hybrid creatures that look and act the part of the ape-human, but no one can explain demonstratively how one species actually gives rise to another. Even the tidy tale about how *homo habilis* was superseded by *homo erector* and then *homo sapiens* frayed when researchers found that the first two species coexisted in same area for about a half million years. One was supposed to have spontaneously appeared, through accidental mutation, and quickly driven the former version to extinction, according to the Darwinist model. Such vast discrepancy in dating evolutionary changes remind us how ephemeral all these reconstructions are.

Our bodily origins are a permanent mystery. There exists in effect a missing stretch – "link" is no longer fashionable – between humans and other primates, insofar as a plentiful supply of straightforward, developmental evidence is simply not available. In the end, it is irrelevant whether the first man and woman emerged from the womb of an ape, a *homo* variant, or some other sentient creature. Suffice it to say that our physical frames are born of this earth, which is *very good*. (Genesis, 1:31) Even more miraculous and inexplicable is the origin and development of our minds, souls, and spirits. No skeletal evidence will ever account for that. Even if one simply grants that apes at some time in the past gave rise to humans, one can quite reasonably ask, "Why?" The simplest answer is that God willed it.

Plenty of bones dug up from the ground indicate that humanity appeared on the scene one to a few hundred thousand years ago. No one knows when they started to make fire and tools, but estimates range from 25,000 to 164,000 years ago. We generally assume that they lived as nomads, hunter-gatherers living in caves or on the move, mainly because we have found no vestiges of villages or towns older than 10,000 B.C. or thereabouts. More importantly, these people, these males and females, lived as families.

If there is one universal truth that applies to human history, it is that the family is a biological reality that is prior to any and all governments, states, and societies. The family is the first society; it is there that we first learn about love and trust, the pain they involve, and how necessary they are for happiness. In the family we learn how to be compassionate, literally "to suffer with" others. We are all creatures of the family. No one is a totally independent individual. No one created, raised, and formed himself alone. It is obvious, but it needs to be said: since the advent of humanity, each and every one of us has a mother. We all have fathers too, whether connected to our mother till death parted him from her, or more briefly associated.

In human history, all women and men are equally God's creation and therefore of the same worth, yet seldom treated that way. They grow out of the same miniscule earthly origin, no matter how manipulated, and their lives follow the same divine thought. Love is the logic of motherhood, marriage, and the family. Everyone throughout all history began life as a very small child, and until rather recently, perhaps a majority never made it to adulthood. To this day, grown-ups remain rather close to the children that they once were. Their bodies grow and their capabilities increase, but the person is still the person. Works of written history tend to ignore children, unless they are specialized studies in field of "family history." If we were truly democratic in our interest in history, we would have to admit that the past belongs more to families, and to the little ones, than to great and powerful individuals, just as does the future.

Paleo- to Neolithic

Archaeological evidence from caves and excavations suggests that families of *homo sapiens sapiens* lived in varying associations with each other in far-flung parts of the world a very long time ago, anywhere from one to four hundred thousand years ago. This vast period of time is called the Paleolithic, due to the crude quality of the surviving stone tools. But implements of stone are only part of the story. From the Paleolithic period, we can see that the human is an interdependent being; communitarian living is fundamental to our nature.

The one human race naturally lives in communities of families, males and females, adults and children, and makes its way through life collectively. Males in the Paleolithic period tended to do more of the hunting, fighting, and large animal husbandry, while women tended to gather, nurse, and nurture. Gender roles stemmed from natural aptitude and local, cultural necessity. The division of labor was meant to increase the chance of the community's survival, and populations were small. Little statuettes of rotund female figures indicate the significant value placed on fecundity and fertility.

Grave sites and cave art suggest that these people sought God, believing in a spiritual realm, an afterlife, a happy hunting ground. They might have worshipped with music and singing. Excavators have found bone flutes in caves, and a musicologist established that people often painted images on the rock walls in the cave chambers with the most resonant acoustics. If the cave-dwellers were literate, vestiges of their writing have vanished, but they certainly used language, however simply. These mysterious "early" people, in their simple, basic way, showed a capacity for spiritual understanding and expression. They very likely believed there was more in the world than met the eye. At least some of them were aware of divinity in and beyond life, and they strove to meet it at death. They were no less human that we are.

We should not forget that nomadic, illiterate peoples who lived and worked with simple tools could be found all over the globe until the nineteenth century, when expanding states and world empires increasingly won them over or wiped them out. There are a few left even today, in the tropical forests, great deserts, and Arctic regions. They are living witnesses to the wide diversity of human life in the world.

Towards the end of the last Ice Age – no one can say for certain how many or how regular these have been – which lasted roughly from about a hundred thousand to ten thousand years ago, archaeological evidence reveals a shift, noticeable in a few regions. Historians commonly refer to the change as the Neolithic (*new stone*) period, again in reference to the quality of the edge on stone axes (chipped or ground and polished) that turn up in scholarly digs. But there is much more to it than that: more people settled down.

In some parts of the world, over thousands of years, it seems that groups of families began to abandon their nomadic ways. They domesticated more animals, such as chickens, goats, sheep, cattle, and pigs, and planted grains. They built more permanent settlements, mostly of mud brick, dwellings, storehouses, and forts. They settled on hilltops, lake shores, river banks, and open plains, always near a source of fresh water. They irrigated to keep their fields and gardens green and fruitful. They learned how to fire pottery, make and use sturdy, more elaborate tools and weapons, and weave baskets and clothing. In some areas, they made wheeled carts to transport their surplus goods to trade with neighboring settlements. They constructed walls of wood and stone where natural defenses failed to keep out animal predators and human enemies. Survival motivated them, but the inspiration, the source of the ideas and capabilities, is a mystery.

Human settlements usually leave behind more evidence than nomadic cultures and enable us to divide history from prehistory. Evidence of occupation at Jericho on the Dead Sea goes back to 12,000 B.C., and by 8,000 B.C., a lengthy stone fortification surrounded eight acres of urban dwellings. Somewhat later, the population of Çatal Hüyük, in modern Turkey, might have reached 6,000 souls, living in multi-level houses of mud-brick, decorated with paintings and sculptures. In parts of Europe, people moved and erected massive stone menhirs, dolmens, and circles, such as at Stonehenge, for purposes that are not clear to us today. And at some unknown time, somehow, people began to record their thoughts, words, and numbers using symbols.

How did the shift from Paleolithic to Neolithic come about in certain places? Why did some people change their way of life and others not?

Theories abound, but the answer comes down to a choice of two: it was either accidental or intended. Either the human brain mutated at random over time and bumbled into greater processing, planning, and acquisition of skills, which in turn afforded those people a higher chance of survival, or the enhanced capacity for settled, community living was a gift of the creator, part of the divine plan for human history.

Without these Neolithic novelties, history would have remained static, circular, directionless, and locked in a single age, incapable of greater unity. Humanity would have remained in caves, dugouts, and tents, close to nature and bonded to it, subject to her vicissitudes, but still fully human nonetheless. God, however, wants the human story, in the West and throughout the world, to go forward. Human cultures and civilizations, especially those with literacy, build and acquire new things, skills, and knowledge at a higher rate, and pass them on to future generations more reliably than by word of mouth. But above all, beyond the buildings, tools, and weapons, the coming of writing gave God a new way to reveal himself to us, using his beloved human agents, with all their inadequacies, in order to teach us the truth about who he is, who we are, and how we are to be.

2

The Gift of Civilization

They said to one another, "Come, let us mold bricks and harden them with fire." They used bricks for stone, and bitumen for mortar. Then they said, "Come, let us build ourselves a city and a tower with its top in the sky, and so make a name for ourselves; otherwise we shall be scattered all over the earth. (Genesis 11:3–4)

Babel

All existence comes from God and is headed back to him, according to his will and plan, not ours. It is the same with human history. Several thousand years ago, mankind developed civilization on earth, in accordance with a loving gift from the creator with the freedom to do with it as we please. God enables human civilization and culture, lets us develop them, and together we propel human history in a forward direction.

From our perspective, the millennia of civilized living seem part of a gradual, developmental process, but in comparison with the eons that came before, civilization came to us spontaneously late last night. If *homo sapiens sapiens* has not changed structurally in a couple of hundred thousand years, the appearance of the capacity for civilized patterns of behavior is a truly dramatic, totally unprecedented occurrence in the immensely long history of the earth. Our challenge, then and now, is to do justice to the giver.

Civilization relies on order and reason, as does the universe and nature, and humanity needs the same if it is to approach God. All known peoples in the ancient world made concerted efforts to reach the divine, to know, please, and appease it, in any number of ways and forms; this yearning attests to the divine presence in the universe, not in spite of the diversity of human religions, but because of it. Difficult as it is for us to comprehend and accept, God's way is unity in diversity, and this way, as manifested in the early millennia of human civilization, points to God's truth and the eventual coming of Christ.

The story of civilization is a set of variations on the theme of the Tower of Babel. People come together, amass resources and economic and military power, build cities, and take pride at their achievements. In their self-congratulation, they start to imagine that they can compete with God, live without him, and fashion law, morality, and truth as they please. Leaders especially, kings, princes, and high priests, fall most often for this temptation and commit wrongs on an appalling scale.

But God only tolerates grave injustice for so long. In time, he lets empires disintegrate, regimes collapse, and the ambitious fail. If he did not, then *nothing will later stop them from doing whatever they presume to do.* (Exodus 11:6) He created us to adore, obey, and serve him, not ourselves. Human freedom culminates in love of God, not in the delusion that we can create ourselves. In the several-thousand-year-old story of civilization, God's will is just as prevalent in the beginning as today.

The "First" Civilizations

The term "civilization" has many uses and shades of meaning. Primarily, civilization is a way of life, no less or more human than the nomadic, the cave-based, or the rural, but distinctive nonetheless. Civilized peoples concentrate population, resources, and institutions in villages, towns, and cities. Civilization reflects peoples' resolution to settle and work with nature to satisfy the basic needs of their families and the rest of the community. It relies on a capacity to learn techniques of construction, agriculture, production, and organization, to improve them as the need or opportunity arises, and to pass this knowledge on to the next generation. Civilization is a choice that partially reveals the breadth of the chasm between humans and other members of the animal kingdom. Where animals act out of instinct in making their dwellings and finding their food, human beings have the privilege to choose how they live. The greatest choice of all, and the most purely human, is to love God.

Civilization also involves a "civilized" mentality and "civil" behavior, matters of the human mind and soul. *Civilization* evokes standards of behavior, of education and upbringing, of peaceable decency and refined politeness, not for the sake of oneself, but for one's neighbor and the wider human family. Civilization implies a kind of elevation; God calls humanity perpetually to rise above itself, to look to him and his ways, to leave all selfishness and brutishness behind. The constant challenge in all of history, for each human being, is our answer to the divine invitation to self-betterment. Apes, for all their sentience and intelligence, can never ponder the difference between the way the world is and the way it ought to be.

The world's first known civilizations, while displaying all the same essential elements, were unique and nearly unrecognizable to one another. In some cases geographical separation prevented sharing even the most basic mutual awareness. As the story proceeds across the millennia, however, successful civilizations, those that grow and last, come into contact with each other, and, despite their mutual conflicts, take steps toward unity.

Human civilization may have actually first begun in the Holy Land, but we will never know for certain. In the region commonly called the Middle East, along the Nile River, the eastern Mediterranean seaboard, and Mesopotamia (between the Tigris and Euphrates Rivers, in what is now Iraq), archaeologists have unearthed evidence of pockets of civilization from 8,000 B.C., give or take a few millennium. Civilization in China might have arisen around 4,000 B.C., and in India and the Americas in the following millennia. The dates vary so much as to seem whimsical. It may be tempting to argue that people of the first civilization, whoever and wherever they were, exported their know-how across the globe, but the theory lacks supporting evidence. Civilization is a mysterious, miraculous gift, wherever and whenever it commenced. Suffice it to say that the people in these far-flung regions, who spoke wildly different languages and knew next to nothing of each other, developed civilization by their own efforts, using the God-given capacity to do so.

These civilizations and others all show a similar set of characteristics. In their effort to live in one place, people built villages, towns, and cities near a sufficiently reliable supply of water and close to their dwellings and fields. In many places they baked and brewed combinations of local grains, fruits, and honey, for consumption, preservation, and pleasure. They organized politically and stratified socially according to variations of strength, ability, and expertise. They worshiped God in the way they knew best. They traded goods domestically, with neighboring areas, and sometimes over greater distances. In some places, they developed simple metallurgy, mixing copper and tin to produce bronze, which is harder and more durable than both. They paid taxes to their authorities and kept records of these transactions, which seems to have been an occasion for developing the art of writing. They defended their people and possessions by means of defense works and personnel. In short, they had everything they needed for settled, communal life.

While building foundations, ruins, pottery shards, some inscriptions and artwork from this distant era have been uncovered for our examination, very few human bodies have survived intact. But in 1991, high in the Tyrolean Alps, hikers made a truly spectacular find. There, freshly thawed from the ice, was the body of a young man, 25–35 years old, who had died in about 3300 B.C. The corpse had dried and mummified naturally in its icy encasement, and so was perfectly preserved. He measured five feet two inches tall, and had weighed about 110 pounds. He was only marginally smaller than British soldiers in World War I, whose average weight was 125 pounds.

This man, dubbed Ötzi, was just as real and fully human as all people today. The tint of his teeth showed that he had mainly lived on milled grains. He wore clothing of sewn animal skins, a thick cape of grass (similar to those worn by shepherds in that region until the turn of the twentieth century), and a fur cap with flaps to cover the ears. On his feet were sturdy, laced, leather boots stuffed with grass for insulation. He carried a long bow of yew wood (an excellent choice for such weapons), a quiver with flint-headed, feathered arrows, a wood-framed backpack, two canisters made of wood bark with shoulder slings, a flint dagger, and a copper-headed axe. He had everything he needed for survival in that mountainous area, but the story has a dark side. An arrowhead lodged deep in his upper-left shoulder, as well as the broken nose and fractured ribs, suggests that he had been murdered or killed in battle. Whether he died fighting or was shot in the back and fell to his death is unknown. Ötzi testifies that mankind has always used its best technologies for violent ends. We are no different. Despite living over 3,000 years ago, Ötzi's way of living and dying demonstrates how much all human beings share in all periods of history.

Mesopotamian Diversity

God loves a beautiful bouquet, as nature on his earth amply demonstrates, and human civilization shares the same love of variety. Each of the supposed "firsts" shows unique characteristics to counterbalance the overarching commonalities. These differences usually reflect local natural environment. God creates us to live in his garden, in accordance with nature, so that we can work with it effectively, for the sake of our families and future. While nature always changes, she is usually less threatening to human civilizations than we are.

Mesopotamia, a flat region cut through by rivers and tributaries, hosted a number of prominent civilizations, such as the Sumerian, Akkadian, and Babylonian, in close proximity to each other, mainly in the area between Baghdad and the Persian Gulf. Royal dynasties from these appear to have succeeded each other in dominance from the fourth to the second millennia B.C. Each group of monarchs assumed power over their people, over-awed or conquered their neighbors, and came to a violent end in due time. Most of the details are lost in the sands and layers of mud, but the basic pattern remains constant. The flowing rivers brought life to the desert, but occasional, sudden, destructive floods in the stormy season kept things in the arid region uncertain for common farming families. For generation after generation, the local people endured storms and warlords alike.

Mesopotamian peoples display a remarkable range of achievement, using inventiveness and reason in their efforts towards order. They developed full systems of writing, such as wedge-shaped cuneiform, beyond the needs of simple record-keeping, and thereby preserved their works of literature. Some of the earliest known epic poetry hails from the Sumerians. To keep order between the various elements of society (the nobles, the free common people, and the slaves), they established law codes for civil society, criminality, legal procedure and business dealings, land tenure, and family matters such as marriage, divorce, and inheritance. The most famous is the code of Hammurabi, that detailed retributive justice ("an eye for an eye, a tooth for a tooth") for the orders of society. This system was not egalitarian. Members on the lower level of the social scale suffered heavier, more brutal punishments. Those who establish systems of worldly justice, in spite of their merits, usually show more mercy to the moneyed. Even in our best attempt to imitate God's justice, we always fall rather short.

Aspects of Mesopotamian civilization show people searching for God, for Love in the face of death, often sadly frustrated by their own efforts. The great *Epic of Gilgamesh,* one of the earliest known surviving works of literature, concerns a mighty king and hero, who "had seen everything, had experienced all emotions, from exaltation to despair, had been granted a vision into the great mystery, the secret places, the primeval days before the Flood." Gilgamesh is the epitome of power, privilege, and pride. "I alone rule, supreme among mankind." In the epic, he travels across the world, conquers all, and builds the greatest city on earth. He knows no limits and does whatever he likes to his people. They, however, cry out to God, who hears their woe and sends him a rival, Enkidu, a man wild and free, hairy and terrifying, every bit as powerful as the king of civilization. Gilgamesh counter-attacks, sending a woman who seduces Enkidu, makes him fully human, and brings him into civilization. Gilgamesh wins him over in a contest of strength, and the two become fast friends. They travel far and kill monsters as awful as fear itself, but Enkidu takes sick and dies in agony. The account of Gilgamesh's great mourning at the loss of his friend remains timeless. For the rest of the epic, he travels on, trying to find a way to get back at death, but he fails, and returns, an old man, to his splendid city of Uruk. The hero's story ends in the civilization where it began. The *ziggurats* of Mesopotamia, massive monuments of ascending mud-brick terraces, once topped with temples aimed toward the heavens, only went so high.

While kings and rulers came and went, God allowed human life in this region to flourish. For thousands of years, these peoples took joy at marriage, births and feast-times, suffered through dearth, disease, and the plague of war, and all mourned at death and loss. The vast majority of the population was peasant farmers, agricultural laborers, and shepherds, who tried to do their best for their families and insure the survival of the next generation. They begged their gods to spare them pains and grant them success in their endeavors, and a few people did their best to predict the future through the dubious arts of divination and animal sacrifice. No matter what happened from day to day, the flaming sun always rose and fell over the life-giving land and waters.

The Mesopotamian legacy lives on today in a number of ways, good and bad. Traces of the Sumerian talent for mathematics and organization still survive in the world's sixty-minute hour and 360-degree circle. Many things have changed in the region – the old cults dedicated to numerous gods have long since disappeared, and the old languages are dead – but the rhythm of human life is basically the same. Violence and instability still plague Mesopotamian cities; foreign powers vie with local strong men for predominance. Dictators and other governments will come and go, but the people who live there still strive for life and peace in their homes. *Gilgamesh* largely ignores the simple life and focuses instead on warriors' exploits, but the epic's emphasis on human qualities, such as friendship, adventurousness, and grief, rings across the centuries.

Unity in the Nile Valley

The Egyptian civilization that grew up in the Nile Valley presents the same complete manifestation of human civilization as in Mesopotamia, but the differences could not be more obvious. Only a few hundred miles to the west of Mesopotamia, Egypt appeared to be a land of comparative tranquility. With little rain during the year, the weather was more stable. Every day the sun rose over the forbidding, lethal desert in the east, blazed its way across the blue sky, raining light and heat over the Nile Valley's fertile soil, to set again over the all but lifeless ocean of sand, the Sahara, in the west. The surroundings inspired a daily appreciation of God's distinct gift: the cycle of life and death, the human drama between earth and heaven.

The Nile itself was mystery to the Egyptians for thousands of years. It came out of nowhere, out of the desert in the south, and if the valley's denizens ever ventured into the African highlands to locate its source, there is no record of their having had this geographical knowledge. The Nile they knew was a gift of God, the source and sustainer of their lives. It flowed gently (except in the southern cataracts) through all of Egypt, nourishing both the valley and the northern delta with rich and black silt. The annual flood, due to seasonal rains in central Africa, was a gradual, predictable affair. As the waters retreated, a thick layer of fresh, fertile mud covered the fields and made them perfect for planting. Even the rocky desert hills showed their generosity with veins of gold and other minerals, so near the surface in some cases that mining was an above-ground affair. Protected in the north by the Mediterranean, in the west by the vast Sahara Desert, and in the east by the desert and the Red Sea, there were few opportunities for incursions and attacks by predatory neighbors.

Roughly three thousand years of Egyptian history before the birth of Christ show long stretches of independence and a remarkable degree of cultural and political stability, under a regime that readily united religious faith with governing order. The pharaoh, a monarch whom people worshipped as a living god, led an administration of local governors and temple priests who managed the vast stretch of fertile land and its fruits both for the security of the regime and the sustenance of the people it was charged to protect. The duty of all was to uphold *maat,* the sacred harmony of the universe, here in their kingdom on earth. The preference for symmetry and adherence to form in Egyptian art indicates cultural continuity and consistency rare to be found among human civilizations. Their mythology held the afterlife as a potentially pleasant option, which partially explains the elaborate preparations made for the passing into death.

Yet this stable sheen had many disfiguring blemishes, placing Egyptian history firmly in the wider story of humanity. More than thirty dynasties of pharaohs came and went in the passing centuries. We can only imagine the level of injustice involved. During the so-called Old, Middle, and New Kingdom periods (each lasting for about half a millennium), the pharaohs kept the country unified. Some extended their power through conquest, south into Nubia and northeast into the Holy Land. Between these phases, however, during rather unimaginatively named "Intermediate Periods," internecine fighting revealed that kings cannot be God, despite their best intentions and efforts. The Egyptian regime suffered from disunity, either because of civil war between rival dynasties or the rare, successful foreign invasion. It is debatable whether the turbulence granted the common people a respite from exactions or increased their burdens as a result of war and violence. But in any case, peace and unity eventually won out. The Egyptians allowed themselves and their country to draw together again and again, until 30 B.C., when the Romans annexed it. For generations thereafter, Rome mercilessly exploited the Egyptians as the grain suppliers for the ravenous capital city of the enormous empire.

In Egypt, respect for divinity and its gifts to nature and humanity inspired the artistic and architectural achievements we all know so well, from the mountainous pyramids to the subterranean tombs once laden with gold and treasures more extravagant than we can imagine. All these testify to Egyptians' belief in the reality of an eternal afterlife. In addition to the three famous stone pyramids at Giza, which survive to this day, dozens more were built along the west bank of the Nile to the south of ancient Memphis. These were cheaper constructions, mounds of earth, sand, rock, and mud-brick, encased in stone so that they mimicked Giza's pyramids in appearance. Almost all of these were smooth and white-washed, and the cap-stones at the top were covered with sheets of polished bronze. Standing in a high place in the city of Memphis a few thousand years ago and looking toward the south, one would have seen a series of unearthly, geometrically perfect, glowing white mountains, each topped with a star of reflected sunlight. Probably the most expensive component of these immense projects was the maintenance of the workers, their food, housing, and pay. Archaeologists have uncovered their on-site villages. Builders probably used slaves as well, but it is hard to say how many and how often. The monuments' exploitive, ugly side pales in comparison to the pharaohs' military ventures, which periodically oppressed the peoples of Nubia in the south and the Holy Land to the northeast.

Description of the cultural wealth of Egypt could fill the rest of this book, but this remarkable civilization came to an end as have many others. The pharaohs' empires expanded and collapsed. Home-grown cults, art, and writing withered and died, and the language, religion, and government rolled into other forms. The myths, stories, poems, songs, and prayers, which witness to all aspects of the human condition, gave way to other, new expressions which aspired to the same eternal truths. A few intellectual achievements, however, like the number π and the 365-day calendar, survive intact, along with the ancient ruins and myriad museum pieces. Today Egypt is one of the most populous, prominent countries in the Middle East, at once profoundly ancient and yet as contemporary as the rest of the world. A Christian interpretation reminds us that God will not let humanity fail, even if its most venerable empires prove ephemeral over time. God's mystery, his gift of life, love, and peace, reigns till the end of history.

Egypt *is* her people, kept alive and strong in her families. As in Mesopotamia, we should never forget that through the millennia the overwhelming majority of the populace lived in simple poverty, working in the fields and on building projects in order to sustain their families. They spent much time baking their bread and brewing beer from the grain they harvested. Almost none of them could ever have afforded a tomb and the trappings we associate with ancient Egypt today. Their concerns were local, mundane, and deeply personal; their hearts were as human as ours. Their simple, local culture had its high points, but records from its law courts show that conflicts and quarrels proliferated. One court case about a sizeable jar of lard dragged on for eight years. And times were terrible when the Nile ran low or failed to flood at all, sometimes for years on end. Then people were trapped, starving in a barren trench, surrounded by dead desert. Egypt, for all its gifts, at times was a hell-hole. But this is true of every place on God's earth. Nature, while beautiful, can ravage human civilization.

Around the World

God planted and nurtured flourishing, original civilizations across the world in the thousands of years before the birth of Christ. They waxed and waned, one sometimes giving rise to another. Historians have named some only recently. All show us that while God wants humanity to thrive in history, he gives no monopoly to any one form of worldly order. Around the Mediterranean basin, the Minoans on the island of Crete and the Mycenaeans on the Greek mainland built their palaces, fortresses, villas, towns, and villages in the latter half of the second millennium B.C. Further to the east, peoples we call the Hittites and the Assyrians developed their civilization, acquired empires through conquest, and fell apart, all in a matter of centuries. The seafaring Phoenicians at the eastern end of the Mediterranean and the Persians, in what is now Iran, showed more staying power, relatively speaking. The Phoenicians established numerous commercial colonies across the Mediterranean seaboard, and the Persian kings built an immense, land-based empire, imposing their authority on both Mesopotamia and Egypt in a mere two decades. To the north and west of the Mediterranean, archaeological finds, including the body of Ötzi the Ice Man, shows us that civilizations prospered in northern Europe in the millennia B.C., although we can only give names to a few.

Civilizations sprang up on the Indian subcontinent, first perhaps in the valleys of the Indus and Ganges Rivers, and spread across that expansive and varied landmass. Like those of the Middle East, the Harappan and the Aryan peoples in northern India and the Dravidians in the south built cities exhibiting all the essential elements of civilization. Many different kingdoms arose, coexisted, and vied for dominance over the centuries, while the culture thrived in spite of their mutual destruction. To this day, the multi-faceted spirituality of Hinduism continues to withstand modernization, and the caste system, an ancient arrangement of social and economic differentiation based on birth and reinforced by religious belief and practice, stubbornly persists as a force to be reckoned with. Despite recent economic growth, in thousands of villages, the ox-pulled cart, the wooden plow, and the woven basket serve, as they have for the last five to six thousand years, as standard farming equipment. India's spiritual fertility also gave rise to Buddhism, a religion that proved to be influential in lands near and far from India itself.

Civilizations developed with apparent spontaneity, across land and sea, at their own pace and each in its own way. The vast region we know as China, separated from India by the Himalayas and neighboring mountain ranges, saw agriculture come by about 5,000 B.C. and other features of civilization soon after. Although most reliable lists of kings only go back to the first millennium B.C., archaeology suggests that rulers called the Shang took control over China's northern region in the mid-second millennium B.C. The presence of writing, the distinctive Chinese characters carved on pieces of bone and turtle shell, shows that civilization had long taken root. Kings ruled over diverse regions with the assistance of a literate elite, whose unique and difficult calligraphy helped to unify and standardize the administration. For centuries kings fought to keep down rebellious peoples. They also faced repeated incursions from the north and west, which helped to insure that no dynasty would dominate for too long. Extensive wall building beginning in the fifth century B.C. helped to stem the tides of warriors, but it never proved totally effective. China became a land of her own, the Middle Kingdom, that tended to assimilate new arrivals culturally, even if she succumbed to them militarily.

Distinctive forms of civilization appeared in Korea and Japan, Indochina and across southeast Asia, and in the central parts of the western hemisphere, such as among the Olmec and the Maya. Their diversity is dizzying, but the commonalities win out all the same. All the world's first civilizations were primarily agricultural, peasant societies, where people lived in villages and small cities, organized by families, clans, and tribes, worked for their living, and prayed for their dead. Cities were a symptom rather than a cause of civilization; at best ambivalent creations, they actually guaranteed neither prosperity nor independence for most people.

In the hands of self-serving, self-loving people, cities entrapped more than they liberated and took more than they provided. Often parasitic, cities lived off agricultural production and sometimes gave comparatively little in return, especially if elites institutionalized oppression instead of justice. Using prisoners of war as slaves was normal, and it was arguably more merciful than outright massacre, if owners observed limits on use and abuse. Debt-slavery, the self-sale of the impoverished, starving peasant to a creditor, was just as awful, especially when bad weather, diseases, and pests decimated the harvest, but it was better than starvation. In both cases the elite benefited from other people's misfortunes. In many capital cities, kings sometimes terrorized their people, even if they carefully propagated a fatherly image. They concentrated military power and compelled the peasants to sustain it with the fruit of their labor, even when imminent threats were lacking. Leaders of armies and navies exploited the best achievements in metallurgy and technology and put them to use in slaughter, all in the name of the leaders' particular terms of peace. Cities could be used for evil as well as good.

In all peoples, ancient and modern, civilized or nomadic, we see more than random biological and behavioral variations; God's hand is working. In the same way that gravity and other mysterious, as yet unknown forces shape the breathtaking galaxies and nebulas of outer space, so God forms all the peoples of the earth, imbuing them with talents and capabilities which raise them above all other creatures. He grants them the freedom to attempt to control nature or to let it be, according to their needs; all people, whether on camel-back or in multi-story apartment blocks, alter their surroundings to ensure their survival. But the universal human drama is not so concerned with where we live as the fact that *we live*. When it comes to human worth, it is irrelevant whether one scratches one's sustenance out of the Kalahari or works to support a luxurious, urbane lifestyle. The former case, social anthropologists claim, actually involves fewer hours of work per week and significantly less stress, although the Bushmen do not live as long and have fewer things to show for their work. Suffice it to say that God reveals his preferred paradox in humanity as well as in the cosmos, that of unity in effusive diversity.

Civilization is a great human achievement, inspired by God, and just as great is human culture, a word closely related to "cult," meaning worship. The human heart yearns for love and purpose, which are the source of meaning, just as the body needs food and movement in order to maintain its health. Across the world, in almost all ancient cultures we know of, civilized and otherwise, we find a nearly universal belief in the divine origins of the universe: that the earth and the sun and the heavenly bodies and all living things come from spiritual beings at work. These beliefs are not the result of ignorance, but of human reflection. Even if we now know, through science and technology, that there is a lot of material behind the little lights in the night sky, we still do not know why they are there in the first place. God created us to be questioners, to seek him in every aspect of reality. He reveals the answers, through faith and reason, through research, prayer, and contemplation, as he sees fit.

Israel

And now enters one of the most fascinating, tragic, and uplifting characters in humanity's story: Israel, the Hebrews, a unique people in the history of the world, and the West particularly, in all times, ancient to modern. The Hebrews' specialness lies not in any significant technological achievement but in their religion, in the primary cult of their culture and civilization, their Yes to God. While no different from anyone else in their humanity, the Hebrews appear to be the first of few peoples to have worshipped the one God directly – if others did the same somewhere in the world, we know nothing about them.

The Hebrew monotheistic faith in God set them apart from all other peoples who exercised polytheistic cultic practices. God gave this small, otherwise insignificant tribe a special identity and a unique path to follow him; he revealed himself to them and gave them a covenant. In time, their religion took on the name Judaism. The irony is that the Jews, who profoundly influenced all of Western Civilization, join this history as nomads, having left the great imperial cities of Mesopotamia behind them. In saying No to civilization over three thousand years ago, the Jews, bearing their gift from God, would shape the West and the world. This should remind us that God, not civilization, is the source of all true good.

The Bible tells us that sometime in the second millennium B.C., a visionary known as Abram, later Abraham, took his family and followers away from the area near Ur, in Mesopotamia, leaving that civilization behind them, beginning the marriage of God and Israel. In terms of the wealthy and powerful of his age, Abraham was a nobody, but he was a true prophet; he opened himself to God and let him take over his life. He felt with God, spoke to God, and listened to him. In a mysterious way, Abraham shared God's experience of humanity and history, and God loved him back. *I will make of you a great nation, and I will bless you; I will make your name great, so that you will be a blessing. I will bless those who bless you and curse those who curse you. All the communities of the earth shall find blessings in you.* (Genesis 12:2–3) God promised to make Abraham *the father of a host of nations.* (Genesis 17:4) In light of the flourishing of Abrahamic faiths around the globe, history shows the prophecy about Abraham's spiritual fatherhood is as true today as in earlier times.

The covenant God articulated included no guarantee for riches, might, prestige, and perfection. After Abraham and his descendents finally settled in Canaan in the interior of Palestine, perhaps during the 1200s B.C., they established a civilization of their own. Just after 1000 B.C. Hebrew tribes united and established a kingdom with Jerusalem as its capital city. Jerusalem soon divided into two, Israel in the north and Judah in the south, and both parts went to war against each other. The Assyrians, a neighboring imperial power, trounced the kingdom of Israel in 722 B.C. and expelled many of its people. Judah met the same fate in 586 at the hands of a Babylonian king, Nebuchadnezzar II, who savaged Jerusalem and destroyed its holy temple, devoted to

God's glory. After the Persians conquered Babylon in 539, some Jews received permission to return to Jerusalem and rebuild the city and the temple. Five hundred years later, however, Roman imperial armies once again wrecked what the Jewish people had built. Again and again in history, one might be tempted to conclude that God's covenant means more trouble than anything else.

The Hebrews, though few in number and repeatedly subjected to foreign, imperial powers, carry a special light of love in the world. God, who revealed himself to them, is all-powerful and transcendent; he acknowledges no rival deities. He participates actively in life; he communicates with people, prophets in particular, and at times conveys his messages through them. He loves his people, preserves and sustains them, as they love and obey him. The covenant is not a negotiated agreement, no symmetrical pact between equals. God ordained the relationship, yet another gratuitous gift from the Creator who is love. God gave humanity monotheism and declared, first to the Hebrews, the law and the way through life that lead back to him, allowing, as always, for individual free will. Among the Jews who kept the faith, God's name was so sacred, it was not to be pronounced; in writing, however, one could use the four-letter symbol, YHWH. They called him Lord, *Adonai*. A daily Jewish prayer said, *Hear, O Israel: the Lord is our God, the Lord alone! Therefore, you shall love the Lord, your God, with all your heart, and with all your soul, and with all your strength.* (Deuteronomy 6:4–5)

In this monotheistic faith, God's word created the universe and everything in it, set history in motion, and guides it always. God inspired the Torah (i.e., the Pentateuch, the first five books of the Bible) and issued a law of righteousness. His prophets made it clear that God judges people according to their conduct, in life as well as in worship and sacrifice. God is just, and not arbitrary; he punishes according to our transgressions and rewards those who follow him, on this or the other side of eternity. Scripture tells us his justice reigns always and everywhere. *Before the mountains were born, the earth and the world brought forth, from eternity to eternity you are God. A thousand years in your eyes are merely a yesterday....* (Psalm 90:2–4)

God inspired the human authors of the Bible, so we must listen to their words. Jewish Scripture entails a diverse group of texts, composed at different times by different people. While neither a disciplined theological treatise nor an empirical transcription of past events, the Bible has elements of both. Similarly it is neither a novel nor a textbook, neither continuous narrative nor a catalogue from beginning to end, but it relates many stories and teaches truth through them. So, with respect to history, for example, it does not make a difference whether Abraham did and said exactly all that is recorded in the Bible. His existence in time can be neither proven nor measured empirically, but his message, his relationship with God, lives forever. Scripture echoes, reverberating God's history with his chosen people. The Bible presents many images and tales, in which we can find truth. Scripture shows us the highs and the lows, the struggles and the periods of peace, and it shares with us the way to God's greatness even in the midst of our failures.

Scripture shows that the Jews had a terribly difficult time following God as he stipulated. The texts offer many instances where people grew apathetic and forgot or neglected him, where they grew resentful about their sufferings and lost patience in the hope of his deliverance. Time and again, they transgressed his love by devoting themselves to objects of idolatry, foreign and man-made, giving into their own passions and treating their neighbors unjustly. Scoffers, skeptics, know-it-alls, and the proud all made the same error: they talked themselves out of God's loving righteousness.

> *For they reasoned unsoundly, saying to themselves, Short and sorrowful is our life, and there is no remedy when a man comes to his end, and no one has been known to return from Hades.*
>
> *Because we were born by mere chance, and hereafter we shall be as though we had never been; because the breath in our nostrils is smoke, and reason is a spark kindled by the beating of our hearts. When it is extinguished, the body will turn to ashes, and the spirit will dissolve like empty air.*
>
> *Our name will be forgotten in time, and no one will remember our works; our life will pass away like the traces of a cloud, and be scattered like mist that is chased by the rays of the sun and overcome by its heat.*
>
> *For our allotted time is the passing of a shadow, and there is no return from our death, because it is sealed up and no one turns back.*

Some people tried to alleviate such pessimistic thoughts with ruthless, consumerist hedonism:

Come, therefore, let us enjoy the good things that exist, and make use of the creation to the full as in youth.

Let us take our fill of costly wine and perfumes, and let no flower of spring pass by us.

Let us crown ourselves with rosebuds before they wither.

Let none of us fail to share in our revelry, everywhere let us leave signs of enjoyment, because this is our portion, and this our lot.

Let us oppress the righteous poor man; let us not spare the widow nor regard the gray hairs of the aged.

But let our might be our law of right, for what is weak proves itself to be useless.

(Wisdom, 2:1–11)

This text displays the perennial struggle of man between love of God and love of self that characterizes the story of the West. For the author's own day, possibly as late as the first century B.C., the text articulates the tension between the Jewish faith and the beliefs and attitudes of a neighboring, predominant culture, that of Hellenistic Greece. Skepticism, hard-line empiricism, and nihilism directly challenged faith in the Lord and his covenant. Some denied the mystery of love eternal, because they could not buy it, grab it, or measure it. In the twenty-first century A.D., when it comes to human nature, we still find nothing new under the sun.

Wisdom allows the human being to discern God behind materiality's screen. Scripture speak of wisdom as a person. *The Lord begot me, the first-born of his ways, the forerunner of his prodigies of long ago; from of old I was poured forth, at the first, before the earth.* (Proverbs 8: 22–3) Wisdom comes to earth, builds a house with seven columns, and hosts a banquet feast, calling out over the city, *Let whoever is simple turn in here....* (Proverbs 9:4) Wisdom is from God; it is the way and the truth. But it is also humble in that it comes from on high, past time and all measure, and comes to dwell among the simple people who endeavor to be and do right and good in their lives. But we all know that each of us has the freedom to reject wisdom, and temptations to do so abound, especially for the rich and powerful, the rulers of the world, the builders of many Babels, as the rest of history makes amply clear.

Israel is different from all other cultures and civilizations in that her heart, soul, faith, and wisdom, as opposed to her technology, money, and power, have not only survived the passing millennia but grown far beyond their initial proportions in terms of world historical prominence. God gave the message and hope of salvation to the Jews, to the people in search of a home in a world marked by violence, injustice, and anger. The Jews, who suffered so much at the hands of greater worldly powers, hoped that God would intervene again in history and send them a Messiah, an "anointed one," who would end their sufferings and lead them forward to God's justice and salvation. In history, through Christ, God's extends his invitation to all the nations of the earth. Abraham's faith in God has literally billions of children in spirit.

3

The Greeks Thought of Everything

Now all the Athenians and the foreigners who lived there spent their time in nothing except telling or hearing something new. So Paul, standing in the middle of the Areopagus, said: "Men of Athens, I perceive that in every way you are very religious. For as I passed along and observed the objects of your worship, I found also an altar with this inscription, 'To an unknown god.'" (Acts 17:21–23)

God has a special place in his heart for the poor. Power-hungry dynasties during the first few thousand years of human civilization amassed great empires and untold riches through brute conquest, but God endowed tiny Israel, which was poor in every worldly way, with a distinctive spirit. The people of Greece also received a special gift in human history: a language with an extensive vocabulary, perfectly suited for philosophy and literature, and a number of great minds, mouths, and hands to match. Greece lacked wealth such as bullion, precious stones, high agricultural productivity, and political consolidation, but she abounded in beauty and brilliance for centuries, unsurpassed, in some cases, down to our day and age. Unlike the breathtaking pyramids and great temple complexes of Egypt, or the light of Israel's unique faith, the greatness of

Greece, in the story of the West, lies in the life of the mind, in speculation, analysis, and research in accordance with human reason. How and why did this come about? The story shows more spontaneity than progression, and the ultimate author of Greek glory is God.

In and Out of Ignorance

The last chapter briefly mentioned the Minoans and the Mycenaeans of the second millennium B.C., two civilizations that left behind extensive ruins, palace complexes on the island of Crete and fortresses and tombs on the Greek mainland, but little in the way of literature and record-keeping. Relying on clay tablets that have survived, scholars have managed to decipher one of their two main scripts (writing systems), called Linear B, but the other one, Linear A, remains obscure. These clay tablets are scarcely more illuminating than any inventory of supplies and goods. Linear B, found more in mainland Greece than on the island of Crete, indicates that people of the time spoke a language related to ancient Greek, but the fragmented texts do not tell us much about them. Archaeological digs show that both the Mycenaean and Minoan civilizations came to an end during the twelfth century B.C.

No one knows what wiped them out. Historians have hypothesized years of savage warfare, plague, drought, famine, maybe even a couple spectacular volcanic eruptions, earthquakes, or tsunamis. People, however, are much more adept and thorough at annihilating civilizations than are natural disasters. Greek oral tradition, however, written down centuries later, speaks of a new arrival, a people from the north called the Dorians, who appear to have settled mainly in the Peloponnese, the southern part of the Greek mainland.

Historians usually call the four centuries from 1150 to 750 B.C. the "Dark Ages," or in some cases the Greek "Middle Ages," but neither term is satisfactory. The sun bathes the Aegean in light for much of the year, to say nothing of 400 years; "dark" can only refer to our ignorance about the people and their way of life during that time. Historians also tend to consign certain periods of history to middle or intermediate status when they either do not know much about them or do not like them as much as what came before or after. At any rate, after about 750 B.C., we have more archaeological evidence of increased population, settlement, trade, art, political organization, and, most importantly, the re-emergence of writing, this time using a phonetic alphabet, adapted from the Phoenician. Civilization, in other words, mysteriously rebounded, and enables us to relish the amazing story of these remarkable people.

Greek bards composed and sang the most important literary inheritance from the centuries following the end of the Minoan and Mycenaean civilizations. The *Iliad* and *Odyssey*, written down in the eighth century B.C. and attributed to the blind poet Homer, draw on centuries of oral epic poetry and tell tales of gods and war heroes of the Mycenaean age. Although both works are set in the cultural context of the so-called Dark or Middle Ages, they spoke to Greeks for centuries afterwards of things human and divine as did no other works of literature. They speak to us still, if we take the trouble to listen.

Homer's heroes were rugged individualists with corresponding ideas and values. Achilles, Odysseus, Menelaus, Agamemnon, and others, were aristocrats, members of an elite defined as much by a belief in its inherent superiority as by its political, military, and economic status. While most were petty kings and chieftains, Homer shows the characters as having less interest in governing their people than in maintaining and defending their personal honor at all costs. Honor was something for which these aristocrats lived, fought, killed, and died; they fought not only for their own honor, but the honor of their family and friends as well. Competition was their way of life, whether in sports or on the field of battle; moral behavior among these people consisted of helping one's friends and destroying one's enemies. The sum of all virtues in ancient Greece was *arete*, a word used when an archer's arrow hits right on the mark, denoting general excellence and manly bravery. There was little energy left for modesty and self-restraint. These men entitled themselves to indulge in sensual pleasures with whomever they found suitably attractive.

Homeric, aristocratic women, on the other hand, best exemplified by Odysseus' wife, Penelope, enshrined the virtues associated with quiet domesticity. While the Greek warrior kings ventured on military and sexual escapades, their wives were to remain at home and maintain the family and its possessions with unfailing chastity. Such women provided legitimate male heirs, managed their husbands' estates efficiently and vigilantly, and gave them no cause for complaint. For centuries, Greek literature graphically portrayed the terrifying opposites to this ideal, in characters such as Clytemnestra and Medea, murderers of spouse and children, destroyers of the family, who threatened to plunge society into chaos.

For hundreds of years, Greeks referred to Homer merely as "the poet," and quoted *Iliad* and *Odyssey* in almost every imaginable kind of discussion. The young memorized portions of the text, and bards performed the works in their entirety during religious festivals throughout the year. For the Greeks, the two epic poems were not comparable to Hebrew Scripture – no deity issued Homer a covenant – but many perhaps attributed his great talent to the appropriate muse. The works are profoundly religious in the sense that divine powers are real and interact with humanity. None of the heroes are secularists. Personifying human strengths and weaknesses, the Greek gods quarrel amongst each other, pick their favorite human heroes, and help them to wreak havoc on their rivals. Such a form of faith virtually insured that the Greeks were almost never at peace with one another.

Archaic and Classical *Poleis*

The history of Greek-speaking people offers a remarkable example of the search for unity amid dizzying diversity. Almost as if by nature, during the early centuries of the first millennium B.C., the Greeks began to organize themselves into small, independent, poor, and competitive city-states, or *poleis* (singular *polis*). By 550, in the so-called "Archaic" period, these *poleis* may have numbered as many as 1000. They appeared on the Greek mainland, around the rim of the Aegean Sea and the Black Sea, and in southern Asia Minor (what is now western Turkey). Greeks traveling in ships founded *poleis* in southern Italy and Sicily (so much so that the Romans called that region "Great Greece"), the north coasts of Egypt and Libya, and along the Mediterranean seaboard of modern-day Spain and France. Each *polis* could have had its own particular legal traditions, weights and measures, religious practices, military, political, and economic organizations, but this does not mean that each one differed sharply from the others in all ways. Many borrowed ideas and practices from their founding metropolis as well as their neighbors, and the weaker often fell under the influence of the stronger.

Greek *poleis* developed a variety of political constitutions that one finds around the rest of the world today, denoted in words that are direct

Greek borrowings: monarchy (rule by one person), oligarchy (rule by a few), or democracy (rule by the many). By no stretch of the imagination did the Chinese or the Inca model their monarchy after the Greeks, but for the West, the Greek *poleis* composed the grand themes, on which the rest of political history is a set of variations. The Greeks most likely did not create these systems, perhaps not even democracy, but they began a tradition of study and analysis of political forms and processes that is still going on to this day.

Poleis were mainly agricultural communities, glorified villages in some cases, more often situated for easy access to farmlands than for trading or defensive purposes. For many centuries, the overwhelming majority of Greek men, women, and children, citizens of the *poleis,* toiled under the hot Mediterranean sun to scratch their living out of what little fertile land they could occupy. Greece is mostly mountainous; only about a quarter of the land was arable at the time. They mainly lived on barley and other hardy grains. Farmers also grew legumes, fruit, and vegetables, and their goats and sheep provided milk and cheese. The wealthy lived on wheat and mutton, but the rest of the population seldom tasted meat or fish. The Aegean, though stunningly beautiful, is poor when it comes to food. The Greeks did their best for their families, acquiring a slave if they could afford one, usually a prisoner of war, to supplement their labor. Their year was divided into phases of plowing, planting, and harvesting, tending vines, making wine, and pressing olives for oil, surviving the winter's damp chill and the summer's brutal sun, and partaking in community celebrations of numerous religious festivals, with processions, sacrifices and feasts, performances of dance, theater, and song, and athletic contests.

If the farms were successful, families grew in wealth and number. If their crops failed, the people faced debt slavery or loss of lands. But even success could be a double-edged sword. In some cases, if a *polis'* population outgrew the fecundity of its lands – this happened on some of the smaller islands in the Aegean Sea – the community would resolve to send away some of its young people to start a colony, another *polis,* of their own. Surviving inscriptions tell us that those who refused to go, who went into hiding, or dared to return without authorization, could face the death penalty. On the mainland, war was a way to acquire more land at the expense of unloved neighbors. For the competitive Greeks, especially for the land-holding elites steeped in Homeric morality, the summertime war became almost routine.

In Western history, two *poleis* stand out from all the others, Sparta and Athens, but these two famous Greek city states were the exception rather than the rule. Athens' fame may be due in part to the fortuitous survival of Greek texts. Some 90 percent of extant works stem from Athens and its authors, so it is no wonder that people often come to associate Athens with all of ancient Greece, even though this is a false impression. Athens was the *polis* of an entire region called Attica, roughly 1,000 square miles, which supported a large population relative to other *poleis*, extensive, fertile fields, and silver mines. Athens also was a center of the ancient pottery industry, a chief exporter of olive oil, and a participant in a wide trade network, but she was a predominant power in the Greek world only for a brief period of time. When it comes to raw force, we must give precedence to Sparta.

Sparta embodied Homeric values like no other *polis*. The community loved war and military dominance above all. From the eighth century B.C. to the fourth, Sparta's warrior elite was the most outstanding, and terrifying, in all Greece. Early on, the Spartan *polis,* located in the southern Peloponnese, conquered Messenia, the fertile region to the west, enslaved the entire population – the so-called helots, who outnumbered the Spartans ten to one – and guaranteed the flow of grain and other supplies to the militarized city. Spartan leaders decided whether infants should live or die, educated young boys for war and girls for childbirth, and kept young men, even the married ones, in the barracks, until they had attained the age of thirty. Thereafter, men still ate with their military comrades in the mess halls and were liable for military service until the age of sixty, although few men lived that long. Women managed estates, serviced by helot labor, and raised children on behalf of the brutal Spartan state. As part of coming of age, young Spartan males traditionally ventured into Messenia unarmed, with the goal of murdering a helot. If the Spartan were caught and killed, it was his own fault. It made for a lethal population, but we should not imagine the Spartans as a bunch of wild-eyed assassins. Spartan choirs and pipers earned high regard among other Greeks. Spartan warriors usually grew their hair long, and would let it down and comb it out before annihilating their opponents.

Sparta helped her friends and hurt her enemies. She established the Peloponnesian League for the mutual defense of all *poleis* in the Peloponnese (except for her old enemy, Argos). Members had not much choice in the matter. In return for the freedom to run their own domestic affairs, League *poleis* accepted that Sparta would determine foreign policy, which basically meant that she could make final decisions about when and where to make war and then count on League members' support. Whenever her fighting men left on campaign, they always kept a nervous eye on the oppressed helots, whose occasional rebellions proved Sparta's perennial Achilles' heel. The Spartans, like all people, yearned for peace, but on their own terms, granting themselves license for the low-grade reign of terror in Messenia.

The Spartan constitution reflected a similar desire for stability. Neither monarchy, nor oligarchy, nor democracy, it entailed elements of all three. Two kings presided over religious festivals and alternated leading the troops in war so one could always be at home. The *Gerousia,* a council of twenty-eight men who had lived for at least sixty years, discussed various policies and judged cases; members served for life. An assembly of Spartan citizen-soldiers, the "equals" who had served in the military until they turned thirty, voted on the *Gerousia's* policies, and sometimes was permitted to choose between alternatives presented to it. The assembly also elected five *ephors,* one-year-term officials who served as a kind of check on the *Gerousia* and the kings, in addition to managing foreign policy and keeping tabs on the helots. The constitution made sure that nothing changed or happened very quickly, unless an emergency situation absolutely demanded it.

The system persisted for centuries, until the Spartans wore down their ranks with excessive wars so that the helots could throw off their yoke, and bring the exploitation to an end. During the centuries of Spartan supremacy, however, *poleis* often sent emissaries to the Spartans, asking for their help in their struggles with their neighbors, or for protection from foreign invasion. The Spartans tended to win these battles when they got around to sending their army. For such *poleis,* the Spartans were the guarantors of Greek freedom, the heroes, the most excellent of men, and women. Spartan soldiers were supposed to die before turning to flee and throwing away their heavy weapons. Mothers supposedly said farewell to their sons with the choice, "Come back with your shield or on it." Victory from raw might made them honorable, and no other group of Greeks, or any other people, could tell them what to do. Achilles would have approved.

While Sparta was the picture of solidity, Athens, only about 100 miles away, was, by comparison, in a constant state of flux. The Athenians considered themselves the aborigines of Attica, unlike the Dorian invaders (*i.e.,* the Spartans) who had settled in the Peloponnese. To make a long and very complicated story short, from the eighth to the sixth centuries B.C., Athens developed the most famous democratic constitution of the ancient world. When the written record begins, an oligarchy of the wealthiest families ruled over a large mass of humble farmers, laborers, and craftsmen. As more of these fell into debt slavery and suffered deprivation, an enterprising aristocrat would harness the people's frustrations and topple the government, establishing himself as a *tyrannos,* literally a "boss," who would rule alone in the best interest of the people and the *polis,* so he said. He would definitely check the power of the aristocratic oligarchy, but oftentimes his rule, or that of his successor, would be oppressive in its own right. It did not take much for a group of disgruntled aristocrats to arrange for coups of their own, supported by various tribes and clans of Attica. Such political history makes for turbulent reading.

But Athens headed in a democratic direction, by one means or another. In 594 B.C. all rival factions agreed to appoint a single man, a poet named Solon, to reform the state and preserve them from civil war. Solon cancelled all debt slavery but did not redistribute landed wealth. He reorganized the state based on classifications of wealth and military service, but unlike in Sparta, he allowed for the participation of poor adult males in the general popular assembly. Solon's reforms only held for a few decades before the state fell into the hands of another *tyrannos,* Pisistratus, who put down the aristocrats and elevated the common man in support of his government and the *polis* in general. When his son proved a tyrannical disappointment, an exiled aristocratic family called on the Spartans for help. Ironically, a Spartan army installed Athens' most famous and radical democratic reformer, a man named Cleisthenes. Cleisthenes broke up the political power of clans and tribes and set up a system of popular voting groups, the *demes* that spanned the whole of Attica. He also made the popular assembly the supreme authority in the land. All free adult male citizens were members and had the right to suggest legislation and contribute to debates. The degree of popular participation in a *polis* of such a size was unprecedented, although women, slaves, and foreigners could not take part.

In terms of values, the Athenians aspired to follow Homer as much as the Spartans did. Although democratic, Athens was hardly peaceable. Her patron goddess, Athena, goddess of wisdom, fine handcrafts, and strategy and discipline in war, features prominently as a supporter of heroes in *Iliad* and especially *Odyssey*. Athens often went to war against her neighbors, such as Megara and Thebes, and she even managed to pick a fight with the massive, mighty Persian Empire to the east. A surprise victory over the Persians at Marathon in 490 B.C. boosted Athenian self-confidence, which soared even higher after Athenians joined forces with thirty-one other Greek *poleis* under Spartan leadership, and repulsed a massive Persian invasion of Greece in 481–479 B.C. The Spartan sacrifice at the battle of Thermopylae lives on in Western popular memory to this very day. The Hollywood spectacle, *300*, released in 2006, is merely the latest manifestation of its memory.

But aside from democracy and a glorious military history, Athens made long-term contributions to Western civilization itself. She adorned her city with standard-setting art and architecture. Classical Greece inspired great movements in Western art for more than two millennia. These architectural forms invoke qualities of nobility, grandeur, and uplifting solemnity in building. Classical Greek statuary, with its emphasis on perfect proportion, strength, and beauty in male and female figures, nude or adorned in drapery, remain impressive representations of human bodies in three dimensions. Greek portrayals of human beauty, balancing simplicity and honesty with idealized perfection, will never lose their appeal.

Even greater, and more important, perhaps, for the history of Western civilization is Athenian literary and philosophical achievement, which actually spread beyond the Athenian *polis*. The Aegean basin, so beautiful in its interplay of sky, sea, and island, of mountain, valley, and coastline, served as a crucible for the Western philosophical tradition. Although the Spartans seem to have had limited interest in literature and elaborate discourse – from their region, Laconia, English derives "laconic" – many important thinkers came from other *poleis,* islands, and regions in the Greek-speaking world. And Athens was the hot-house of such activity, especially in the fifth and fourth centuries B.C.

The Birth of Western Philosophy

The miracle of Greek philosophy proves that there is nothing new under the sun. Graced with a language rich in vocabulary and nuance, Greek thinkers show us human reason in full maturity; they basically thought of all the fundamental tenets of philosophy, and to some extent of science as well. This is not to say that other peoples in other times and places did not come up with similar ideas, but the fact is that certain souls among the Greeks had a special calling to fulfill. Where the Israelites turned away from polytheistic religion to faith in the one God, Greek philosophers looked beyond the vagaries of their gods' pantheon for reasoned answers to basic questions. They sought knowledge of things for knowledge's own sake, not with an eye always trained on industry, monetary wealth, or material gain.

The story of Western philosophy, as far as we can put it together, begins ironically in Homer's region, Ionia, on the eastern coast of the Aegean Sea, many miles from the Greek mainland, with a materialism that leaves little room for God. Here a few particularly inquisitive minds, beginning in the sixth century B.C., called for rational, natural explanations of natural phenomena; they were more interested in the physical causes of lightning than in stories about Zeus hurling about bolts in fits of anger. Thales, a philosopher from Miletus, studied the heavens, charted the movements of the heavenly bodies, and even was said to have predicted an eclipse in 585. He considered the nature of things: how everything changed, how all life experienced birth, growth, decay, and death. He and other Ionian thinkers sought some sign of permanence, a basic, universal matter, behind life's constant instability. Thales said that water, with its special forms of mist, liquid, and solid ice, is the substance that brings unity to existence and yet provides for its great diversity.

Another man from Miletus, Anaximander, agreed with the principle of some universal substance, composed of particles, but did not accept that it could be water for obvious, observable reasons we can all think of. Anaximander was content to leave the particle undetermined, even if he argued for its existence through abstract reasoning. Anaximander also theorized that man was descended from other animals, who in turn came originally from the sea. So much for Darwin's originality. Another thinker from Miletus, Anaximenes, said that the primary matter was air, from which came all things, and yet another, Heraclitus, from Ephesus, said fire was the answer to the mystery. A century later, Leucippus of Miletus explained material diversity by the collisions and combinations of an infinite number of tiny particles, called atoms, which are indivisible and undetectable by the human eye. Even today, having long split the atom, nuclear physicists working at linear accelerators are trying to find the smallest, most elemental particle. They blow up quarks, neutrinos, and anti-neutrinos, carrying on the same project, and yet always finding something new. Some at CERN, the new particle collider built in a circular seventeen-mile tunnel in Switzerland, hope to find evidence for the "Higgs boson," which some call "the God particle," and which supposedly bestows mass on all other particles. This thought comes from the Ionians, actually, and the quest to understand the nature of matter will go on forever. God, who is certainly more than a particle, has insured that humanity will never solve the mystery of existence through purely empirical experimentation, even in its material substrate.

In their hypotheses, these Ionians were the first known materialist philosophers, and they were probably well pleased with their conclusions. They did not, however, persuade other thinkers, particularly those of the sixth century B.C. who conceived of the cosmos in more than material terms. One group in southern Italy saw more in being and spirit than in matter. The so-called Pythagoreans stated that souls were real, that they existed along with living, material bodies, and that at death these souls transmigrated to other bodies—reincarnation in so many words. Texts concerning this group say they were vegetarian, promoted silence, played music, and philosophized about numbers and math as the best way to maintain the health of their souls. Things, they said, were actually numbers, and reality was made up of units. Pythagoreans claimed the earth was round and not the central point of the universe, an idea which took another two thousand years to come into its own.

Still other thinkers kept to material explanations for natural phenomena, but saw order instead of chaotic action and random occurrence. Again, it was Heraclitus of Ephesus who argued that there is more to fire than heat and flame. Fire, he explained, is energy itself, the reason for all growth, retraction, tension, relaxation, coming to be, and snuffing out; fire is the reality behind the flux. In addition, he saw "the One" in all oppositions and differences. He called "the One" God, wisdom, *logos,* and law. This God was very real, if impersonal and rather abstract. Heraclitus championed the idea that there is unity, an order, a system, in the apparent chaos of nature's diversity. Furthermore, he held Homer and the Greek polytheistic cultic practices in low esteem. "Homer should be turned out of the lists and whipped," he snarled. "The mysteries practiced among men are unholy mysteries."

Heraclitus represented a minority, of course – the military elite loved its bard, and the mass of farmers were busy with their basic livelihoods – but he was not alone. Xenophanes of Colophon in Asia Minor also dismissed the Greek gods as anthropomorphic fantasies. "If oxen and horses or lions had hands," he said, "and could paint with their hands, and produce works of art as men do, horses would paint the forms of the gods like horses, and oxen like oxen, and make their bodies in the image of their several kinds." Xenophanes taught about a single, transcendent, unknowable deity, the One who was God, "the greatest among gods and men, neither in form like unto mortals, nor in thought"—total Otherness.

The great search for truth, for the solution to the mystery, continued in the fifth century B.C. Parmenides of Elea in southern Italy rejected the ideas of the Pythagoreans as a bunch of eccentric opinions. Parmenides sharply distinguished between *being* and *becoming*. Being, he said, is simply all that *is*. It is therefore the One. Becoming, on the other hand, which is tantamount to all forms of change and diversity, is mere illusion, and so no reflection on appearances and the senses can yield the deepest insights. Human reasoning about being is therefore the only means for attaining truth. Although he had little interest in souls and other non-material objects, his strong division between becoming and being had a tremendous influence on later philosophers and theologians, who struggle to distinguish between what is eternal and what is fleeting or temporary.

Other thinkers put together ideas consonant with modern science. The famous Hippocrates of Cos dedicated his life to studying diseases and their medical treatments without attributing them to this or that god or goddess. And Empedocles, a Sicilian supporter of Parmenides, thought up something akin to the law of the conservation of matter, a fundamental principle in chemistry. Material things, he said, cannot come in and out of existence. When humans die, their bodies merely separate into component parts. Against Thales and Heraclitus, he hypothesized that four eternal elements – water, fire, earth, and air – serve as the "roots" of all other substances. Each of the four cannot become like any other, but they can combine and separate endlessly. Together they make being an unchanging, material reality. But Empedocles did not deny spiritual reality; he attributed the tremendous diversity of life on earth to cyclical actions, where Love, "a blessed god," joins the elements together, and Hate, which is always lurking around, tears them apart.

Finally we come to Anaxagoras, a fifth century philosopher, who grew up in a Greek city in Asia Minor and fled to Athens during the Persian Wars. He accepted what Parmenides had taught about being's changelessness, but instead of Empedocles' love and hate, Anaxagoras proposed that *Nous,* or Mind, originated the earth, the cosmos, and all existence, set all things order and motion. Mind is "infinite and self-ruled," "the finest of all things and the purest, and it has all knowledge about everything and the greatest power." For Anaxagoras, Mind is not necessarily immaterial; it is omnipresent, "the thinnest of all things," akin to space.

In a Christian narrative of the West, these heady, intellectual ponderings are part of God's on-going revelation to humankind and his plan for our history. We search for him in his mysteries, and he enlightens us for our efforts to find truth, the light in the dark, as he sees fit. Early Greek philosophers raised the problem of reality, of the One and the Many, of unity and diversity, and came up with a host of possible solutions, many variants of which will always be with us. But above all the rest, three philosophers in particular, Socrates, Plato, and Aristotle, set the agenda for Western philosophical thinking, which underlies culture and civilization.

Socrates, Plato, and Aristotle

Philosophical inquiry is only worthwhile if it serves God by searching for truth. Socrates, his student Plato, and then his student Aristotle, all devoted their lives to learning about truth in its many forms at any cost. But before we turn to their contributions to philosophy, we must first begin with the law courts and lawyers of Athens, which played an indispensable and decisively negative role in this wondrous story.

The wealthier or more ambitious citizens of Greek *poleis,* especially in the larger democracies such as Athens, rapidly realized that an important way to protect and increase their fortunes was to convince the popular assembly of their positions during legislative debates and their innocence and righteousness in lawsuits. This required training the males in persuasive public speaking; the rich sought the quickest minds and loudest mouths at a price. Teachers, the sophists, akin to many law professors today, trained their pupils for high fees to argue first one side of an argument and then the other. Justice, for them, was a game, a contest, where victory is the majority vote of whoever showed up at court that day. Sophists subsumed any interest in objective truth to the more compelling goal of defeating one's opponent in a public forum. Armed with words, their values were Homeric, and they quoted the bard readily, whenever it suited them. They were relativists and skeptics with expert knowledge of custom, culture, and civilization, and they enjoyed high prestige in society and the political establishment. Only brilliant eccentrics like Socrates endeavored to put them in their place.

Many Athenians thought Socrates was just another sophist, but he was not, although Aristophanes, a comic playwright, lampooned him as such on the Athenian stage. Indeed, Socrates was the exact opposite, an unpaid visionary in search of true, universal definitions, with more interest in humanity than natural science or cosmology. In his youth he fought for his *polis* against the Spartans, married later in life, and raised a family with humble means. After a kind of conversion experience, a special spirit, or an inner voice, drove him to search for truth and steered him away from erroneous conclusions.

In Plato's writings, Socrates is the short, pug-nosed gadfly who roamed about Athens, in the central squares, marketplaces, and training grounds, and questioned all those who considered themselves wise, or authorities of this or that, never claiming to be one himself. Socrates was a merciless critic, not in the sense that he attacked others and their ideas, but in that he relentlessly questioned people to the limits of their knowledge until they had to admit their own ignorance. For Socrates, this was the beginning of wisdom, the sibling of virtue. He targeted the sophists in particular, because they stank of pride, claiming to know virtue and teach it, while preferring relativism to truth. According to Socrates, people could acquire virtue through rational thought and examination, and no money needed to change hands.

As we can imagine, a man who routinely humiliated Athenian elites attracted the attention of the younger generation. Socrates had a profound influence on Plato, a young Athenian aristocrat, one of his student-followers, who learned to discriminate between might and right, goodness and badness, logic and falsehood, beauty and all that lacks it. Perhaps the key difference between the two men is that Plato wrote, where his teacher does not seem to have bothered. Socrates is the main character in several Platonic dialogues, basically short plays that invite the reader's intellectual participation, rather than deliver a lecture or a set of abstract statements and maxims. Each of these marvelous works of literature is a treasure unto itself, showing the range and wealth of Plato's thought about politics, metaphysics, astronomy, mathematics, and ethics. They will never lose their inherent relevance in any serious field of inquiry. Almost miraculously, every dialogue he is known to have written, at least two dozen, has survived the vicissitudes of time.

Plato's dialogues enshrine Socrates' search for truth in the objective reality of ideas—idealism. Human knowledge is much, much greater than the gleanings of sense-perception. For Plato, ideas and ideals actually exist, even if there are no absolutely perfect examples on earth, as in the case of geometric shapes. We can learn about these eternal ideals through reason and contemplation. Ideals such as beauty, goodness, and justice – he called them "forms" – had their own realm, Plato said, which only the human mind, spirit, and eternal soul could access. But there was an inherent danger in such learning: once people contemplate the forms and come to know them, they come back to life on earth, and understand how illusions blind us and deceive the senses. Contemplation enlightens, but it intensifies the darkness we live with, and leads others to hate us for what we have seen.

Some dialogues feature sophists and undermine their typical view of things. *Protagoras* and *Meno* consist of a grand debate about virtue—what it actually is and whether it is teachable. *Theaetetus* looks at objective versus subjective truth and exposes the error in the statement that "man is the measure in all things." While this may be true with sensory objects, it is not for ethical values. *Gorgias* runs against the widely held notion among Greeks that might is right when it comes to morality; the dialogue argues that the worst evil befalls a person when he or she does wrong, not suffers it. The dialogue ends with Socrates relating a myth about the reality of divine, eternal judgment after death. His inner voice and his God-given reason told him that this "myth" was true.

Plato's other dialogues go far beyond the sophists and their predilections, clearly anticipating and participating in God's revelation.

Timaeus examines the natural world and its many life-forms, and argues that God, the "Demiurge," crafted living beings out of mere matter, according to the eternal forms. For Plato, the cosmos derives from the intelligence of a divine mind. *Symposium* and *Phaedrus* examine the essence of beauty and love, which Plato calls "heaven's greatest blessing." In *Phaedo,* Plato uses the theory of the forms to prove the immortality of the soul, and he reiterates his belief in divine judgment, the soul's reward or punishment. The *Apology* and *Crito* tell the story of Socrates' sham trial and unjust execution in 399 B.C., and explore what the righteous person is to do in the face of persecution. The Athenian popular assembly had tired of the self-proclaimed gadfly and needed to strike at someone for the failure in the long war against the Spartans. Socrates, who refused to change with the times or in response to the wounded pride of the masses, was a casualty of democracy.

Plato is one of the greatest philosophers ever to have lived, whose system for understanding existence and the human condition stands on its own and serves as a foundation or departure point for all serious thinking. But just as the human eye has blind-spots, Plato's philosophical genius could not always see clearly through the thick veil of human frailty. (We are a fallen race, after all.) Plato wasted years trying to turn two Sicilian tyrants into philosopher kings, modeled after those in his utopian *Republic*. After his resounding failure at changing the ways of the world, he returned to his native Athens and founded an association of philosopher and students, the Academy, in 386 B.C., which lasted for 900 years. In a grove of shady trees beyond the Athenian city walls, he lectured his pupils and led discussions, hoping to elevate leading members of the Athenian citizenry in virtue. One of his pupils in particular may have surpassed him.

For centuries people referred to Aristotle as "the philosopher," but today he lacks the reputation he deserves. The texts that survive, mainly lectures notes and lengthy summaries, do little justice to Aristotle's ancient fame for brilliant writing and lecturing. We can hear Plato's voice in his dialogues, but we have only a few quotations from Aristotle's own prose and poetry. Also, there are some silly things in his philosophy. For one, he shows almost no understanding of women. To him they are merely botched males, comparable to children and dogs in character.

Nonetheless, in Aristotle's methodology, we might venture to name him the grandfather of Western, empirical science.

Aristotle was a stupendous intellectual; his mind was a miracle unto itself. He researched, wrote, and taught about biology, botany, zoology, anatomy, medicine, mathematics, astronomy, physics, logic, ethics, metaphysics, music, psychology, politics, rhetoric, literature, and aesthetics. He established a detailed system of rigorous, formal, logical argument, as a method to differentiate right arguments from those that merely seem sound. His technique and terminology persist to this day. He referred to his teacher, Plato, in glowing, respectful terms of awe, and he always agreed with him that goodness, true happiness, is impossible without wisdom and virtue. Like his teacher, Aristotle tutored a monarch's son, Alexander the Great, and later founded his own school in Athens, the Lyceum. But in his philosophy, Aristotle moved away from Plato's idealism. In addition to contemplating the forms, Aristotle gathered all the specimens he could find and subjected them to rational analysis. Following Plato's lead, he believed the key determinant in the nature of things was their ultimate goal, purpose, or end—their teleology.

While Plato attributed phenomena to the transcendent, universal forms, Aristotle attempted to take seriously sensory perception, people's direct experience. He believed in the reality of both matter (component, physical elements) and form (essential characteristics); but matter, in living things, he said, tries to match the form according to teleology. Take an acorn. It is certainly not an oak tree, but it has oak tree potentiality. It *wants* to become an oak tree; that is the purpose of its existence. According to its nature, the acorn tries its hardest, given the resources of the surrounding environment, to actualize itself and attain the form after which it was modeled.

Of humankind, Aristotle said, "All men by nature desire to know." Those who aspire to wisdom endeavor to understand the causes behind things and the underlying nature of reality. They can attain such knowledge through study and analysis. The human being, he also stated, was a communal creature that wants to live in a *polis*, which is comprised of families, its most basic unit. Aristotle gathered descriptions of 158 different *poleis'* constitutions and analyzed them according to their success and failure. The best *polis* to him was the one that fulfilled the human end of happiness and virtue, its true teleology. Moderation, or the Golden Mean, was the key to success in this most important enterprise as well as many others, such as determining correct ethical qualities and behavior.

Aristotle, to some extent, brings Greek materialist and idealist philosophies together. He had limited interest in God, and considerably more in the things of this world. For Aristotle, *being* is unchanging reality itself, and not material. Being is God. God is the Prime Mover, the first cause of movement in the universe, but he is only a spiritual or intellectual force as opposed to a physical one. Aristotle defined God as "Thought of Thought." Material things, however, are dynamic, change all the time, and such change is certainly not illusory, as for Parmenides, but kept in order, according to Aristotle, by matter and form. Not a fundamentalist in his empiricism, Aristotle allowed metaphysics to inform his science. Aristotle firmly believed in universal truths, and his theories never lost sight of teleology. The things he studied, living and inert, had *intentionality*. All forms of motion point to a specific end. Even tossed rocks fall down to earth because that is where they belong.

Much in Aristotle we readily dismiss because of what we now know about gravity, magnetism, electricity, physics, biology, and other technical fields of study, but all scientists have to contend with his theories in some way. A prominent neurobiologist once said in an interview, "I have studied nerve cells for decades, and can tell you just about everything that happens when one of them grows from the spine all the way down to a hair follicle on the lower left calf, but I do not know how *it knows* to go where it goes and do what it does." We are left with a simple choice. Either that nerve cell bumbles its way down the leg, so to speak, according to a random series of bio-chemical processes and reactions, or it does, somehow, mysteriously *know* what to do. The further neurobiologists delve, the more wondrous complexity they find. Ultimately, life is one of God's many mysteries, and empirical science will never get down to the bottom of it.

Anyone pondering the great, timeless questions about life and existence must contend with what these three Greeks had to say. It makes no difference that many in their own day regarded them as mere eccentrics, or, in ours, as totally irrelevant. University professors can teach the entire corpus of Western philosophy as a dialogue between Plato and Aristotle. That fact alone is the sign of a rare, enduring gift to history.

The Greek Legacy

The ancient Greeks gave much more to the West than its philosophical agenda. Having already mentioned their art and architecture above, we cannot neglect the poets, lyric, elegiac, and epic, Homer, Hesiod, Sappho, and Pindar, whose words and images have moved hearts for thousands of years. The playwrights of Athens, the great tragedians, Aeschylus, Sophocles, and Euripides, and the comic Aristophanes, developed dramatic art and simultaneously brought it to a climax. Their work fundamentally concerns the nature of humanity and its place in the order of things. These plays pose questions and present problems that concern families, governments, religious practices, social arrangements, gender roles, birth, growth, and death. Whatever parts of them may strike us as arcane or archaic, they will always be relevant because they address the human condition.

Finally, ancient Greece gave birth to the twin strains of Western historiography, one open to the divine, the other closed. Herodotus, the so-called "father of history," wrote an extensive account of the Persian Wars and their complex causation. He carefully included myth, legend, and oracular pronouncements in his narrative, and critiqued them, along with human deliberation and institutional influences. Thucydides, one generation later, followed Herodotus but went his own way. In his great history of the Peloponnesian Wars, he dismissed what poets and prophets had to say out of hand, attributing the causation of events to exclusively human decisions, good and bad, and the unknown factor of pure chance. While he strove for scientific accuracy in his narrative, he also took the liberty of composing speeches and debates as he imagined them to have occurred, for the sake of demonstrating the ideas and reasoning at work. While Herodotus included the words of prophets and poets, Thucydides frequently indulged in historical fiction. Both wrote for all time and have much to teach us today.

Such Greek geniuses were visionaries, one might say, but of a different variety from those of the Hebrews. They sought truth, beauty, and goodness, but had no faith in a single, personal divinity to enlighten them. Most poets and playwrights clearly found inspiration in the Greek gods and goddesses, but the God that appears in Plato and Aristotle neither gives nor accepts love. He is more a distant, though active, concept than a father to people of faith. Nonetheless, the Greeks used their God-given reason and talent to produce a brilliant body of art, ideas, and texts, a cultural achievement that should serve as a standard for all that learn about them.

The Hellenistic World

While the ancient Greek intellectual and artistic tradition transcended the pandemic Homeric chaos of Greek politics, the unfailingly quarrelsome Greek *poleis* squandered the vitality of their culture on pointless wars. Greek culture gave the West a share of its identity, but when it comes to political practice, they offer little to emulate. Athenian democracy degenerated into mob rule, and Sparta sank under the weight of her own system of oppression. People who love worldly, military might savage themselves as much as their victims.

Sparta had joined Athens in fighting the mighty invading army of the Persian Empire in 480, but the two turned against each other after they had vanquished the foreign enemy. After the Persians retreated from Greece, Athens put together her own league of allies and built a great navy to clear the Aegean Sea and the Ionian coast of any Persian presence. When that project was complete, Athens refused to allow any member *poleis* to quit. She turned her defensive league into an oppressive empire, subject to the whim of the Athenian popular assembly; her subject peoples had no rights to speak of. Meanwhile, she tightened her citizenship requirements; only those with two Athenian citizen parents could be citizens themselves. Athens imploded on her own arrogance.

The Spartans, for their part, who were just as exclusive if less oppressive – apart from the helots, of course – watched all this from the Peloponnese. Their own league members, especially those who had to deal with Athenian interference, constantly complained about the rising threat from overweening Athens. In 431 B.C., the Spartans threw down the gauntlet and charged into Attica. By the beginning of the fourth century B.C., the two had exhausted each other in a terrible series of useless conflicts now known as the Peloponnesian Wars, immortalized in Western memory by Thucydides. His overarching theory was that Athenian restlessness and overconfidence, inherent in popular democracy, was bound to intrude on Spartan hegemony in southern Greece. When

Spartan confidence turned to fear, war was inevitable. However that may be, the wars were still an unqualified tragedy for all involved.

Internecine violence weakened the Greeks and allowed a new conqueror to enter the fray and subjugate them all. Although Sparta defeated Athens in 404 B.C., dismantled her empire, tore down the city's defensive walls, and deprived her of her great navy, she still bounced back, and by the mid-fourth century, the two were at it again, struggling for dominance along with a new powerful *polis,* Thebes. None of these three could give a knock-out blow to the other. A king from the north, Philip of Macedon, invaded and subdued all of mainland Greece by 338 B.C., something which neither Athens nor Sparta had been able to accomplish in their entire history. The irony is that while the Greeks of that time never considered Philip a Greek like themselves, his son, Alexander, projected Macedonian power and Greek culture much farther than any *polis* or *poleis* had ever done before. He established what historians call the Hellenistic World, and killed the traditional *polis.*

In about ten years (334–323 B.C.), Alexander conquered the whole of the vast Persian Empire, replacing the Persian rulers with his Macedonian followers, careful to leave the imperial system intact. One robber band replaced another. Alexander was a young military genius who accomplished his goals in way that were utterly repulsive. He gave full reign to his savage temperament and knew no peace unless he was on the warpath; he basically lived for blood, drink, and sex. Only after a full mutiny of his forces in India did he turn back and face the task of consolidating his rule. He drank himself into a stupor and died of a fever, at the age of thirty-three, in Babylon. His conquest of Asia Minor, the Middle East, Persia, and western India was in vain; after his death his generals immediately carved up the great empire and set to making war against one another. But even from such totally unnecessary slaughter, God can find a seed of good to sow.

Alexander's most enduring achievement in all likelihood never crossed his mind.

From the eighth to the early fourth century B.C., Greeks and Hebrews had almost nothing to do with each other, apart from some light trading. Alexander's rampage changed all that. His new capital of Egypt, Alexandria, became an intellectual capital in the eastern Mediterranean on par with Athens. There "Hellenic" philosophers, scientists, and writers kept the Archaic and Classical Greek cultural legacy alive and added to it according to their ability. The city was beautiful, wealthy, and blessed with a cosmopolitan population of Greeks, Egyptians, and Jews, in roughly equal proportions. In Alexandria, Jews engaged intensely with all aspects of Greek culture; the quotation from the Book of Wisdom at the end of the previous chapter testifies to the tension in that encounter. Within a century or two, Alexandrian scholars produced the Septuagint, a translation of Hebrew Scripture into Greek. The Septuagint is the fruit of the intellectual and spiritual traditions of diverse peoples. This fusion of faith and reason helped to lay the way for the coming of Christ in the history of the West and the world.

4

The Romans Did Everything

Let all the earth fear the Lord; let all who dwell in the world show reverence.

For he spoke, and it came to be, commanded, and it stood in place.

The Lord foils the plan of nations, frustrates the designs of peoples.

But the plan of the Lord stands forever, wise designs through all generations.

Happy the nation whose God is the Lord, the people chosen as his very own.

(Psalm 33:8–12)

God wants to redeem humanity, and he has to power to do so in one fell swoop, just as he created the universe and all existence; but that would entail the end of our story, the great adventure of human life on earth. In history, God shows a distinct preference for drama; momentous developments often come from very, very small beginnings. Rome is one example, but the best of all is Jesus of Nazareth. The West, in many ways, derives from both, and, for good and for ill, it will never escape either.

The history of Rome defies modern scholarly explanation. No political scientist could ever have predicted that a single city in central Italy would conquer and unite the whole of the Mediterranean basin and all of Western Europe, and no mechanistic theory of history, no contrived system of forces, factors, geography, minerals, proteins, and microbes can satisfactorily explain this almost unimaginable fact. Rome, the eternal city, is a mystery. The Romans did everything good that any regime has ever done, and everything bad as well. Rome, despite her many flaws and errors, brought the West together in a way that the Greeks never could. Rome built up a great and terrible empire that unified many different peoples whether they liked it or not, usually by violence, but at the same time she provided an opening for God's mysterious, human entry into the world. With this paradox, Rome set the course for the West and its unique calling in world history. Roman history shows us what God can do with the great on behalf of the little.

Splendor and Squalor

Italy is a beautiful place. She offers mountain ranges of all sizes, green valleys and parched ravines, flatlands and rolling hills, rivers, lakes, and easy access to many hundreds of miles of Mediterranean coastline. No one knows how long people have lived there. Ötzi the Ice Man (see chapter 2) hails from the fourth millennium B.C., and Greeks colonized much of southern Italy in the first. Rome enters the archaeological record in the eighth century B.C., as a group of villages scattered across several hilltops alongside the Tiber River, about fifteen miles inland from the sea, where the coastal flatlands meet the rising Apennine mountains. Mosquito-infested marshes by the Tiber separated the villages and kept their populations small. The inhabitants were people who spoke Latin, a direct, simple language better suited for farmers and soldiers than philosophers and artists. The Latins planted their crops, tended their flocks, tried to placate their many gods, suffered inevitable trials, and lived in humble poverty.

Historical memory of Roman civilization begins with foreign domination. A people from the north, the Etruscans, who spoke a language largely indecipherable to us today, conquered the region (we do not know when) and established a line of kings who ruled until

509 B.C. These monarchs exercised *imperium,* which is basically power over life and death; the king could inflict fines, imprisonment, corporal and capital punishment. The king was also the chief priest of the city's cults and the leader of military campaigns. His aristocratic supporters met in a council called the Senate when the king needed them, and an assembly of the common people gathered at his behest to approve his decisions and to grant him *imperium* at his accession, ceremonially at least. The Senate really had no legal authority as an institution, and the assembly had even less. The petty kings of Rome ruled over a poor populace, but they also united the humble villages into a single city. Under Etruscan leadership, common laborers and slaves installed drains in the marshes, paved the area with stone, and built the Forum, a central square, all of which allowed the city to grow and prosper. But worldly success could not excuse moral turpitude.

According to Roman oral history, written centuries later, Etruscan abuses of power led to rebellion and Roman self-rule. A son of the reigning king, Tarquin II, raped a virtuous Roman matron, Lucretia, who in her shame and humiliation committed suicide. This tragic scandal inspired an uprising of aristocrats and commoners against the king, who fled to a neighboring principality for protection. The Romans established a republic, based largely on the political order they had before, but theirs became one of the most influential constitutional arrangements in Western history. The monarch's power was divided and checked. Instead of a king, Rome had two consuls, elected for one-year terms, who served as generals and high priests and exercised *imperium* limited by law. Consuls could not execute Romans in their own city without the agreement of the popular assembly. The Senate became the bedrock of the republic, making law, handling foreign policy, and controlling the purse strings. In moments of great emergency, the consuls and the Senate could agree to appoint a dictator for a period of six months only and grant him unrestricted *imperium,* for the salvation of the state, they hoped. The goal of the republic was to achieve harmony and cooperation between commoners and the elite, and to protect all citizens from the tyranny of foreign monarchs.

The Roman republic's basic order remained in force for nearly a half millennium, and Rome grew, from a humble, rustic city to a glittering multicultural empire, through a combination of tenacious self-defense, wise policy, and greedy, aggressive war. In the fifth century B.C., she repulsed attacks from the exiled Etruscan king and his allies, and she survived internal struggles between the privileged elite, the so-called patricians, and the plebeians, the general populace. Rival constituents made compromises in the interest of self-defense, survival, and expansion. By 450 B.C. the law of the city had been codified and written down for all, with legal protections for the citizenry and brutal punishments for transgressors. Over time, the distinction between patrician and plebeian melted away, and the popular assembly won greater legal authority and influence in governance. Two tribunes, popularly elected officials whose bodies were deemed sacrosanct or inviolable, sat in the Senate, and although they were not to partake in debate, they could veto any action, magistrate, or law. Roman checks and balances brought a measure of equilibrium to the republic, but Roman society never became egalitarian.

In the fourth century B.C., Rome conquered her neighbors, one by one, in fits and starts, not as part of a consistent policy of imperial expansion, but in the repeated use of a policy of reconciliation. Some fights Rome picked, others were foisted on her, but when she won, she did not always burn down cities and slaughter whole populations. Instead, she either annexed the territory and made a blanket offer of citizenship, with its legal rights and privileges, or she invited the defeated foe to become an ally, granted independent home rule, and extended citizenship to the local leaders. Treaty terms were varied and negotiable. Allied cities and states paid neither tribute nor taxes, but provided troops if the Romans dispatched an army on campaign. The city of Rome gave people the venue and a chance to have a stake in their republican constitution. Roman political leadership realized what the Greek *poleis* like Athens and Sparta could not get into their heads, that unity can be found amid diversity.

One after another, Rome subdued and incorporated the other Latin-speaking peoples, then the Samnites, Etruscans, Gauls, and Greeks. By the mid third century B.C., the city of Rome more or less controlled all of central and southern Italy. When she moved into Sicily, she clashed with the Carthaginians, a Phoenician people with an empire around the rim of the western Mediterranean, and met her match. Roman armies suffered appalling, total defeats, the worst in Rome's history, but the republic held together. Almost all of the allies stuck to Rome, in spite of the terrible presence of Carthaginian armies ravaging Italy for several years on end. This set of long wars came to a close at the end of the third century B.C. when the Romans and their allies were able to send an army to the north coast of Africa and challenge the Carthaginians on their own soil. In these so-called Punic Wars (from Latin *Punici* for "Phoenician"), Rome learned how to fight at sea as well as on land, and the western Mediterranean became a Roman lake. In the late third and early second century B.C., the Romans turned to the east and took on Macedonian kings who had allied with Carthage. Rome sent her armies into Greece to help rebellious Greek *poleis* against their Macedonian overlords, but the Greeks quickly turned against their newfound supporters. The Romans had no patience with such behavior, no matter how Homeric, and soon gained control of mainland Greece and all of Asia Minor. Rome was then the greatest imperial power in the Mediterranean.

An empire is a political arrangement where one people or government dominates and exploits others, and all throughout history it ultimately proves poisonous for all involved. At first, Rome's overseas empire was merely the reward for the republic's military victories, but with time it gradually sickened the state at home. The infection really began with the islands of Sicily, Sardinia, and Corsica. The Romans made these into provinces, not allies, and instead of citizenship, these foreign peoples received a Roman army garrison to keep order, a governor to rule them with unrestricted *imperium*, and tax officials, similarly unchecked, to gather local tribute for the new order and reward themselves for their services. The system invited greed and abuse; it imposed strains everywhere even as it enriched the Roman elite.

No one suffered more than the local people of the provinces. Next in line were the simple Roman citizens, the rank, file, and backbone of the Roman army, who left their farms to go fight Rome's wars during the summer campaigning season, after plowing and planting, hoping to return before harvest. These independent farmers faced longer and longer terms of service, in faraway places, and did not receive enough remuneration to make ends meet. More and more families could no longer support themselves on their small plots of land; many fell into debt, sold their assets to speculators or larger landlords, and moved to the city of Rome to search for a means of survival. Roman senators, meanwhile, became enormously, fantastically rich, in land and booty plundered from conquered cities. Legions of slaves, also the spoils of war, worked on the great estates for as much as it took to keep them alive, allowing for reliable profits in the agricultural markets. No small-time farmer could compete with them. Historical documents of the time say next to nothing about the women, children, and men living in destitution.

The empire became more violent and ruthless as it grew in size. In 146 B.C. the Romans inflicted the ancient equivalent of the nuclear bomb on two great cities: Corinth, in Greece, for having rebelled, and Carthage, the old enemy, for having rebuilt after the Punic Wars. Roman forces attacked, won, and then slaughtered nearly every living thing (apparently including animals). The army saved some people for the profits of the slave markets, emptied both cities of all movable goods, destroyed the buildings, and cursed the very soil. The barbarity was gratuitous and totally unnecessary, and it marked the beginning of the end of the republic.

From Republic to Principate

In the century 133–27 B.C., the Roman Republic, which had withstood numerous growing pains, was racked with tumors, cancers, and gangrene. Attempts at land reform and redistribution on behalf of the ailing citizen-farmer-soldier and his hungry family turned into occasions for mob violence and slaughter within the city's precincts, where no one was supposed to carry a weapon. Reformers such as the Gracchus brothers claimed the senatorial elite were starving the state for the good of their own insatiable gullets. While the self-proclaimed defenders of the good old order condemned the land reformers for conspiring to scrap the constitution and replace it with demagogic, mob rule, the ambitious fleeced the provinces and fought for the prize of political dominance in Italy. One general after another, men like Marius, Sulla, Pompey, Crassus, and Julius Caesar, raised armies beholden to themselves, not the republic, and used them to "pacify" Italy and "rescue" the republic from her enemies.

While the republic ailed, the empire spread its tentacles over what is now France and the regions west of the River Rhine. Rome controlled the land around the whole of the Mediterranean except for Egypt and a stretch of the north African coastline across from Spain. On two occasions, a trio of obscenely rich, powerful, and violent men, a triumvirate, agreed amongst themselves to run the empire, and the institutions of the republic, as they saw fit. The first triumvirate was a secret arrangement, and it ended in civil war. The second triumvirate was open for all to see, but it too led to war among the members, which should not have surprised anyone who knew what was going on, given the three personalities and their megalomaniacal self-love. The bloodshed culminated and came to a halt in 31 B.C. with the victory of Octavian, the grandnephew and adopted son of Julius Caesar, over Mark Anthony and Cleopatra, the Hellenistic queen of Egypt. Octavian added Egypt to his personal fortune, one of the greatest the world has ever seen, and went back to Rome.

In 27 B.C. Octavian carried off a fascinating charade. Appearing in the Senate house, he lay down all his official titles and gave up his powers, having saved the republic once and for all. "No, Caesar, no!" his dutifully prepared supporters probably cried out. The prostrate Senate – Octavian had repeatedly culled its ranks of all opposition – granted him powers equal to and above both consuls and tribunes. He was granted personal control over the provinces that contained the lion's share of the Roman military, and was given even a new name, "Augustus," with a month in the calendar to match. Augustus graciously, humbly complied with their wishes, alleviated their burning fears, and relieved them of their burdensome freedom. When it came to the calendar, he picked a month with thirty-one days as his own, so as not to appear inferior to his adopted father, Julius. While Augustus referred to himself, in false modesty, as *princeps,* or "first citizen," and "the champion of republican liberty," and did rule through the republic's old forms, institutions, and officials, in reality, he was the unquestioned, all-powerful Emperor.

Historians call Augustus' new order the principate, and despite the inherent oppression, it was hardly worse than the civil wars that raged before. On the whole, Augustus proved a capable monarch who kept the empire intact and himself in check. In keeping with the farce, he lived relatively simply, as far as hopelessly rich emperors go, shunning luxurious adornment and fatuous adoration. After defeating remaining pockets of his enemies throughout the empire, he scaled back the monstrous military and provided his veterans with generous land grants. He professionalized the ranks, making the military a viable career option. Still, it is false to say he brought peace, except to Italy. Fighting continued in all directions, against the Germanic peoples living between the Alps and the Danube River, against the Berbers and other nomadic tribes in northern Africa, in the northern parts of Spain, and against the Parthian Empire which lay beyond Asia Minor, Armenia, and Syria. Augustus showed little tolerance for corrupt provincial governors, especially those who inspired more instability than they resolved, and he courted the Roman urban populace with a steady supply of clean, drinkable water, a generous grain dole for the needy, rudimentary arrangements for protection against fire and for the maintenance of public order, and massive building projects that boosted urban employment for decades. In his own words, "I found Rome brick and left it marble." Wealth in coin and kind, extracted from all parts of the empire, paid for the magnificence.

But the elegant white marble squares, monumental temples, and majestic aqueducts should not blind us. The city of Rome was cramped, loud, dingy, and dangerous, with as many as a million residents, most of whom lived in misery, just trying to make ends meet from day to day. The vast majority settled in squalid tenements that were often badly built and prone to collapse, crushing and smothering the unfortunate inhabitants. Augustan administration of the empire was small and lean by our standards – only a couple thousand official bureaucrats kept track of an immense geographical area with a total population of about 50 million – but the nature of the system was every bit as oppressive as it was participatory. It routinely relied on cooperation with local elites, who received power, authority, and Roman citizenship for their collaboration with Roman might. Many regions managed their own affairs on the whole, and had to pay Rome for the privilege. Some, like Egypt, which supplied the massive city with grain, were essential to upholding the Augustan order and were ruthlessly exploited. If Egyptian peasant farmers went hungry in satisfying Roman demand, it was too bad for them, and if they acted up, Roman legions were all too ready to put them down. Augustus ruled there with the authority of the living god, *pharaoh*, and no Roman Senator was allowed to visit Egypt for any reason without his permission. Empire is a wonderful enterprise for the rich and upwardly mobile, but for simple peasant families, it is rarely worth the burden.

Why did all this occur? What accounts for the century of upheaval that perverted and brought down the republic?

Roman historians from that time period, despite their different approaches, respond practically unanimously: morality was paramount. Morality, the fundamental values and beliefs that influence the decisions people make in freedom, mattered immensely in the ancient world.

People chose their morality and ran the world accordingly. Few if any in the ancient world believed in mechanisms or structures, economic, social, and so on, that made up people's minds without their knowing. People interpreted their times in personal, not mechanistic terms. Indeed machines of any kind were relatively few, and there were none that seemed to function on their own accord, as became commonplace in the twentieth century. Men, women, children, and beasts of burdens performed almost all forms of labor. Men who opposed each other in battle used basically the same armaments, so discipline, skill, and valor were paramount in bringing victory. People embodied political order, ruling in accordance – one hoped – with established law and custom. The common view was that the gods usually caused the unexpected, good and bad, and misfortune served as the true test of human dignity and virtue.

Sallust, who wrote during the mid first century B.C., a senator who knew corruption from his own expertise in it, argued that elite greed, ambition, and addiction to luxury and violence came with the acquisition of empire, beginning after the defeat of Carthage. Selfless civic virtue among the natural-born leaders declined, Sallust said, weakening the republic against the depredations of conspirators aiming at universal power. The poet Lucan, who was born after Augustus' death, wrote, "when fortune poured through Roman gates the booty of a world, the curse of luxury, chief bane of states, fell on her sons. Farewell the ancient ways!" Tacitus, a brilliant historian writing later in the first century A.D., who could not stand elite slavishness toward the Emperor, said that the state under Augustus "had been revolutionized, and there was not a vestige left of the old sound morality." Polybius, a Greek intellectual writing back in the second century B.C., attributed the Romans' superiority in virtue to their religious belief. "[A] scrupulous fear of the gods is the very thing which keeps the Roman commonwealth together." The elite, he said, used the threat of divine retribution to keep the general populace in order. Even within the magistracy itself, he claimed, Roman officials, "men [who] have the handling of a great amount of money, ...from pure respect to their oath keep their faith intact."

Something happens to people when they decide that nothing, no deity, state, or worthy cause, is higher or worthier than themselves. Such individuals almost of necessity spread dissension and destroy communal peace rather than establish and nurture it. Add tremendous wealth, military might, and unrestricted legal power to that scenario, and a hellish situation is almost guaranteed. *Where does one's first allegiance lie? Who says what is right and wrong? For whom does one live or die?* These are the great questions in the life of every person, and the answers reveal what and how he or she truly loves.

Western Convergence

According to Christianity, the one God is love, the source of justice, truth, goodness, and beauty. Rome, in this light, was only as good and great as she built, reconciled, and gave, freely and fairly. Her history had to be messy, bloody at times, because she is human, and therefore frail, for all her vast territories, riches, and men of war. In this regard she is neither alone nor unique among the world's empires, living and dead. But God gave Rome a special role in history. Rome is a venue, a vehicle that brought the West, and the world, into a new eon. Rome enabled the convergence of the best of Greece and Israel. Polybius, writing about the Roman republic's constitution in the second century B.C., theorized that "the tendency of all is toward unity."

While the acquisition of empire killed off the Roman republic, it opened Roman state and culture to Greek influence, not all of which was welcome or good. From the third century B.C. on, after the Roman conquest of Greek *poleis* in southern Italy, the Roman elite readily adopted or simply copied Greek art and literature. One might say that the Greeks, defeated by the Romans in battle, overwhelmed their conquerors' culture. The Roman well-to-do began to educate their children to be bilingual, exposing them to Greek rhetoric, literature, philosophy, mathematics, astronomy, and music; a Greek philosopher was a trophy-slave in any rich Roman's home. Latin writers and poets followed Greek examples and mimicked their literary art forms. Roman sculptures and painters assiduously copied Greek originals, while Roman architects followed Greek styles and ornamentation. There was always room for local Latin and individual expression in these endeavors, but the Greek influence was so pronounced as to seem inescapable. In religion, the Romans adopted the Greek pantheon, retold their myths in Latin, and welcomed some but not all of their cultic practices. The cult of Dionysus, Greek god of wine, with its encouragement of inebriated, frenzied fits of sex and violence, did not initially pass Roman moral muster, and the republic handled it as it did other problems. In 189 B.C., it banned the cult in the city, stopped its activities, and executed its recalcitrant devotees. The Senate trounced the cult again in 139 B.C., but by the time of Augustus, such behavior was normal for the Roman elite.

After the Roman conquest of Greece and Asia Minor, the Roman adoption of Greek culture continued. While the Greeks had pioneered the rounded arch, concrete, and the grid pattern for city streets, the Romans applied them on a massive scale. The Romans built many theaters, amphitheaters, and colosseums in Greek architectural style, and staged plays written according to Greek models, but they also used these great buildings for gruesome gladiatorial battles and bloody hunting shows. In the eastern Mediterranean, Rome left Hellenistic civilization intact and solidified it. The cities in that region were well established, more sophisticated, and richer in terms of material wealth than those on the western side of the Mediterranean. The language of Roman imperial administration was Latin in the West and a Greek dialect in the East, *koine,* which was commonly used among the diverse peoples living in the area from Greece, Macedonia, and Asia Minor, to Syria, Palestine, and Egypt. This lingua franca, *koine,* while not as elegant and complicated as the Attic Greek of the fifth and fourth centuries B.C., eventually helped to spread Christianity as the language of the New Testament.

Few outside of Italy felt much love and loyalty to Rome and her emperor, apart from collaborating elites and the various colonies of discharged veterans. For the vast majority of her people, Rome was a distant, though terrifying, threat, made real by the expensive and repressive presence of her military forces. Provincial governors and client kings must have felt Rome's underlying warning to keep the peace at all costs, lest she have to take matters into her own hands. The Roman Empire was basically a system of military garrisons installed in cities, connected by well-built roads, to facilitate the projection of her power, lubricate the flow of required resources, and enhance commerce. And the closer one came to the center of power, the person of the Emperor, the more perverted and lethal the situation became. The successors of Augustus – Tiberius, Caligula, Claudius, and Nero – showed, each in his own unique and horrible way, the depths to which a man can sink when he knows he can do anything to anybody. Outside of the hellish little world of the imperial court, millions of humble commoners, the vast majority living modestly as peasants in the countryside, benefited from Roman peace where it was to be had, but also paid a heavy price. In many places, people yearned for liberation, for a special person who could cast off their burdensome yoke and lead them to a better life. Such a wish is universal, one might claim, regardless of where or when.

Just as the Romans established their all-powerful cosmopolitan regime, God kept history moving forward, introducing a miracle, something totally new and unexpected, although the way had been well prepared. The coming of Christ and the Christianization of the West drew upon the monotheistic faith of Israel, Greek philosophy, and Roman organization, discipline, and morality, such as it was. God's appearance this time was tinier and even more silent than ever before. About two thousand years ago, people generally acknowledged that the divine made life rather unpredictable, and that deities interfered in human affairs all the time, fathering and giving birth to demi-gods. God's entry into the ancient world as a full, complete human being was a surprise, but entirely within the realm of the conceivably possible for the people of the time.

Jesus of Nazareth

Leaving the city of Rome in its awful might, the story of the West goes to the eastern reaches of the empire, to the province of Palestine, in particular a client kingdom called Judaea. The reigning king was a practiced collaborator called Herod the Great, a member of the Hasmonean dynasty, an unexceptional line of rulers and priests. Herod's predecessors had kept taxation flowing to the Macedonian kings and easily shifted allegiance over to Rome when the newcomers conquered the region in the first century B.C. The Temple in Jerusalem was a prime center for making money, mainly through its thriving market of sacrificial animals and religious accessories. It is fair to say that Herod's royal line had more interest in money, power, and their own security than in the Jewish faith.

Judaism as religion generally lacked organization; practices and beliefs were so diverse and diffuse that the term only loosely applies in the time of the birth of Christ. Three prior centuries of Hellenization had taken their toll on Jewish distinctiveness. The common tongue in Judaea was no longer Hebrew but Aramaic, a Syrian import. Worship of the Greek god Zeus and/or the Syrian god Baal was normal in some areas. Not all, however, were content with the assimilationist trend. A group called the Zealots wanted to throw off foreign, imperial rule and reestablish the old independent kingdom of Judah. Another, the Essenes, left corruption behind them and took up residence in the desert, living ascetically in strict adherence to the Torah. These were the people who left us the Dead Sea Scrolls, the oldest extant versions of Hebrew Scripture, written in the second century A.D. and discovered in 1947. The Pharisees accepted Roman rule in the region and profitable practices at the Temple, but they rejected Greco-Roman culture, living according to the letter of Jewish Law. The Sadducees, a group of priestly aristocrats, were similar to the Pharisees except that the Sadducees did not believe in the afterlife or a resurrection of the dead. Based on Hebrew prophecies, many hoped that God would send them a savior, a Messiah, whose justice would reward the righteous and punish the wayward. Exactly how he would do this was open to debate.

In Christian history, something happened that changed everything in 6 or 4 B.C., or sometime between 1 B.C. and 1 A.D., depending on how one counts. In keeping with God's preference, it started very small and seemingly insignificant, a private matter between a poor young couple in a little village called Nazareth, about eighty miles north of Jerusalem as the crow flies, in Galilee. Beginning as we all do, as a virtually invisible, single cell, one small step away from nothingness, God entered history as a human being. At first it was a family matter; Jesus' conception was Mary's business, and then Joseph's, her betrothed. Both experienced something, received some kind of message, to let them know that everything would be all right, and both said Yes. The biological law is that women are equipped to have children entirely on their own, needing nothing from men apart from a single sperm cell to fertilize the egg. Unisex reproduction is common in lower life forms, but it does not fit God's preference for complementarity in higher species. He who created the universe could easily arrange for one of Mary's eggs to have a complete set of DNA and be ready and set to grow when the time was right. The question is not so much how the virgin birth could have happened at all, but why it does not happen more often as the exception to the rule for billions and billions of human births. The only other option is that Mary and the first generations of Christians, including the evangelist writers, were lying, or badly deceived. The option is the same for the rest of Christian belief and history: it is either God's wondrous truth or an unfortunate falsehood.

The stories about Jesus' birth and youth are well known, and all attempt to explain the unexplainable: how the Almighty, whose name was not to be spoken, could deign to join humanity on earth, and yet let almost no one notice. It is a colossal joke, actually, characteristic of God's sense of humor, similar to his packing the earth with bounteous life in a dead, barren universe. The idea that God could have let himself be born as a defenseless baby occurred to virtually nobody. Perhaps even his parents persuaded themselves of their doubts while Jesus was a child and youth – but things changed when he began his ministry.

Jesus was a largely self-trained Jewish rabbi, with utterly remarkable abilities. All the people around him tried to make sense of what was happening according to their understanding and inclination. To some he was a wise teacher, to others a demon, and to still others, the Messiah, the Christ, the son of God. He was Love, and love is always a challenge. Jesus revealed his special powers publicly, and significantly, at a wedding. Shortly thereafter he assembled a diverse group of twelve followers, but even they could not quite comprehend and accept what they saw, heard, and felt, what he was doing for them, and with them. They disagreed among themselves, tested him, and often failed to understand his teaching. He stayed with them, abandoning none, not even the one who betrayed him. He was Love.

What did Jesus look like? Deeply tanned by the sun, no doubt, and wind-whipped, but spared the toxic effects of smoking, drugs, immoderate consumption of food and drink, and useless worry, stress, bitterness, and hatred, Jesus probably looked about as old as his thirty-odd years, at the most superficial level. Artistic renditions and mysterious relics usually depict him shortly before or at death, suffering the burden of unjust punishment, born out of merciful love for humanity. The four gospels say nothing about Jesus' appearance, probably with good reason. Our eyes only see the barest surface of what actually is. Can our human visual organs, even when enhanced by technology, really see what lies beneath the physical surface, and truly discern the nature of beings? The man who was God is a matter of the heart, mind, and soul, as well as the senses.

The miracles: the healings, feedings, storms, transformations, voices from on high, the flames above people's heads – how can one explain them? In brief, these are textual images, and we can never fully recover or recreate the true, historical context of lived, human experience. The evangelists never tried to produce exact, empirical renderings of what could have been recorded if audiovisual technology had been available; they did not limit themselves to terms from the five physical senses. The story-tellers and writers recorded and recast the stories about the man that had changed the hearts of so many among the community of his followers, of those who believed in him and his astounding, completely revolutionary message. This is not to say that the four Gospels are made up, empty tales from deluded minds. The stories and words about and from Jesus convey truth and meaning; they transcend physical details, much as they make use of them.

The four Gospels and the rest of the Christian New Testament stand as testimony to the ministry of Jesus and the experience of his early followers. What the Bible shows is that something, many things, actually, truly remarkable and unprecedented happened in Palestine in the years around 30 A.D. Many, many people experienced things that jostled commonly held notions and stirred up every kind of human emotion in a powerful way. The events frightened many, although Jesus always told people not to fear but to have faith. He traveled throughout Galilee and Judaea, preaching in towns and synagogues, on hillsides and beaches, or even in a boat. He spoke to Jews and non-Jews and paid special attention to the weak: the sick, the broken, widows, and children. He admonished those who were rich, powerful, selfish, and domineering, and he reserved his most dire warnings for those who harmed children and led them astray. He told everyone to live and love simply, as do children.

Jesus often spoke of the Kingdom of God – the term appears 122 times in the New Testament – that it is coming, and that it is here now. The phrase means not only that God exists, but that he is present, aware, and fully in charge. History comes from him and culminates in him, and Jesus told people to open their hearts, adapt their minds, and change their lives according to it. This is his good news, the happy tidings his heavenly Father had appointed him to convey to all alike. But the Kingdom Jesus spoke of is unlike any other. In it there is no power structure, no forced exactions, and above all, no crass violence, but definitely order nonetheless. Justice comes according to individual choice. Those who live in love of God will find joy in their sufferings and new life with him after death. Those, however, who indulge in whim, lust, and rage at the expense of their neighbor, those who despise the creator for daring to limit their selfish pleasures, they separate themselves from God their father in death as in life. God's Kingdom is one of love, which Jesus often described in conjugal terms. Humanity is his chosen bride. But in his goodness, God grants us the freedom to reject him and his love for whatever we happen to find more attractive at the moment.

Jesus, a man of the so-called ancient world, instructed people how to redeem human civilization for all time: they had to turn it upside down and inside out, but through love, and not with violence of any kind. Jesus cited Hammurabi's law code – eye for eye and tooth for tooth – but instructed listeners to do the opposite: accept punishment and abuse and offer to take more. He cited the essence of ancient Greek, Homeric morality – help your friends and harm your enemies – but asked for the opposite: *Love your enemies, do good to those who hate you, bless those who curse you, pray for those who abuse you.* (Luke 6:27–8) This Kingdom of God was and is obviously nowhere on any map, but there it was, and is, in the mysterious person of Jesus the Christ. God's self-revelation is bigger than any book, even the Bible; his love is all-powerful and all-knowing for all time. If we let Christ into our hearts and love him without fail, then God's Kingdom lives in us, regardless of what history may send our way. This is as true in the first century A.D. as it is in the twenty-first.

And then it all seemed to come to a sudden end, just as Jesus said it would, much as his twelve chosen followers were loath to accept it. One of them, Judas Iscariot, decided the rabbi's time was up, that he was too radical, perhaps, with regards to the Temple's power structure, or maybe, on the other hand, not radical enough, because he would not lead a military uprising or provoke a regime change. We will never know, but Judas decided that Jesus no longer fit his needs. He changed according to how he read the times and the mood, and took a fat profit on betraying Jesus to the local and Roman authorities. All but two of Jesus' twelve ran, probably out of fear for themselves, when he was seized; two returned to the fringes. A young man named John, with connections to the high priest's court, secured access for himself and the fisherman named Peter. During Jesus' interrogation and condemnation, neither Peter nor John said a word in his defense. For the moment, hatred and fear had the upper hand.

What happened next is an excellent, detailed example of the Roman, imperial version of justice. Jesus was a local problem, a small-time, unarmed critic of Jerusalem's Temple priests. The priests' tribunal, the Sanhedrin, wanted him dead but would not do the deed, probably for fear of reprisal from his followers or the Romans or both. The Sanhedrin sent him to Pontius Pilate, the prefect or governor of the Roman province of Judaea. Pilate was not of senatorial rank, commanded a low-grade garrison of maybe three thousand auxiliary forces, and the last thing he wanted was trouble. Pilate did not see much of a revolutionary in Jesus and sent him to the client king, Herod Antipas (son of Herod the Great), who happened to be in Jerusalem at the time. Herod was the ostensible ruler of Galilee, Jesus' homeland, and it was common Roman practice to leave local matters to the local rulers, unless disturbances became threats to Roman supremacy. Herod seems to have shared Pilate's assessment and probably enjoyed sending Jesus back to the man who held the real power in the land.

Pilate, knowing the desires of the Sanhedrin, turned to the people, to let them decide upon the death sentence; it was a moment in which a vestige of Roman republicanism coincided with a traditional act of mercy at the Jewish Passover. But the assembled Jerusalem mob preferred to liberate a real revolutionary, Barabbas, who was probably the more dashing character, a man with Roman blood on his hands. Pilate had Jesus flogged, with real Roman savagery, and crowned with a wreath of thorns, and presented the bloodied, battered man to the people, but they called for more, not less. To Pilate, it made no real difference, as long as the Temple priests had the lion's share of popular support to keep Jesus' followers quiet and in line. A moment of real democracy in a province of the Roman Empire resulted in the crucifixion of Christ. Roman barbarism killed the greatest advocate of human civilization.

The Resurrection and the Church

The resurrection of Jesus of Nazareth is part of the historical record, a foundational story in the world – billions of people know about it – and in the West it cannot be avoided. The event is something completely unprecedented, something all empirical science and learning will never be able to explain adequately. It seems crazy to believe it, but it makes sense of what came before and after. Everyone ever exposed to Christian teaching must grapple with the same crucial issue: we are all free to believe that Jesus' resurrection either did or did not take place. For those who say Yes, if we believe that a man triumphed over death, then that man must be totally unique among humans. Human life itself must then be different from what it may seem. For those who say No, however, they must entertain the prospect that all Christianity is essentially an assumed lie, a 2000-year bout of individual and mass psychosis. For many, the choice is daunting, and the stakes extend into eternity.

The resurrection proves that everything Jesus said, did, and was is true. It shows us that God is God, and for him, nothing is impossible. God kept his promise to Israel, and now offers his salvation to all people who love, hope, and have faith in him. In Christ, God manifested himself in the world, to show all humanity the way, the truth, and the life. In the time after the resurrection, till this very day, people wonder, ponder, and argue about what Jesus' life meant, from its first, mysterious beginnings to his wondrous ministry, and horrific self-sacrifice. The resurrection of Christ shows that God is the supreme power and true light for humanity in the world, the God who revealed himself to Abraham, Moses, and prophets, visionaries, and seekers. The resurrection shows us how all earthly powers, with their litigiousness, rancor, and brutality, pale before the God who did not call for revenge for Christ's sacrifice.

Jesus conquered death and assumed a new kind of life. No one witnessed his departure from the tomb where his body was laid to rest, but many people experienced him in different ways in the days, weeks, months, and years afterwards. The Gospels tell us that he came to individuals such as Mary Magdalen and Peter alone, and to groups large and small, of the twelve and hundreds of others. To some he was a vision, to others a voice, and to others, a living, breathing body. With some, he conversed about the right way to read Hebrew Scripture, with others he broke bread. For the rest of history, God remains, as before, hidden, except to those who meet him in prayer from the heart. The amusing paradox is that God, through his continuing self-revelation in history, creates as many mysteries as he clears up, and yet he wants us to keep things simple. Christianity is the belief that divine love is supreme in and after life. In this faith, all human beings are equal before God.

Jesus fully intended for all of humanity to hear this faith throughout the world. His Gospel of life was not meant for an exclusive group, locked in time and bound by institutional regulations, destined for demise. Like most good things, Christianity began small. His twelve, later called apostles, led the effort, joined by many supporters, those who had experienced Jesus and his message, directly or indirectly, and let him change their hearts. One in particular, a Hellenized Jew and Roman citizen named Saul, who lived in Jerusalem among the Pharisees, who might never have heard or seen Jesus, viciously persecuted his followers and their new, Christian movement. Saul even appears to have presided over the stoning of Stephen, perhaps one of the first of Jesus' followers to suffer death for his alleged offenses against God. On his way to wipe out Christ's movement in Syria, Saul was overcome, blinded, a thundering voice in his ears: *I am Jesus, whom you are persecuting.* (Acts 9:5) In time Saul came to understand that God had come to him, as a person, not an ideology. Saul became St. Paul, who spread the Gospel to Jew and non-Jew alike, mostly in towns across the Roman Empire's Greek East. Through men like Paul and women disciples as well, Athens, Jerusalem, and later Rome came together through faith in Jesus Christ.

Sometimes the moral wisdom of Socrates and Plato appears in Christian teaching. *For it is better to suffer for doing good, if that be the will of God, than for doing evil.* (1 Peter 3:17) Greek regard for human reason also bolsters Christianity and detracts nothing from it, and Christians must be able to defend their faith with rational argument, in humility, not out of pride. St. Peter exhorted his flock: *Always be ready to give an explanation to anyone who asks you for a reason* [logos] *for your hope, but do it with gentleness and reverence.* (1 Peter 3:15–16) The commonly used Greek dialect, *koine,* rapidly became the lingua franca of Christian communities in their communications, literature, song, and liturgy. The Gospel of St. John and several apostolic letters in the Bible show the importance of Greek thought in understanding Jesus. The meeting and mingling of Greek philosophy and Jewish faith in Christianity imparted to the new religion both novelty and venerability in history. Christian faith is a gift of the one God, who is love and reason, not an assembled or contrived thing entirely of human making.

The same goes for the Church, a community of prayerful followers, the living manifestation of Christ's resurrection in human hearts. Jesus created the Church and showed its members what to be and do. Imbuing his closest followers with his and God's Love, the Holy Spirit, he told them to spread faith in him to the ends of the earth. After his death and resurrection, the apostles spread Jesus' word, building communities and breaking bread with them as Jesus had directed. They coordinated their activities, ordered their shared message, and sought solutions to problems. Many died horribly painful, violent deaths for their efforts, but their sacrifice and fortitude won over still more souls for Christ. The apostles replenished and expanded their ranks through careful, prayerful selection of leaders, laying on hands and invoking the Holy Spirit. With the passage of time, the numbers of Jesus' eyewitnesses diminished, and the Church became a movement of converts alone. From the beginning, Christian culture distinguished itself from the Roman imperial regime by bestowing its special love on the weak, the sick, the poor, the very young and the very old, the people who lacked power in the empire. But the revolutionary novelty of Jesus and the all-too-human element in the Church brought discord as well as God's peace.

The apostles' preaching about Jesus brought wonder and outrage, relief and turbulence to the communities they visited. Some Jews thought it the worst kind of blasphemy, and some polytheists loathed the idea that their gods, idols, festivals and sacrifices were worthless, or even demonic. Philosophers thought it preposterous that a god should suffer. In places, Christian enthusiasm certainly gave way to zealotry, anger, and proselytization under duress. More than a few seem to have made the error of taking excessively literally Jesus' words about his imminent return and the rapidly approaching end of the world. Jesus did not lie; the world will end in a flash, but on God's time, not ours. And the greater truth is unassailable: we should all live as if this day were our last, avoid sin like the plague, make speedy amends for our transgressions, and love immediately from the bottom of our hearts. Disagreement always accompanies the human quest for truth, and the Bible itself shows numerous examples of how Christianity in history is no exception to the rule.

Among Christians, there was a wide array of opinions, predictions, and actions, but knowing Jesus' wishes, the people strove for unity. Some work was fully consonant with Jesus' message and intention; other projects were manipulative and exploitive. From the very beginning, apostles faced many questions and challenges to the Christian movement. They met periodically in council to formulate common responses, and many deferred to a leader, Cephas or Peter, the "rock," commissioned by Jesus to feed his flock. The apostles developed a shared understanding of who Jesus was and what he taught. This orthodoxy, or "right teaching," took shape and found expression in hymns, letters, forms of worship, and creeds. The apostolic succession, self-selecting Christian leadership, endeavored to maintain orthodoxy amid the inevitable changes in culture, society, and politics.

The Christian Church, always aspiring to unity in prayer and faith, though logistically divided into various communities, established a new age in Western history. With good reason, for many centuries people divided time into B.C. (before Christ) and A.D. (*anno Domini,* in the year of the Lord). In the Christian era of history, a fresh, living seed, planted by the God of Israel, took root in the Greek East and unfolded its delicate tendrils, eventually branching across the whole of the Roman Empire and beyond. Some of its fruits were pristine and gave rise to more new life, while others in time filled with the worms of human weakness and rotted. But still there is no denying that Christianity united the best aspects of the West. Pilate's sign on the cross of Christ, *Jesus of Nazareth, King of the Jews,* written in Hebrew, Greek, and Latin, intended to mock, but it proved prophetic. (John 19: 18–20) Since then, the identity of the West depends on a merging of Judeo-Christian justice and love, Greek rationalism, and Roman order, each challenging the other, in new and unexpected circumstances.

5

The West Diversifies

*A king is not saved by a mighty army, nor a warrior delivered by
great strength.*

   Useless is the horse for safety; its great strength, no sure escape.

   *But the Lord's eyes are upon the reverent, upon those who hope
for his gracious help,*

   *Delivering them from death, keeping them alive in times of
famine.*

(Psalm 33:16–19)

L ooking at the first thousand years of Roman history, from
   roughly 800 B.C. to 200 A.D., one might be tempted to conclude
   that Western history is the story of human progress, toward a
multicultural, governmental unity confirmed by its power and wealth, its
stability resting on the successful ordering of the strong over the weak.
Rome rose from obscure, humble, rural origins to surpass and subdue
Greek, Egyptian, and many other civilizations under its network of
garrisons and wealthy cities. At the empire's apogee, Rome's supporters
considered it open, fair, and tolerant of all matters not directly relevant
to its monetary and military superiority.

   But the next several centuries revealed the hollowness of such a point
of view. God raises up peoples and casts them down according to his
ultimately inscrutable design. Success by any worldly measure means

nothing to him. When the time was right, different peoples entered the lands of the former Roman Empire for reasons unknown to us but perfectly comprehensible to God. At least a dozen identifiable Germanic peoples crossed the Rhine and the Danube and dismantled the imperial order in the western half of the Roman Empire, replacing it with arrangements according to their warlike tastes. But they, too, in time succumbed to the Roman temptation, and made a bid for universal empire, only to be toppled in turn by Vikings, Magyars, and internecine strife. The Roman Empire survived intact in its Greek-speaking eastern half until armies of Arabs and converts to a new monotheistic religion, Islam, sharply reduced Roman influence in the Holy Land and Egypt, areas the empire had dominated for several hundred years. Roman uniformity, always in part an illusion, gave way to a new wave of diversity.

Faced with these great upheavals, one can rightly ask, if there is an all-powerful, participatory God, what on earth is his design for history? The answer is simple enough: History confirms Christ's message. Worldly measures of success, such as money and power, are empty. Money is always crass, seductive, and ultimately worthless: a mere medium of exchange. Power, in the world's terms, cows and destroys; it moves by intimidation and violence. Loving them is the wrong thing to do. God always confirms the falseness of worldly loves, periodically on a grand scale. Also, in the first several hundred years A.D., God revealed that he would spare his people nothing in history, just as he did not spare Jesus. He did not send and sacrifice his son for the sake of utopia on earth. Lovers of God must suffer the same temptations and pains as all other members of the fallen human race. But nonetheless, Christianity in history, the Church of the faithful, is a real force for good, for bringing peace in times of crisis. Committed to loving God above all, inspired by Christian love, the Church struggles and sometimes succeeds in pacifying, reconciling, and unifying lands where only hatred, thievery, and bloodshed previously reigned.

God has another message that history makes totally clear: nothing can put an end to his people. No tragedy, disaster, catastrophe, war, famine, revolution, or cultural, ideological, sociological, political, or economic paradigm shift can or will ever remove true faith in the One who is Love. Crises come, one after another, but when the noise subsides and the dust clears, those devoted to him will always be there to go on working in his vineyard. It makes little difference whoever claims this or that imperial power at the moment, nor does it really matter whether one dies young or old – death, when it comes, is usually a painful, isolating experience. As long as one loves God above all, and one's neighbor as oneself, and lives life accordingly, nothing else matters. The competition is with and against oneself, one's weakness for other, lesser loves. The prize is the afterlife promised by God and confirmed by Jesus Christ.

The Roman Imperial Temptation

As said before, Rome offered a venue for God's human entry into history. The Empire provided stage, backdrop, and theater for Jesus, the most scintillating character in the story of the West, but his movement, the Christian Church, did not need the empire to survive; far from it. In the first and second centuries A.D., Rome seemed a Goliath, while the Christians were at most a gadfly that only on occasion compelled the emperor's terrible attention. Rome, meanwhile, increased her dominance over her many peoples. Her borders expanded yet further and solidified in some areas such as Britain, while others saw repeated bouts of warfare, as in poor Mesopotamia. Roman towns and cities grew, her merchants and emissaries traveled to lands near and far, and within the empire, the emperors reigned supreme, no matter how foul or ephemeral each proved in turn. But the empire staggered in the third century, recovered miraculously in the fourth century, and collapsed in the fifth.

Despite its appalling abuses and ultimate failure, the Roman Empire of the first two centuries A.D. has seduced students of history. Some, one might say, adore her to the point of worship. Historians and filmmakers painstakingly reconstruct her massive, majestic city for museums and movies, highly praise her might, and downplay or perversely glorify her atrocities. Raw Roman power and ruthless, use-and-abuse culture still fascinates after well over a dozen centuries. Members of the Greco-Roman literary elite first crafted this imperial idol with fine words, and numerous intellectuals for centuries afterwards have added to the litany of myth, none more than Edward Gibbon, a brilliant scholar of the eighteenth century who turned imperial Rome into a bygone paradise.

In the second century of the Christian era, the Empire of Rome comprehended the fairest part of the earth, and the most civilized portion of mankind.... If a man were called to fix the period in the history of the world, during which the condition of the human race was most happy and prosperous, he would, without hesitation, name that which elapsed from the death of Domitian to the accession of Commodus. [96–192 A.D.] The vast extent of the Roman Empire was governed by absolute power, under the guidance of virtue and wisdom. The armies were restrained by the firm but gentle hand of four successive emperors, whose characters and authority commanded involuntary respect.... Such princes deserved the honor of restoring the republic had the Romans of their days been capable of enjoying a rational freedom.

Gibbon attributed the collapse of the Roman Empire to the spread of Christianity, which spoiled the supposedly happy situation described above, and eventually ushered in the so-called Middle Ages, in his terms, "the triumph of barbarism and religion." Christianity, he claimed, ruined Roman culture by imposing superstition, fanaticism, and intolerance on the populace, just as the Jews had done in their own vicinity, he added. Gibbon, very much a man of what is known as the Enlightenment of the eighteenth century, also airily dismissed several centuries of Byzantine (Greek Orthodox) culture and rule, as "a tedious and uniform tale of weakness and misery," all of which shows more prejudice than knowledge on his part. Gibbon's ironic, witty ridicule of Christian hypocrisy is devastatingly funny, and, on those grounds, his text deserves many admirers among those who relish a good, spiteful joke. Gibbon had converted to Catholicism earlier in his life, but afterwards he changed his mind, and became a proud, unwavering devotee of the Roman imperial ideal, one of many over the past twenty centuries.

The Roman Empire in the second century may have been quite marvelous for the Greco-Roman elite who composed eulogies to its awesome grandeur, but revolts and wars raged repeatedly in regions around the empire's periphery. Its economy weighed heavily on the backs of peasant farmers who paid rents and provided free labor service in return for permission to occupy and work the land, and the empire simply could not have survived without slave labor. Appalling spectacles of public bloodshed and wanton prostitution kept the urban populace entertained. Cities and military camps were essentially parasitic and relied on the labor and productivity of the countryside, where the overwhelming majority of the population lived. Family, food, shelter, and clothing were the preoccupations of the many.

Rome nursed the seedlings of her own destruction. God's law over history states that earthly imperial orders do not last forever. Their hearts sicken, their minds warp, the extremities go wayward, and their bloated bodies inhibit necessary reform and quick reactions. No empire or state is a fairyland, no matter how rich and self-satisfied. Even the United States after World War II, when it enjoyed many years of fantastic economic expansion, struggled with poverty, corruption, and violence at home while it engaged in numerous wars and revolts abroad. In terms of abuse and wrong-doing, empires are just as fallible as any other political arrangement. Government regulates but does not redeem humanity.

The Growth of Christianity

For all its flaws, the Roman Empire had a special purpose in the Christian history of the West. Despite its cruelty and rampant inequity, the unified system allowed faith in the one God to spread, much as the emperor's men tried to stamp it out. The empire formed a kind of loose social, economic, and cultural community, with systemic evils that almost invited belief in Jesus and his Gospel, although the political leadership periodically saw this belief as a serious threat. The prevailing, Greco-Roman culture held that the strong should rule over the weak. Leaders valued war as something natural and indispensible. Victory brought glory, while defeat deserved humiliation. Many scoffed at the idea that the meek, the hungry, and the downtrodden could actually be blessed and happy. The Christian tendency to reject all Greco-Roman gods and refuse to participate in public sacrifices, the elite believed, indicated a deeper obstinacy which could readily manifest itself in disobedience to imperial power. Some Christians who declined to cast some incense on an altar dedicated to the emperor's spirit received the death penalty for their convictions.

Prevailing Greco-Roman attitudes, values, and beliefs, on the other hand, made peace with the governing principle that might is right. Epicureanism, an Athenian philosophy from ca. 300 B.C that flourished among the Roman elite, argued that even if the immortal gods existed, they did not concern themselves with humanity. Pleasure was good, and pain bad, so the good life consisted of enjoying the simple pleasures such as a drink of clean, cool water on a hot day and the company of friends, and avoiding pain wherever possible. People should not fear death, Epicurus argued, because death was merely the disassociation of the atoms that made up the body. The world was eternal, not the soul, so nothing mattered in life beyond a human's own pleasure and pain. In the face of the inexorable, arbitrary power of an Alexander or a Rome, Epicureans recommended seeking an easy, humble life in one's own garden. Lucretius, a Roman poet of the first century B.C., turned Epicurus into an advocate for rational, materialist atheism, "wherefore religion now is under foot." The mind and the soul, said Lucretius, were the one and the same and merely a bodily function. Everything ended at death, and all speculations about the afterlife were the nonsensical projections of idiots. Life then, for Lucretius, was sensation, neither more nor less, without point or meaning.

Much in Epicureanism reads like a self-help program for those materialists who could afford to indulge in it. Such an exclusively material view of the mysteries of life has never proven uplifting. Theognis, a poet who lived in Megara during the sixth and fifth centuries B.C., reacted to Greek materialist theorizing about changeability in nature with dejection and rejection: "The best for man were not to have been born and not to have seen the light of the sun; but, if once born (the second best for him is) to pass through the gates of death as speedily as may be." Arthur Schopenhauer said as much in the nineteenth century A.D., and one might include twentieth-century existentialists like Jean-Paul Sartre. Materialism always ends up infatuated with death.

Stoicism, another Romanized philosophy, originally from Athens in the third century B.C., resembled Epicureanism but was a bit more open to loving God. As with Epicureanism, Stoicism recommended quietism in the face of unpredictable, willful powers, but was guided by virtue, not pleasure. Virtue, these philosophers argued, consisted in controlling the emotions in accordance with nature's designs. If one's child dies, the virtuous thing to do is to make an act of will to accept the lot nature handed out. It must be so and no other way. Happiness is therefore a choice to accept nature as she is and does. The situation could be as commonplace as going to the baths and getting jostled about in the pressing crowds; then, too, one can choose to be in harmony with natural occurrences. For Stoics, the world is material in part, but divine in its agency. They prized reason, *logos,* the universal logic that explains nature's workings. The wise, they taught, dedicate their lives to being in harmony with nature. Stoicism added an intellectual layer to the old-fashioned Roman stiff upper lip.

Not many people seem to have cared very much about traditional Roman polytheistic worship, except perhaps for the free meat, drink, and fun at festivals. Roman polytheism was civic, led by aristocratic priest-politicians, who slaughtered animals, inspected entrails for omens, and burned things to placate the gods. Augustus tried to revivify the old cults, but in the early second century A.D. under Emperor Trajan, a provincial governor wrote to him complaining that the temples were empty and no one was buying sacrificial foodstuffs. Of course levels of piety must have varied greatly over such a vast area, but one thing is for sure: people then, as now, sought more than mere survival. The human heart naturally yearns for love – you can see this in little children everywhere – but Rome offered precious little of that. Unwanted babes were exposed to the elements, or tossed away. The mainstream culture made little room for inherent human dignity, preferring a wide variety of exploitation instead.

Jesus' teaching about love, repentance, salvation in him, and eternal life with him challenged everyone who heard it and everything about the empire, and it appealed to people of wildly diverse backgrounds. While in some ways unprecedented and new, it drew on ancient faith, philosophy, spirituality, and cultic practices. Next to Christianity, Epicureanism rang flat and hollow, and Stoicism fell as short as it reached. Above all, Christ's Gospel gave as much meaning and hope to the suffering, the humble, and the disenfranchised as to the rich, educated, and powerful. The ennobling stories of martyrs such as Felicity and Perpetua helped God's word to spread. With such stories went belief, throughout the Empire's Greek East, and also to Rome itself, the area around Carthage, and parts of Italy and Gaul (later France).

Especially during the period 100–300 A.D., little Christian communities sprouted in all parts of the Empire, mainly in towns but also in country villages, in spite of periodic, intense persecution. Missionaries carried the faith beyond Rome's borders, across the Rhine and the Danube to diverse Germanic peoples, across the channels to Ireland, beyond the Nile and the desert to Ethiopia, over Mesopotamia to the Indian subcontinent. The process is still going on today. Christianity is a missionary movement of God's word; those who love God above all simply must share with their neighbors. That the Church survives all disasters and continues to move is proof of God's love for her.

God's Church suffers much—attacks from without and scandals from within. Celsus, a second-century polytheistic philosopher, assaulted Christianity for being new-fangled, unreasonable, divisive, and politically and socially subversive, largely due to its inclusion of the simple, the uneducated, and the poor. Greek philosophy, after all, was never meant for such low, boorish persons. In some ways, Celsus was right, even if he missed the point: the Church is always in one crisis or another, and she will never be totally free of them. Where the Church is militant, excessive fervor can lead to error, superstition, and real abuses perversely committed in the name of faith. And where she loses interest in conversion of hearts and busies herself with purely institutional functions, the bureaucratic side of religion, as it were, she opens the door to flaccidity, self-satisfaction, stodginess, and corruption. God wants it that way. Only true love for him alone can achieve unity.

Loving God as One

More than anything, God wants his people to love him, with their whole selves, in all aspects of their lives. A great challenge for those who profess faith in God is how to live up to Christ's prayer just before his arrest and crucifixion: *That they may all be one, as you, Father, are in me and I in you, that they also may be in us, that the world may believe that you sent me.* (John 17:21) As love is more than mere sentiment, unity rests on God's revealed truth, summed up in a common creed. Not everything people say about the New Testament, about what Jesus said and did, can be right, because in their freedom and weakness, people can and will say just about anything imaginable. A body of right teaching, orthodoxy, must be catholic (from the Greek *katholikos*), which refers to beliefs generally or universally held over time, not just at a given moment. Early on, Catholic orthodoxy settled on and forever held to the Holy Trinity, the mystical union of God the Father, Jesus Christ the human and divine Son, and the Holy Spirit, as an answer to the question: who was Jesus the man and what is his relation to God? Nothing exemplifies unity in diversity better than the Trinity. Trinitarian, Catholic orthodoxy, the original creed of the Church, must stand constant and firm against attempts to diminish or discard it, against other, newer, constructed creeds, known as heresies (from the Greek *hairesis*, meaning "choice").

The main heresies of the first four centuries A.D., such as Gnosticism, Arianism, Donatism, and Pelagianism, show the same characteristics of all the rest for the next two thousand years. With the best intentions, heresies endeavor to mitigate or evade pressing, immediate problems besetting the Church. People choose them according to their given time, place, and circumstances, which can be very compelling. But Jesus never told his followers to believe what they want and change as they see fit. Quite the opposite. Believers are to wait patiently for Christ's coming and work on reforming themselves. They must repent of their wrongs and sin no more. They should unite themselves in prayer with all believers, living and dead, who await final reunion with God. They may not relativize Christ and his salvation. The paradox is that Jesus, a real person and yet a mystery, left his followers with parables, commandments, and prayers, but no codifications or systematic explanations of what he is all about. There has been disagreement about Christ and Christianity from the very beginning, as the New Testament letters show us, because of human freedom and fallibility and God's hiddenness. Ultimately, however, God knows what is right and wrong. Heresies come and go, but orthodoxy stands in its simple, childlike devotion to God.

Bishops, the Church's overseers, were men who literally were supposed to have vision from above. Their task was to show their people how to love God, to work for unity in that love, and to take care of the Church's many spiritual and logistical needs, including fostering unity with their brother bishops wherever they might be, living and dead. It was a near-impossible task: to protect the flock from local and imperial persecution, allocate resources for charitable and other ends, discipline the wayward, settle disputes, curb abuses, guarantee right teaching, and provide spiritual inspiration. Many men and women assisted in God's grand task, presbyters ("elders"), deacons ("servers"), priests, teachers, and care-givers. In the first centuries, communities were mainly small and underground, but limited size did not make them any easier.

Loving God takes many forms. Unity does not by any stretch of the imagination mean uniformity. There are about as many ways to love God as there are people, and some individuals are particularly adept at inspiring others to join them in loving God in a radical way. Communitarian forms of Christian living appeared in the first century A.D., very likely with the apostles themselves. Christian communities continued to develop, especially beginning in the third century A.D., with the rise of monasticism, which refers to a wide range of traditions for prayer and life devoted to loving God. Most notable among monastic leaders was Antony, a young man living in the Nile Valley in the later third century, who sold off the lands inherited from his family, gave the proceeds to the poor, in accordance with the Gospel, and took to the desert. Antony lived in bare poverty, endured self-imposed fasts and a great many physical trials, and lived the contemplative life. His experience, however, was anything but peaceful. Antony was a spiritual warrior, experiencing terrifying visions of battles between good and evil and enduring their effects. Although a hermit, he was hardly alone. People came from near and far, the humble and the powerful, even the Bishop of Alexandria, to ask Antony's advice about matters of the spirit and faith. Soon a group of hermits gathered around him, each living separately, but in the association of a spiritual community.

God inspired monasticism, a loving orientation of humanity toward divinity, which in turn inspired love of God in others. Monastic traditions proliferated and diversified spectacularly. Some preferred spiritual athleticism in devotion. One of the most famous and extreme examples comes from Syria. St. Simeon Stylites lived for thirty-odd years atop a column, perhaps as high as forty-five feet, existing literally between earth and heaven, yearning to see God's face, but even there he was not alone. Pilgrims came from near and far and asked for his advice although he was totally uneducated and spoke very simply. He championed orthodoxy, and others followed his example. Such ascetics commanded immense spiritual prestige among Christians. Most monks, however, were not so spectacular. They lived in humble communities, usually but not always separated according to sex, devoted to loving God. Some lived at home with their parents and siblings. Others lived away from their families, professing vows of chastity, poverty, and obedience to the Church and her chosen spiritual leaders. Such communities took root in towns, in the countryside, and in the wastelands, among forbidding mountains, in the forests, on rocky coasts, and in deserts. These communities lived and worshipped according rules developed by Christianity's great early exponents, Origen, Basil, Jerome, and Augustine.

Monasticism, like parenthood, when done well, requires constant self-sacrifice for the sake of others. God handed the human family the responsibility for sustaining the human race. He gave monasticism, this form of intense devotion to God, a unique calling during this period of Western history. Although diametrically opposed to the beastliness of Greco-Roman culture, Christian monasteries preserved its languages and key texts for the sake of knowledge and learning, whether or not they supported Christ's teachings. No historian would debate something so obvious: monasticism kept the cultural and intellectual achievements of the Greco-Roman world alive even as the empire fell to pieces.

Rome's Miracle

Rome's worldly achievement was to dominate her massive empire for as long as she did. A half millennium or more might seem long, but it is not unmatched in world history. The greatest change, which came late in imperial Roman history, involved the Christians. In a mystifying series of highly unlikely developments, the Church, the community of believing followers of Jesus in the lands of the West, transformed from a small, oppressed minority into the only institution able to hold together the diversifying parts of the expiring empire.

In the third and fourth centuries A.D., the Roman Empire was anything but happy and prosperous. For the sake of internal security, the regime slowly tried to turn the empire into a giant military prison, in effect. Foreign peoples and powers attacked the borders in the north, south, and east. Whole regions broke away from Roman rule for a period of time. Military expenditure soared to meet the threat, and taxation with it. To pay for troops and campaigns, the government devalued its coinage by mixing in cheaper metals. Inflation slammed artisans, merchants, and urban dwellers; small farmers foundered; and wealthy people left the towns for the countryside. Historians generally agree that the empire's economy waned in the third and fourth centuries, along with its gross population, although the estimates are darts thrown from a huge distance. Corruption and tax evasion increased, and society

divided into two: those in the military establishment and those out of
it. The summit of power, the imperial office, tipped and reeled; from
235–285, seventeen of twenty emperors were murdered by factional
infighting.

Diocletian, a talented, ruthless emperor (reigned 284–305) who
had fought his way up through the ranks of the army, established a
stability that proved temporary at best. He divided the empire into four
regions under the control of four military monarchs, the tetrarchs, each
with his own capital near the area of greatest instability. None chose
the city of Rome. Diocletian slapped on price controls – this never
works for long – in order to maintain the buying power of a soldier's
salary, but the move proved a boon only for the black market. He
decreed that poor landless peasants live and work on state properties,
which they could never leave, effectively creating a new kind of slave.
Wealthy landowners quickly followed the imperial example for their
own benefit. The poor gained some protection against imperial tax
collectors, but at the cost of their freedom. Diocletian made himself
the idol of an imperial cult, calling himself "lord" (Latin *dominus*)
instead of *princeps* or *imperator.* He also unleashed a new wave of
horrific persecution to rid the empire of Christianity, but it had the
exact opposite effect.

God in his majesty can make good come from the unlikeliest corners
of misery. After Diocletian's retirement, the four tetrarchs fought bitterly
among themselves for the old grand prize of supreme power, until
Constantine, the one who had set off the contest, eventually defeated
his peers. He credited God, however, the creator of the universe and the
Lord of history, with giving him control of the empire. In 312, facing a
daunting battle at Milvian Bridge on the outskirts of Rome, Constantine
claimed to have seen in the sky a cross of some kind, or perhaps the chi-
rho, a monogram of the first two letters in the Greek spelling of Christ,
and it occurred to him that the symbol would help him win his war. He
had his soldiers' shields emblazoned with the image. His men won the
day, and, like a good, practical polytheist, Constantine resolved that the
God of the Christians was worth his mettle. The new emperor adopted
the chi-rho as his battle standard, ended Christian persecution, and from
then on took a great interest in the Church. Delaying baptism until just
before death allowed him to persist in the murderous practices of his
high office without significant qualms.

Christianity entered into a new age under Constantine. But it certainly was not utopia. With the end of the persecution, Christians everywhere in the empire could finally come out into the open without fear or punishment, but the new freedom brought another set of temptations. Before, Christians had suffered terrible pressures to abandon the faith for the sake of their personal safety and convenience, but under Constantine's regime, people adopted the mantle of Christianity to get ahead in the state and society, particularly at the emperor's court. Many seeking his favor readily accepted baptism and went through the motions of worship. Constantine officially tolerated polytheistic worship, but on occasion he closed pagan temples and transferred their assets to the local churches. The infusions of wealth brought troubles as well as benefits. Christian bishops suddenly became monetary beneficiaries of Constantine's regime and legal collaborators, acquiring special rights, responsibilities, and privileges. In some ways, history shows us, the Church is better off poor and oppressed than wealthy and proud. Whenever she nestles closely to those exercising military and other forms of coercive power, her leaders and followers often make the error of too readily blessing superfluous violence.

Whatever Constantine's failings, God prevented him from corrupting the Church by undermining traditional orthodox teaching. The emperor firmly sided with Catholic orthodoxy against Donatism and the Arian heresy in particular, which weakened faith in the Trinity, divided the bishops against each other, and threatened to weaken the unity of the empire. In the interest of lasting peace in the empire, Constantine wanted the matter settled, so he called all bishops to meet at Nicaea, a town near his new capital, Constantinople (now Istanbul), in the summer of 325 A.D. Hundreds showed up, mostly from the Greek East but also the Latin West, including two legates from Sylvester, the Bishop of Rome – they supported the emperor and helped preside over the proceedings throughout. The result of the gathering was the Nicene Creed, a simple, clear, unequivocal statement of belief in the Trinity, the essential unity of God the Father, Jesus Christ, and the Holy Spirit. Later Councils of Constantinople (381) and Chalcedon (451) confirmed the Nicene Creed, which stands firm for most Christians today, Catholic, Orthodox, and mainstream Protestant. But, as is to be expected, agreement was not universal, nor will it ever be.

The Empire Shatters

Diocletian's reforms, some of which Constantine had followed, proved fleeting in the face of history. As he does with all lords of the world, God decided the empire's time had come. For about a century beginning in 376 A.D., Germanic peoples such as the Visigoths, Huns, Vandals, Alani, and Suevi, then the Ostrogoths, Franks, Burgundians, Angles, Saxons, and Jutes, entered the empire en masse, crossing the Rhine, the Danube, and the English Channel, and in time staked out their own territory. This was a long, drawn-out, and very complex process; it is false to imagine a century of *Blitzkrieg* starting in 376. In the third and fourth centuries, Roman armies, defense posts, and military installations had begun accepting Germans into their ranks. The borders were porous; the bases also served as thriving trading posts. Christian missionaries had penetrated far into Germany, and some of the Germanic peoples who entered the empire in the fifth century were Christian, although usually Arian, not subscribing to the Nicene Creed. Others knew nothing of Christianity and saw in the Church a prime source of plunder.

Rome's military system failed; it simply lacked the strength, resilience, and sufficient popular involvement to stop whole peoples on the move. Some invaders had to fight their way through serious opposition; others faced virtually none. Some were highly mobile, mounted raiders, others were immigrants and refugees, bringing all members of the family, their movable belongings, and livestock with them. Few if any showed much willingness to pay imperial taxes and obey Roman bureaucrats. In areas that had suffered heavy exactions, the Germanic immigrants were sometimes welcomed as liberators. The spotty historical record tells of battles and sieges, but only rare instances of ethnic cleansing. New conquerors came, unseated the old Roman elite, and took away their lands. Those with the most to lose penned dirges to the empire's fall. The vast majority of people, however, the farmers, peasants, and villagers, stayed where they were and forged on for the sake of their families. Over time, the Germans "Romanized," and the Romans "Germanified." The common man struggled as before, probably with fewer exactions to pay, but with irregular security, depending on location. It is likely that few humble people in the West mourned the empire's passing.

In the Greek East, the Roman Empire remained largely intact, but no less oppressive than it had been. The emperors, safely ensconced behind the massive walls and natural defenses of Constantinople, watched the western Latin provinces go one by one. The old capital city of Rome suffered repeated sacks, and Germanic kings took up control in their given areas and quarreled readily with their neighbors. In 476, the Germanic leaders of Rome abandoned the farce of proclaiming a new emperor and dispatched the old imperial insignia to Constantinople. Rome shriveled, its once bloated populace reduced by more than a half, living in more humble circumstances. The Romans in Constantinople – nineteenth-century historians renamed them "Byzantines" – did not want to let the West go, however. In 488, Emperor Zeno gave King Theodoric and his army of Ostrogoths a commission to retake Italy for the empire, but to no avail. Theodoric and his men settled in Italy and established a new kingdom in their own right. Later, Emperor Justinian (reigned 527–565) set out to conquer the West, but only managed to regain control of Italy, Sicily, and parts of northern Africa and southern Spain. His campaigns may very well have outdone the Germanic invaders in terms of raw devastation, but a plague that swept over the whole Empire in 542–543 probably proved still more murderous. The Roman Empire (a.k.a. the Byzantine Empire), with its capital city of Constantinople, persisted on its own trajectory of temporal death, which came in 1453, nearly a thousand years later. (Christianity offers government no elixir of youth.)

The Germanic peoples in the western parts of the former empire did not reduce the area to darkness and savagery. They brought on no "Dark Ages" – whole centuries of human life simply cannot be dark. And Christianity survived, according to God's promise. Germanic warriors could and did treat others with appalling violence, but their atrocities were of basically the same class as the Romans'. Cities and towns, the centers of Roman power, suffered according to their resistance to the new warlords, and later many stagnated and shrank. Living in large urban conglomerations was not a hallmark of Germanic culture, nor were abstract notions like the state or the emperor's supreme authority, but Theodoric the Ostrogoth was a generous patron of literature and the arts and supported a large-scale effort to restore the greatest buildings and monuments in the city of Rome. Towns along the Rhine and Danube, like Cologne, Strasbourg, and Regensburg, continued to thrive during this period, their craftsmen producing pottery, glass, iron tools, weapons, needles, adornments, etc. as before. And the fortress town of Dijon, in the late sixth century, had a full set of walls with thirty-three towers, four gates, and water-wheels in the stream that ran through it to run the mills.

Peace eventually prevailed over slaughter. In many parts of Spain, Italy, and Gaul, local administration was left to function as before, employing Latin as the official language, as long as people acknowledged the authority of the new conquerors. In Gaul, secretaries kept using papyrus for public documents, following an old Roman regulation, until the seventh century A.D. Germanic kings consistently butchered their rivals in competition for the summits of power, but the Romans had hardly behaved better on that account. Only in Britain and the western areas of Gaul did the newcomers destroy Roman government and tear up Roman culture root and branch. Everywhere else the Church survived, and, over time, reconciliation won out over revenge. Gradually, Germanic peoples abandoned Arianism and polytheistic beliefs, and adopted Catholic, orthodox Christianity instead.

The Germanic Age in the West, 500–900

People loving God over revenge, people making peace after war, people forgiving past wrongs and looking forward to new life, people marrying, intermarrying, and raising families together allowed for new unities to form in Europe. Faith in Jesus Christ did not cause wars as much as help to find ways to end them more quickly and cleanly than otherwise. Despite Rome's failure, God's word kept the West together, however tenuously. It preserved the past, and pointed to a common future.

In the sixth to the ninth centuries A.D., Germanic Western Europe united in religion first, then in politics, and finally in culture. Diversity, however, remained the natural norm. The processes took place quietly and slowly for the most part, but also in fits and starts. Stories of some conversions, like that of Clovis, King of the Franks, survive, but most left no record at all. Clovis, rather like Constantine, was primarily interested in winning battles and keeping his warriors in line, and at first he resisted his Christian wife's urgings to embrace the faith. But an unlikely victory persuaded him, and his conversion ca. 500 A.D., along with his warriors, gave the Church protection and the freedom to preach love of God. Christianity, however, thrives on peace, not war; it exhorts former enemies to bury enough of their differences so that they can both get on with life. The Church's creed, liturgy, and sacraments unify people across race, class, and gender. Christianity served as a spiritual, cultural crucible, where the diverse peoples in formerly Roman lands could come together and agree on new ways to meet their needs and give meaning to their lives.

The Greeks thought of everything, the Romans did everything, and Christian monks saved their best achievements from oblivion. God let the West survive by letting it become something new while maintaining the better part of the old. We can see this in the simple fact that those men and women of Europe who devoted themselves most completely to God, who turned away from violence and power, and even marriage and family, who dedicated their lives to searching for God, both in life and in the Word, in silence and in song, saved the Greco-Roman intellectual heritage for all posterity. Without their prayerful, quiet work, all future movements of great importance in the rest of Western history, such as the Italian Renaissance, the Reformation, the Scientific Revolution, the Enlightenment, and ensuing modernism, would be unthinkable.

Many holy men and women, hermits, monks, and nuns, preceded St. Benedict of Nursia, but this one wise man gave a form and order to monasticism that will never die. While truly founded on love for God, it is deeply human. Benedict, born in central Italy ca. 480, studied in Rome amid the wreckage of the empire, and left it all behind him for the mountains to the east of the city. There he lived as a hermit, in a cave, not perched on a column. His spiritual reputation spread, and soon he was asked to lead a group of monks as their abbot. His first followers soon tired of his rigor. Benedict left them and founded new monastic communities, based on the *Rule* that he wrote, devoted to loving and serving God. Benedictine monasticism acknowledges that the purpose of every life is to attain eternal salvation, accomplished through a faith lived through communitarian work and prayer, led by a father figure, an abbot, who is freely chosen by the community. Benedict's *Rule* disciplines the mind, body, and soul, but it includes no extreme bodily abuses in the cause of spiritual asceticism.

Under the abbot's guidance, monks provided for their own needs, working the land like almost everyone else. Although many monasteries had walls for basic security, they were not closed institutions; Benedict's *Rule* required generous hospitality to strangers. Study, mental work, forms the mind, so all monasteries had a library and a school. As God reveals himself, so people must learn God's word as they search for him. Regular, rhythmic prayer, the recitation of biblical text in speech and song, opens the soul to God, leaving time and occasion for silent contemplation of his wondrous majesty. Benedictine monasteries multiplied and gave rise to missionaries, teachers, scribes, singers, and skilled craftsmen. Monks were often pioneers who cleared forested areas and developed wastelands. Their copyists patiently and painstakingly preserved the words of ancient wisdom, Christian and pagan: the writings of Scripture, the early Church Fathers, Greco-Roman philosophy, history, poetry, mathematics, astronomers, medicine, and so on. Jesus said, *My Father is at work until now, so I am at work*. (John 5:17) In imitation of Christ, monks work, too.

The monks of Ireland, the exceptional island in the West, put all other missionaries to shame during this period. The Celtic people of Ireland, whom the Romans had never managed or bothered to conquer, had adopted Christianity during the course of the fifth century, possibly first hearing God's word from a Romanized Briton who came to Ireland as a kidnapped, teenage slave, St. Patrick. After years of tending sheep and spending his days in prayer, he escaped and eventually returned to Britain. But God called him back to Ireland. After a period of study and service, he was ordained deacon, priest, then bishop, and Patrick spent the rest of his life preaching the Gospel all across the Emerald Isle, decrying slavery in particular. Monasticism quickly took root, both hermitic and communitarian, but not Benedictine. Irish monasteries became centers of learning that safeguarded and copied Greek and Latin texts brought from the European continent. In the sixth to the ninth centuries, these Irish communities formed and launched the missionaries who extended the Church to areas of formerly Roman Europe where non-Christian Germanic tribes had weakened it or wiped it out. While it is a stretch to say that the Irish saved Western Civilization, the achievement is no less remarkable.

Christianity eased the reconciliation and merging of old Roman civilization with the new Germanic cultures in the West, allowing for a more personal order to emerge. In time, the Visigoths, Burgundians, Ostrogoths, Franks, etc., ceased their wanderings, and the leaders established kingdoms based primarily on ethnicity. Germanic Europe organized itself according to traditional Germanic bonds of personal obligation. Germanic kings, chieftains, and warriors had little appreciation of abstract concepts and impersonal arrangements such as the state and citizenship, and no use for uniform, codified law and chattel slavery. A king's power was his prestige among his greatest followers, the extent to which they obeyed and followed him. Political bonds were personal, not bureaucratic, from the top of the social scale to the bottom.

Instead of institutions like the Roman Senate, Germanic kings called their followers to give them counsel when the situation demanded. Custom, the ways, rights, and manners of a given ethnic group, replaced universal, imperial law. Rituals of oath-swearing, called compurgations, and terrifying trials by ordeal replaced judges, lawyers, and juries. If more emotional and dramatic than bureaucratic and deliberative, traditional Germanic practices excelled over the Roman in terms of efficiency. Few complained of the law's delay. Judicial practices tried to end conflicts rather than assign punishment. Payments of blood money were meant to stop the feuds that normally accompanied personal disputes and injury. Personal oaths of loyalty, shared among people great and small, rich and poor, powerful and weak, formed the basis of land tenure. While no one could own another person as a piece of property, much of the peasantry lacked the freedom to leave the lands they worked. It was the price for local security.

For the most part, life for the vast majority went on as it had under the Roman Empire and before. No one expected to live long. Death was normal at all ages, from toddlers to forty-somethings. The population was overwhelmingly young and characterized by exuberance and impetuousness. Leaders of kingdoms and the Church had often just entered what we consider adulthood. Precious few completed more than one decade in their positions. Most children saw one or both of their parents die. To live to see one's grandchildren was a great and rare blessing. The world was huge to these people, limitless and mysterious. Most lived local existences in rural settings. All faced the difficult, daily decision about what to love most in this life. This was as true in the west as in the east of the former Roman Empire. From an elite point of view, the two sides had gone in separate directions, but the presence of the Church imparted unity though not uniformity.

Islam: Another Separation?

A greater change perhaps than the collapse of the western Roman Empire was the appearance of a new faith in God. Islam, which stems directly from Judaism and Christianity, is totally unthinkable without either. All three worship the one God, the Almighty, creator of heaven and earth. Rather than depict Islam as a new religion completely separate from the Judeo-Christian tradition, like Hinduism, Buddhism, Shinto, etc., perhaps we should regard it as many did when it first appeared in the seventh century A.D., as yet another Christian heresy, or, in other words, a religious reform movement in the Judeo-Christian vein, led by a self-proclaimed visionary who was also a gifted tradesman, political leader, and military general. But the differences between Islam and Christianity greatly exceed those between Catholic orthodoxy and well-known heresies such as Arianism. The religion founded by Muhammad emphasized obedience to God, not love for him; Islam means "submission to God." Muhammad established a pan-Arab theocratic empire; Jesus and the apostles showed no interest in such designs. However one depicts the development of great monotheistic faiths, one can discern God's hand at work in the story. Unable to be confined or categorized, God prefers to keep us wondering. Even as he placed humanity on earth to marvel at the dark reaches of the infinite universe, he writes human history with us so that it never ceases to amaze. The mystery of being cannot be restricted to human deliberations and writings.

Around 610 A.D., in Arabia, a desert region neither Greeks nor Romans tried or managed to conquer, a man named Muhammad, by then a well-to-do merchant, who had had extensive contact with both Christians and Jews, experienced a series of visions. He related them to others as *suras,* messages or prayers, which were later compiled as the Qur'an (meaning "recitation"). Muhammad proclaimed "the God"—in Arabic, *Allah,* the creator most gracious, most merciful, the protector of the faithful, the giver of the Book, the source of wisdom, the fount of justice and power, who requires our obedience. The Qur'an inveighs against the polytheistic practices normal at that time throughout the Arabian peninsula, and especially against the false loves that plague Jews and Christians, such as prideful rebellion against God's Covenant, hypocrisy, the love of money, oppressing the weak, and others. Some *suras* retell the story of Jesus, the great prophet, confirming the truth of the virgin birth, his miraculous works, and his ascension into heaven, but they condemn belief in the Trinity as an idolatrous error. Muhammad did not believe that God could or would become a human being. Muhammad's Islam is disarmingly simple, and its obligatory code of right behavior – daily prayer, charitable donations, fasting, modesty, honesty, abstention from pork and alcohol, and pilgrimage – has no need for priests or bishops, sacraments, and abstruse theological controversy, inspired in part by Greek philosophy.

Humanity being what it is, however, disagreement, dissension, and conflict beset Islam as they did Christianity and Judaism. Muhammad was a real fighter. After he condemned polytheistic worship at the Ka'bah, a holy site in Mecca, his enemies drove him more than 200 miles to the north in 622, to the oasis of Medina. He and his followers fought back, raiding the caravans headed to Mecca. Muhammad won over more Arab tribes to Islam, raised an army, and conquered Mecca in 630. He purged the Ka'bah of its idols and died two years later. His followers and successors, the caliphs, subdued all of Arabia by 634 and led their forces far beyond. In the next thirty years, they shattered the Roman (Byzantine) Empire in Egypt and the Holy Land, and overwhelmed the Persian Empire as well, in Mesopotamia and all across Persia proper. But the evil of war only leads to more war. Internal bickering among Muslim leaders led to the murder of Muhammad's successor, the caliph, civil war between rival factions, and the establishment of distinct Islamic traditions in existence today, such as the Shi'ites and the Sunnis.

Islamic conquerors pressed on nonetheless. Their war needed no justification in their eyes, and no Islamic religious authority held them back with pleas for peace. There was no divide between mosque and state, so to speak. The division that really mattered was between *Dar al-islam* (literally "house of Islam"), the realm of Islamic peoples, and *Dar al-harb* ("house of war"), the non-Islamic rest of the world. In the east, Islamic armies eventually reached and entered India, and in the West, they took the whole of North Africa and Spain, and invaded the Kingdom of the Franks (now France). Frankish warriors turned the tide near Poitiers in 732 and pushed the Muslims back to the Iberian peninsula. Time passed, and Islam took root in the history of humanity.

Conversion to Islam was not usually forced on new populations by the point of the sword. Muslim conquering forces tended to establish a new capital, basically a garrison with market and a large mosque, separate from the other main cities. They declared local Christians and Jews "protected subjects," who could exercise their religion as before if they paid a tax for the privilege. The new conquerors made it clear that those who supported the new regime needed to take on the ways of Islam. The similarities shared by Christianity and Islam made conversion for many rather easy; adherents to both worship the one God. Many people in Egypt and Syria were glad to see the oppressive Roman and Persian imperial systems fall, and with the centuries, Arabic replaced Greek and Latin as the common tongue for administration and business. In Spain, Egypt, the Holy Land, Syria, Mesopotamia, and Armenia, Christian majorities slowly became minorities, and they survived, with smaller Jewish minorities, enduring occasional crises and persecutions. The twentieth century, and the twenty-first so far, have seen more attempts to destroy them totally than any other that came before. The Saudi Arabian regime is less tolerant today than were the seventh-century caliphs.

Returning to the eighth and ninth centuries, however, language, culture, politics, social norms, and religion seemed to conspire to keep Christians and Muslims apart, but where they lived together, along with Jews, as in Córdoba, Alexandria, Jerusalem, Damascus, and elsewhere, coexistence was the norm. In the daily contact that comes from simple proximity, many saw the obvious commonality: all three groups seek God. While Muslims do not value the Bible in quite the same way as Christians or Jews do, and Jews and Christians do not regard the Qur'an as Muslims do, both groups look to the One for hope, meaning, and salvation. And all three acknowledge Satan as the father of lies and dissension.

While for centuries violence and suspicion were the norm along the Christian-Muslim borderlands (in northern Spain and eastern Anatolia for example), in areas where the three faiths intermingled, peace and understanding seemed to conquer war and hatred. St. Catherine's monastery in the rocky Sinai desert, for example, fared well under Muslim control. No one took the trouble to destroy it, and in the eighth and ninth centuries, when the Roman Emperor forcibly divested Christian monasteries of their wealth and holy images, he could do nothing to ravage St. Catherine's. Its iconic representations of Jesus are among the oldest surviving in the world today. Especially its encaustic icon, "Christ Pantocrator," (ca. 600), some say, is the closest thing we have to a portrait of Jesus, based on an artistic tradition leading back to his lifetime. The Qur'an itself speaks of Christians as "nearest among them in love to the Believers [*i.e.,* Muslims]... because amongst these [*i.e.,* Christians] are men devoted to learning and men who have renounced the world, and they are not arrogant." (Sura 5:82)

Does God want Muslims and Christians separate and hostile? Did the coming of Islam and the spread of elements of Arab culture cleave East from West? While historians have good grounds for declaring human civilization in these areas distinct, we should remember that land and sea provided passage between these regions, and there was no formal Cold War. Borders, such as they were, remained porous, and people traveled.

In the late seventh century, an Irish abbot named Arculf traveled from his monastery to the Holy Land, which was under Islamic control, on pilgrimage. He stayed in Jerusalem for nine months, visiting Jewish and Christian holy sites in Bethlehem, Nazareth, and the surrounding areas. Jerusalem's stone houses, surrounding walls, and great annual market reflected its prosperity. For personal security, Arculf enlisted a single bodyguard and guide, a Christian soldier, a Burgundian named Peter, who "lived the solitary life." Greater security provisions do not appear to have been necessary. Arculf also visited Carthage, Alexandria, Crete, and Constantinople, which he called, "beyond doubt, the metropolis of the Roman Empire." He had a splendid time and returned to Ireland strengthened in knowledge and faith.

Perhaps the West was bigger than the northwestern corner of the second-century Roman Empire. Perhaps our perception of the West as Latin Christendom alone, cut off from the Greek Orthodox and Muslim East, normal in Western Civilization textbooks, is too small. Arculf and Peter would probably agree. Even though the east-west divide became more compelling over the coming centuries, perhaps, if God is willing, it will melt away in the third millennium.

The Franks and the Lure of Empire

In western Germanic Europe in the sixth to the eighth centuries, civilization continued on as before. Cities, long-distance trade, and overall population declined, as did general literacy, but Latin lived on as the lingua franca of the Church in all her manifestations. Urban centers survived, although on a smaller scale. Some towns prospered. Villages and manors dotted the landscape of what was to become France, Italy, Germany, and the Low Countries, and functioned as autonomous, subsistence economies, producing and consuming according to their needs and capabilities. Statements by the manor's steward, prepared for the local ruling count, show the villagers' wide range of activities. Men and women made tools, weapons, pots, nets, cages, bedding, clothing, and shoes. They brewed beer, baked bread, and erected buildings. In addition to houses, there were cowsheds, sheepfolds, pigpens, chicken coops, stables for goats, oxen, and horses. Cultivated lands produced vegetables, herbs, fruits, honey, legumes, and grains. Some manors had fish ponds and others small mines for minerals. Security arrangements, as mentioned previously, were personal, not bureaucratic or legalistic. Where the plague of Rome's massive armies vanished, roving bands of disorderly raiders were the replacement pestilence. For those who would rather fight than work, who love violence over peace, plundering is the temptation that can become a way of life.

As we have seen, one group of thieves and warriors rises above the others in power, taking over, at least for a while. In the eighth century, the kings of the Franks subdued their neighbors and brought a greater measure of peace and unity to Germanic, Christian Europe. These kings built up an impressive cavalry of knights, heavily armed mounted warriors, whose equipment and expenses were covered by a land grant, called a fief or a benefice. Knights swore to protect their royal lord and join him during summer campaigns. A group of counts swore allegiance to the king and kept order in areas in which they themselves held no lands, making sure no rivals emerged. The leaders of the Church, the bishops and abbots, generally supported the Frankish regime, mainly by helping the counts with governance, keeping records, and settling disputes.

Frankish kings and counts usually respected the Church as a place of sanctuary, and protected her clergy and the faithful from grave danger. When a Germanic people called the Lombards invaded Italy in the eighth century, the Bishop of Rome (a.k.a. the Pope), universally recognized as the spiritual head of the Church (especially in the Latin West), called on the Franks for protection instead of the emperor in Constantinople. Southern Italy was nominally under Constantinople's control, but the emperor could not have done much to help. The Franks rescued the city of Rome and turned over a large portion of central Italy to the

Pope's exclusive governance. In return, the Pope anointed the Frankish king, bestowing a sacral character on the dignity of this, the greatest of Germanic chieftains.

This king, Charlemagne (Charles the Great), rose even higher still. During Christmas Day Mass in St. Peter's Basilica in Rome in the year 800, Pope Leo III crowned this tall, imposing Frankish warrior, and proclaimed him "Augustus," recalling the founder of the Roman principate. The imperial title Charlemagne preferred included the words, *a Deo coronatus,* "crowned by God." The Frankish king wanted all Christians to regard him not as a secular warlord but as God's chosen, his anointed leader and protector of the Christian faithful in the temporal world. It is questionable how many actually did. Accounts disagree about Charlemagne's comfort with the new dignity. Some say the pope had taken Charlemagne by surprise, plunking down a crown on his head while the king knelt in silent prayer during the liturgy, while others indicate that Charlemagne knew well what was coming as soon as he arrived in the city. For the rest of his reign, he was careful in his relations with the Roman (Byzantine) emperor who claimed the same, imperial dignity, nor did he wish to appear beholden to the pope for the imperial title.

The collaboration between pope and emperor was an expression of the hope that the confusion of the past centuries could come to a close, and that a new, Christian polity, based on Greco-Roman precedent, but limited and redeemed by Christian love, would reestablish peace and stability in the West – a holy empire. The hope remained unfulfilled for the next several centuries, but Charlemagne did his best in the time he had. He lavished the Church with bounteous generosity, both within his great realm and in the Holy Land, supporting the building of churches, charitable works, and educational initiatives. Through ambassadors he maintained friendly relations, for the most part, with the caliph in Baghdad and the emperor in Constantinople. But then, inevitably, there is the dark side of empire. By 800, Charlemagne had spent three decades subduing his rivals and suppressing rebellions in his borderlands with appalling brutality, particularly east of the Rhine. He greatly expanded the size of his realm and the number of its tributary peoples. He forced mass conversions to Christianity among the Saxons, on penalty of death. After his imperial coronation until his death in 814, the violence continued. The better name for Charlemagne's regime, therefore, is "the

Carolingian Empire," because it was based on Charlemagne's person, and particularly his name in Latin, Carolus. The Carolingian Empire, like all others, proved ephemeral, having given God adequate reason to do away with it.

Nonetheless, some historians speak of a "Carolingian Renaissance," implying that Greco-Roman culture had a kind of revival under Charlemagne. He did attract a circle of scholars to his palace in Aachen, and he ordered all monasteries and cathedral churches to teach reading and writing. He also commanded the monasteries to use a new, clear, legible script, known as Carolingian minuscule, and to produce fresh copies of Greek and Latin texts, which are now the main source of most knowledge of the so-called classical era. But Charlemagne's empire and rule was essentially military. Many of the bishops whom he enlisted in administering his vast realm accepted his regime's violence a little too readily, lived with too much opulence and wealth, and too closely resembled the counts, who were illiterate warriors like Charlemagne himself. (The Emperor spoke a number of languages, but never learned to write any of them.) More than a few bishops suspended a personal commitment to holiness when performing service for the emperor struck them as more compelling. They were merely Frankish warlords in ecclesiastical garb, who at times went into battle wielding maces instead of swords, as if it made a moral difference. Money, raw power, and prestige, while not evil in themselves, always bring with them the same temptations of old.

The Carolingian Empire went the way of all others. Charlemagne's enormous personal influence declined along with his vigor as age overtook him. Before his death, he managed to bequeath the empire as a whole to his son, but the generation after saw it partitioned, after much violence, according to traditional Germanic inheritance practice, which allots to each son a portion of his father's estate. In 843 the empire became three kingdoms, and then fell to pieces in the next century. Frankish quarreling and regional, ethnic rebellion aided the disintegration but were not the only causes.

Beginning in the late eighth century, the Vikings (a group that includes Danes, Norsemen, Northmen, and Normans) left their homes in Scandinavia and sailed the seas in their shallow ships, for reasons unknown. Historians speculate, attributing Viking movement to climate change, overpopulation, general restlessness, greed, or simple blood-lust, but only God knows why the Vikings took to sea. These fearsome fighters struck along much of the European coastline and penetrated as far as navigable rivers allowed, from Russia to Spain, from Ireland to Sicily. Most sought booty above all, and their primary victims were the hapless, defenseless monasteries and then the towns. Although these attacks were probably more destructive than the Germanic incursions of the fourth and fifth centuries, Latin Christendom was not about to go under.

For all the rampant destruction – sometimes Vikings spent the winter plundering entire regions – most people who lived far inland never saw a Viking in their lives. Nonetheless, to make matters worse, in addition to the Vikings, the Saracens (North-African Muslims) attacked Italy and southern France, and the Magyars, the ancestors of the Hungarians, drove deep into Germany and what is now eastern France, killing and pillaging with abandon. The combination of Frankish internecine warfare and Viking, Saracen, and Hungarian attacks inflicted nightmarish misery on many areas of Europe during the course of about two centuries, but the ninth and tenth centuries still pale in comparison with the hideous violence of the nineteenth and early twentieth centuries.

These crises also passed. God, the judge of nations, heard the cry of the poor and relented, punishing vile transgressors of his law. In the later tenth century, the Magyars retreated to the east and settled in Hungary, where their ancestors live today. The Saracen attacks subsided. In the northern reaches of France and England, the Viking invaders made themselves a home. The king of the western Franks actually invited them to settle in Normandy and use the area as a base to prevent other Vikings from plaguing his kingdom; the conciliatory policy worked. Yorkshire and the city of York became part of a dispersed Viking world stretching from Scandinavia over Iceland to Greenland, Newfoundland, and maybe even New England.

The West moved forward, even after it looked as if the world could not go further. Hardworking families with a strong desire to live led the recovery of communities. Despite the temporary reduction in trade, written communication, and coinage circulation, there were definite improvements. Northern European farmers used a heavy plow, drawn by oxen or horses, that cut deep into the clay soil and turned it over, increasing the fertility of the fields. The plows were superior to the lighter, pointed plows Greek and Roman farmers had used to break up the earth. Moreover, the normal system of planting one field and leaving the next fallow, so as not to exhaust the land, gradually changed into a three-field system, where one field had a winter crop of rye or wheat, another a summer crop of barley, oats, or legumes, and the third took a rest. Agricultural productivity rose. Fewer people suffered dearth, and work repaired the damage of war, pushed back the forests, and built new villages, allowing human civilization more room to grow, in new and different ways.

A New Era Comes

The moving peoples of the ninth and tenth centuries made empire impossible. Kings and emperors were simply unable to react with appropriate speed and effectiveness to Viking, Saracen, and Magyar attacks, so local leaders – counts, lords, knights, bishops, abbots, abbesses, and townsmen – took security matters into their own hands. Around the turn of the millennium, castles and fortresses sprang up across the face of Europe, on hilltops and bluffs, overlooking towns, fields, valleys, river mouths, and mountain passes. The proliferation of castles reflects the dissolution of a centralized, imperial order, but such structures also show people's willingness and wherewithal to deal with the heightened threat to security.

Church and secular authorities bestowed benefices and fiefs on knights and warriors for protection in exchange for necessary material support. Free, small farmers offered their goods and services to a lord for the same purpose, becoming vassals. Those who could give nothing but their labor became serfs, who lacked the right to leave their lord's lands as they wished, although they were not his enslaved personal possessions. Lords promised to "aid and sustain," and vassals promised to "serve and obey," for life. Lord-vassal bonds of personal loyalty and mutual support, usually stated in Christian terms of love and commitment and sworn over a Bible or a holy relic, suffused society at all levels, interweaving the spheres of the Church and secular government. Vassals of monasteries often swore allegiance to the patron saint of the institution, the spiritual person vested with real legal rights. If there was an actual structure to the so-called feudal system, it resembled a great web, in three dimensions, with a number of surges and peaks to represent higher concentrations of power and force. No standard, bureaucratic, hierarchical flowchart applied.

The Church, the community of those who endeavor to love God, was there for everybody and grew by virtue of her own spiritual strength. Most lords maintained a church on their lands for their vassals; it was the place for all members of the community to come together, for solace and jubilation, to mourn, give thanks, and praise. Most priests were probably part-time peasant farmers who knew how to perform the sacraments, and not much else. Low literacy limited Scripture reading, but that did not stop people from learning the stories of Jesus, his life, and ministry by heart. Christianity gave meaning to lives that had to suffer sickness, deprivation, pain, and fear. As the Vikings calmed and reduced their attacks, their paganism slowly gave way to the Christian faith of the European lands they conquered. By the new millennium, the Normans in northern France were as Catholic as anyone else in the Christian West. Later, missionaries, not conquering armies, brought the Christian faith to the Vikings' Scandinavian homelands. That great event, the gradual conversion of Europe's polytheistic peoples, left few records and few spectacular moments, but it certainly took place. In that instance, God's word accomplished what the Carolingian Empire could not.

The lesson of the half millennium beginning with the collapse of the Roman Empire in the fifth century A.D. is that God's ways are not our ways, but those who love and obey him will never fail. All across Western Europe, Christianity gave people a way to make amends and move forward into a better age. The faith gave form to culture. Its ardent belief in the spiritual sphere, in divine justice, love, and peace, and its embrace of self-giving, self-denying morality, shaped the West for centuries to come. No human crisis is so terrible as to break the power of prayer and expunge love from God's earth.

6

Christendom Consolidates

Thus says the Lord: You say, "The Lord's way is not fair!" Hear now, house of Israel: Is it my way that is unfair, or rather, are not your ways unfair? (Ezekiel 18:25)
Repay to Caesar what belongs to Caesar, and to God what belongs to God. (Mark 12:17)

From the tenth to the fourteenth centuries, after the recovery from Viking, Saracen, and Magyar attacks, God propelled the West further along the twisting spiral of history, into a period of exceptional growth, vitality, and consolidation, based on Christian faith in him. The population grew, towns expanded, culture flourished in its Christian context, and even the climate turned a bit milder and warmer, conducive to greater fertility on the land. But humanity did not change. Our failure to love God above all resulted, as before, in violence, banditry, and all other failings in state and society. In this period, however, the evil came mainly from within; there were no foreign attackers on whom to blame general wickedness. Christendom's knightly class above all was as much a cancer as a guarantor of local safety. Emperors, kings, and some popes may have made progress in imposing their peace on wayward vassals, but the warlike means they used may not have been worth the effort.

Just as the period 500–900 was not dark, except in terms of our relative historical ignorance because of the general paucity of written sources, nor were the next four hundred years "medieval," meaning middle. Every era in human history is in the middle of what was and what will come to be. The only time truly in the middle is this present moment, which in the blink of an eye moves into the past, making way for the as-yet unknown future. The tenth to the fourteenth centuries stand on their own, firmly connected to the millennia before and the millennia to come. There was no down-time, no muddling hiatus between the glories of "ancient" Greece and Rome and the improvements, both real and imagined, of the "modern era." The tenth to the fourteenth centuries we may call the Feudal Age, because of the distinctive way people ordered their lives. The Feudal Age had taken centuries to come into being and would go out of practice in the era that followed it.

The Feudal Age

The Feudal Age, as people lived it, bears for us an important truth: God uses human history as an antidote to the false promise of political unity. As much as God loves humanity, his gratuitous, unrestricted gift of human freedom ensures that there can be no perfected government on earth, Christian or otherwise. Violence mars humanity in all ages. All forms of worldly power are potentially unjust, and whether government structures are centralizing or fragmenting ultimately does not make any difference in God's plan for human salvation. Wielders of power shape some of the crosses souls have to bear, and most are of our own making. Christians can measure the success or failure of an era according to the fruits of its culture, the extent to which it glorifies the Father Almighty, and the incidence of true devotion, repentance, and forgiveness among peoples. These last are difficult to measure, but that is no reason not to look for them.

Europe's common identity as a continent is a result more of Christianity than geography; Europe is, after all, only the western end of Eurasia. During the Feudal period, the Christian faith brought more unity to Europe than any political or military order could. Christendom, the domain of Christian peoples, widened to the east and north. Even as the Roman (Byzantine) Empire sharply retracted, the Slavic peoples of Eastern Europe and Russia adopted the Christian faith and began to reshape their cultures accordingly, giving them new values, forms, and practices. In the West, Christianity traveled further north into Scandinavia, and in the western parts of the former Roman Empire, a revived interest in Greco-Roman learning brought new life, and new challenges, to the inheritance of Israel. In the tenth to the fourteenth centuries, the West identified itself as Christendom, lands where orthodox Christianity was the religion of the clear majority, Catholic in the Latin West, and Orthodox in the Greek East. The faith nourished a scintillating, vibrant set of intermingling cultures, all devoted to God, in their imperfect, human way.

For Better and for Worse: Church, State, and Warfare

Worldly power in the form of political unity is a primal temptation. In the Gospel story of Jesus' forty-day fast in the desert, the devil offers him *all the kingdoms of the world in their magnificence,* in exchange for his devotion. But Jesus replies, *Get away, Satan! It is written: 'The Lord your God shall you worship and him alone shall you serve'* (Matthew 4:8–11). The story of Babel in the Old Testament tells us the same thing. God filled the world with diversity, and he wants it that way, then, now, and forever. Political unity, it seems, demands blood as its price. The Romans had unified the Mediterranean and western Europe as no other regime had—it was possible to travel from southern Scotland to the Holy Land using Roman roads, post horses and carts, and Latin—but the political order thrived on ruthless oppression. Conquest had built the Carolingian Empire, but she differed with Rome in terms of size and governmental system.

The political history of the tenth to the fourteenth centuries is continued testimony to man's addiction to sin, through misuse of his freedom. The Church was as much a part of the problem as the "state." Leaders of both quite often made horrible errors, due especially to their misplaced desire to renew the Roman Empire. After the Vikings, Saracens, and Magyars unraveled the tenuous Carolingian imperial order, a dynasty of Saxon princes in northern Germany put the Roman Empire back on the pedestal, this time as ostensibly "Holy." In the mid-tenth century, Otto I subdued the dukes of the major German ethnic groups, the Bavarians, the Swabians, the Franconians, and others, and smashed the marauding Magyars at the Battle of Lechfeld in 955. Otto found his greatest support not among the Germans he crushed, but among the bishops and abbots, who longed for a powerful source of authority to protect them, their holdings, and their vassals and serfs against Magyar attacks. The combination of fear and landed wealth made leaders of the Church susceptible to the imperial temptation. When Pope John XII, who had received his office from the local warlord at the age of eighteen, floundered in his effort to expand the papal state at the expense of his neighbors, he dangled the imperial dignity in Otto's direction. The Saxon prince invaded, subdued northern Italy, reasserted Pope John's authority over the city of Rome, and became Holy Roman Emperor.

One could argue that bishops and abbots who supported the new Emperor were merely being reasonable; they wanted peace in the localities and unity across Christendom. The Roman Emperor in Constantinople took umbrage at the notion that there should be one like him in Rome, but there was nothing he could do about it. Emperors and kings of Western Europe, basically warlords blessed, crowned, and anointed with holy oils, attacked their enemies with glee, but showed limited engagement in matters of government in the localities. Their main interest was in ensuring that enough knights and retainers were available for battle. The imperial title was rather limited; Otto may have been the first among Christian kings in terms of ceremonial prestige, but his official position meant little to rulers of different parts of Europe. Other kings, dukes, and counts around Europe paid heed to the Holy Roman Emperor only if he drew near at the head of an army. The Emperor tended to remain in central Europe anyway, where he endeavored to keep the Germans under heel and indulged his greed for more territory in Italy. This was his primary occupation for centuries.

Unfortunately, local lords in the West, the knightly order of society, emulated the violence of emperors and kings. In the tenth and eleventh centuries, the depredations of the roaming Vikings, Saracens, and Magyars seemed to settle and take root in the feudal system. The petty lords and knights abused their power over the local countryside even as the threat from without receded. Skulking in their dank fortresses, some attacked merchant caravans for booty, took prisoners for ransom, and plundered neighboring Church lands, burning down peasants' houses and stealing animals, with relative impunity. Few people minded if the knights spent their energy and spilled their blood fighting each other for honor's sake on an open field. But attacks against the innocent and the helpless were unacceptable. Something had to be done.

Beginning in 989 in central France, some virtuous, bold cathedral priests and bishops came together and proclaimed the "Peace of God" against knightly criminals. Any lord or knight who acted like a thief, kidnapper, or thug toward the poor, the humble, or the clergy, male or female, would suffer excommunication, or removal from the Church, which was a terrible sentence during this time. The guilty could not partake in any of the sacraments and were declared subject to eternal damnation. In a time when virtually everyone believed in the Last Judgment, and when death often cut life short at a young age, especially among full-time fighters, excommunication denied to ostensibly Christian knights their expected heavenly banquet after falling in battle. It also absolved vassals of their feudal vows to serve and protect their lord. Very few thought they could afford to take excommunication lightly.

To drive the point home, Church leaders gathered and displayed all the holy relics they could, bodily remnants of the martyrs and saints, the innocent who had suffered political savagery for the sake of God's word. Bishops invited lords and knights to attend an outdoor proclamation of the Peace, where the knights were to forswear such behavior before the gathered community. Soon Church leaders added the "Truce of God" to the Peace – this was a sign of confidence at initial success – which forbade all knightly fighting on Sundays, holy days, and all of Lent and Advent. For the Church, it was simply intolerable that Christians should mutilate and butcher each other for enjoyment, but the frequency with which the Peace and the Truce were repeated gives us an idea about their general ineffectiveness in pacifying members of the knightly order. They were still formally entitled to attack clergymen, if the latter were armed, and to burn down anyone's house if an enemy knight or noblemen had taken refuge inside.

Knightly greed and brutality in Europe, when mixed with religious enthusiasm, led to the notorious Crusades. Across Christendom, the lords' younger sons knew they would receive none of their fathers' estate and sought fortune in terribly illegitimate ways. Sending these younger sons to drive non-Christians out of Spain and to wrest the Holy Land

from Muslim control seemed a practical and defensible policy, even if
it entailed many, many crimes against humanity. Church leaders played
an instrumental role in fomenting these ugly wars, and thousands of
Christians supported them. In the early eleventh century, Benedictine
monks, who had founded new houses south of the Pyrenees, invited
nobles from northern France to attack the Muslims in Spain. French
knights ended up fighting both Spanish Muslims and local Christians,
neither of whom wanted them there in the first place. In general, Spanish
Christian knights of the kingdoms of Castile, Leon, Navarre, and Aragon
fought each other at least as much as their southern, Muslim neighbors
or the Norman French crusaders. The knights' purpose was to fight; they
did not need or adhere to a grand strategy. Norman knights also threw
the Saracens out of Sicily, and the Pope rewarded the victor with a royal
title. Ever restless, the Normans went on to take control of southern Italy
away from the emperor in Constantinople.

Is this what Almighty God wants of his beautiful, human creation?
Perennial bloodshed among those who ostensibly worship him? Beginning
in 1095, Pope Urban II preached in France the first of the Crusades
directed against the Holy Land. He explicitly cited the need to alleviate
Europe's knightly brutality. He also proclaimed the Peace and Truce of
God, which were undeniably good, but he promoted military assistance
for the Roman (Byzantine) forces fighting the Seljuk Turks, migrant
conquerors from Central Asia who had taken Syria and Palestine. Those
who went, the Pope said, and gave their lives in the effort, would receive
automatic forgiveness of their sins, no matter how odious. "Let those
who have been accustomed to make private war against the faithful
carry on to a successful issue a war against infidels.... Let those who
for a long time have been robbers now become soldiers of Christ. Let
those who once fought against brother and relatives now fight against
barbarians, as they ought." Urban cared more about sending the wolves
into neighboring pastures than getting them under control in his own. He
and his successors with similar views suffered the blindness of the age.

One can make the argument that war can actually be an act of charity,
especially if one wages it on behalf of a neighbor unjustly attacked. But
the Crusades, which continued for centuries in various parts of Europe
and the Mediterranean rim, merely demonstrate that war is in most cases
a useless human folly, a love of the blasphemy of destruction, rather
than love of the God who is love. History is so full of examples that

one would think humanity could learn the lesson. But our fallen nature prevents us. The Crusades were temporary, improvised diversions for the relentlessly aggressive, and base perversions of Christ's teachings. Jesus never recommended resorting to arms. Some Crusades succeeded, in the sense that Christian lords seized control over lands and local people from Muslims, but most failed, because Muslim armies took back the Holy Land. Armies were small in size, rarely in excess of 10,000, and far more died from disease than combat. The fact that so many in the West supported the ventures makes us shake our heads in disapproval, but then again, given recent history, who on earth are we to judge?

The Crux of Centralization

One of the dominant themes in histories of the West is the growth of government after the fall of the Roman Empire and the ensuing five hundred years of alleged darkness. The usual narrative generally implies that Rome's conquest of Europe and the Mediterranean was a good thing, and that what came after was regrettable, in a barbaric, uncivilized kind of way, until the growth of governmental institutions eventually restored the order that had been lost. From the eleventh century on, so the story goes, France, Spain, and England developed more quickly, centralizing authority in national monarchies, which eventually reaped the reward of expansion overseas. Germany and Italy, however, supposedly lagged behind, and their retarded development into nation-states basically caused twentieth-century World Wars. Such a story undergirds the pernicious prejudice that centralization of power and the violence that maintains it is inherently better than its fragmentation. People everywhere and in all times wield power justly and unjustly; they use it as much as they abuse it. Because we cannot match God in his justice, we will forever be unfair even as we mean to be fair; human justice is rough. For good and for evil, power and authority centralized to some degree from the tenth to the fourteenth centuries in Christendom. Greater lords were usually better able to stop relentless squabbling among the lesser, but the more powerful the prince, the more damage he could do.

Beginning in France, which had the largest population of any Christian kingdom, kings slowly built up a bureaucratic administration of justice in their own estates around Paris. Gradually they projected that power over most of the rest of the country, usually in the name of imposing the king's justice on warring noblemen, in the interest of peace. It is difficult, however, to speak of any progress when the whole of the kingdom was torn to shreds by the Hundred Years' War, an extended, bloody quarrel with the kings of England, beginning in the fourteenth century. England, while smaller in area and population, was all the more centralized, especially after William, Duke of Normandy, invaded in 1066, seized the throne, and murdered the Anglo-Saxon nobility in the next few years. William's barons and knights quickly erected castles to overawe the local landowners and peasants. By the fourteenth century, the kings of England put together small armies and rampaged across France, in a long, vain effort to take that crown, too, as if one were not enough.

The popes played an important role in the process of centralization during this period, attempting to take on the role of supreme legal authority in Christendom. From their own standpoint, they were always trying to improve a bad situation. In the tenth century, the papacy reached its nadir as warlords and German monarchs handed the papal office to personal friends, important clients, or submissive flatterers, a number of whom were in their early twenties and showed little interest in either religion or morality. The debaucheries of John XII are the stuff of legend, while a holy pope, such as Stephen VIII, who was devoted to God in public and private life and committed to peace, suffered a horrible, tortuous death for daring to stand up to the emperor and his strongmen. A series of brave, avid reforming popes tried to change all that in the eleventh and twelfth centuries, but their efforts tragically led to gruesome conflict more often than not.

God does not want his Church to lord over nations in the manner of kings and governments. In the late eleventh and early twelfth centuries, popes took on emperors and kings in the so-called Investiture Controversy, a long, terrible fight over the right to invest bishops with authority. Monarchs until and during that time all too often appointed their warlord friends and court cronies as bishops of the biggest, richest dioceses, and handed them their rings and crosiers, the symbols of their special, spiritual authority. This practice was a flagrant transgression of the apostolic succession in practice, the method by which bishops, overseers of the Church, selected their successors and passed on their traditional authority across the ages. And the papacy, reforming churchmen believed, was not a fat prize for the emperor to give to anyone, let alone an adolescent. On the other hand, the dioceses bishops commanded were immense land holdings with vassals, serfs, knights, and castles, and the bishops controlled their finances and administered justice. The bishops had helped the monarch to assert his legal authority over petty warlords all throughout his realm for centuries. This was true for France and England, but more so in the Holy Roman Empire. If the emperor let the pope pick the leaders of the dioceses, he would have literally handed about a third to a half of the Holy Roman Empire over to Rome.

All involved behaved atrociously. Early on in the quarrel, the popes proclaimed the legal right to depose emperors, kings, and other princes who degraded Christ's Church. They triumphantly cited Christ's commission to Peter: *And I say to you, you are Peter, and upon this rock I will build my church, and the gates of the netherworld shall not prevail against it. I will give you the keys to the kingdom of heaven. Whatever you bind on earth shall be bound in heaven; and whatever you loose on earth shall be loosed in heaven.* (Matthew 16:19–20) Popes lacked the armaments to enforce their will with violence, and the emperor and the kings tended to ignore them and proceed with investing bishops of their choice as before. But the monarchs had plenty of unruly vassals, who only too gladly rose up in armed rebellion after a pope slapped on a sentence of excommunication, thereby dissolving all feudal oaths and ties between the condemned monarch and his people. This happened on numerable occasions. Emperors who attacked Rome and kidnapped the pope, installing a fraud on the papal throne in his place, did not help the situation.

The storm finally calmed with a reasonable, obvious compromise that should have been forged in the beginning. At the Diet of Worms in 1122, the Emperor Henry V agreed to keep his hands off the bishop's ring and crosier, while Pope Calixtus II accepted that the Emperor would be present at the consecration and take care of handing over the realm's fiefs to the newly installed bishop in a separate ceremony. Both were to agree on candidates, before, during, and after. Bishops were to be amenable to the reigning monarch, and yet competent and qualified for the spiritual post. The kings of France and England soon arrived at similar arrangements.

This settlement is so natural, so obvious, one can ask what the fighting was all for. In the last years of the crisis, one daring, visionary pope,

Pascal II, suggested the best and most beautiful and radical solution of all: bishops should give up their *regalia,* all properties and legal powers in the Holy Roman Empire, and serve as spiritual pastors and overseers of the Church alone. They should live simply, in their given diocese, and cover Church expenses using the tithe, the church tax, levied on all the faithful, and nothing else. They were not to lord it over territories in the manner of princes. Roman cardinals and German bishops, most of them from princely families, reacted with horrified disbelief. A Church outside the feudal system, without fiefs, benefices, lords, and vassals, made no sense to them, and they were probably too vain, proud, and greedy to live in humble service anyway.

Elsewhere in Europe, centralization took place at the local level, rather than higher up. In the Holy Roman Empire, the German emperors squandered their resources fighting the popes and other Italian rulers for dominance of the Church, Sicily, and southern Italy, while German princes basically disregarded the emperor's authority at home. In 1356, warring parties in Germany settled their differences, for the time being, with the Golden Bull, a document that rendered the imperial title an electoral dignity, bestowed by seven electors within the Empire – a king, a duke, a marquis, a count, and three archbishops – with no voice for the pope at all. While the emperor retained a special legal authority and the highest ceremonial prestige, his power was more akin to a referee than an enforcer. The seven electors ruled their lands as sovereigns, undiminished by other authorities, and the rest of the Holy Roman Empire became a loose association of principalities, bishoprics, monastic lands, and free cities.

Other parts of Europe showed similar, workable patterns for the distribution of governing power. Italy was just as divided, with the pope dominating a large estate in the middle. Poland, which converted to Christianity during the tenth and eleventh centuries, was as diffuse as the Holy Roman Empire, if not more so, and the Iberian peninsula was sharply divided into at least five kingdoms, those of Portugal, Castile, Leon, Navarre, and Aragon, and a county in Barcelona. Ireland, Scotland, and Scandinavia showed a similar pattern of control by local chieftains instead of centralized authority. There are many ways for people to organize communities and divide authority. One form is not automatically superior to another; all depend on local circumstances and culture. None save people from the errors born of misaligned affections.

The Papal Monarchy and the Church

The Church in the Feudal Age tried to follow God's will, but its leadership grew to resemble the worldly monarchies more than the Kingdom of God on earth as Jesus described. The Church in the world lurches from crisis to crisis, making one mistake after another, usually in the effort to right a wrong or stop an abuse. But this is the nature of man, not God, and he will not abandon her, despite all the flaws of her members, until history draws to a close.

Naturally the highest level of authority in the Church had the greatest ability to work both good and evil. In the twelfth and thirteenth centuries, the popes reached the zenith of worldly power and influence, by means of the most "advanced" legal and financial bureaucratic machinery in the West. Popes declared crusades, levied taxes on all parts of the Church, and shaped the papal court into a kind of supreme law court for handling legal appeals from across the face of Europe. It was all well intended. The bishop of Rome wanted to be able to dispense justice to anyone in Christendom suffering oppression. This is, however, humanly impossible. The law's delay and the snares of money all too often turn competence into corruption. Nonetheless, historians today trace human rights theory and other aspects of "modern" law in the work of twelfth-century canon law professors and clerks.

One of the most famous and controversial lawyer-popes of the era, Innocent III, a brilliant, energetic individual, a lover of both justice and the exalted nature of his office, very much a man of his age, makes the case in point. Innocent settled many disputes among princes equitably and peaceably, but others he made far worse. He called and presided over the Fourth Lateran Council in 1215, which for the sake of orthodoxy clarified and codified Catholic doctrine, liturgy, and canon law, addressing the questions and needs of the day. He also instituted the Inquisition to enforce orthodoxy in areas where people had tired of ecclesiastical arrogance and shaped the faith according to their own preferences. In its educational mission, there was nothing wrong with the Inquisition, and in its rational, judicial procedure, it certainly seemed a real improvement over customary, Germanic trials by ordeal. The Inquisition's use of secular authorities, however, to carry out dire physical punishments for the recalcitrant sent it down the wrong road. With awful regularity, when inquisitors and local authorities authorized the use of torture in interrogations, confessions and further accusations multiplied, and heresy crises spun out of control. This is the opposite of what Innocent hoped to achieve. At the same time, Innocent supported two new movements in the Church, led by two truly holy men, Sts. Francis of Assisi and Dominic, for reviving gospel values among the faithful. Innocent's crusades, however, in the Holy Land and Europe, were unmitigated nightmares.

The nature of the papal office at the end of the thirteenth century teaches a lesson about what happens when high moral authority merges with enormous financial and destructive power. But what could anyone do about it? Holy men who loved God above all struggled terribly in that position. At the close of the thirteenth century, after the death of the reigning pope, the assembled cardinals could not decide on a successor for over two years, because the usual local Roman aristocratic rivalries divided them. Finally, the cardinals heard word of a holy hermit who had prophesied the direst consequences if they left the Church without a leader. They elected the hermit unanimously. The eighty-five-year-old Celestine V left his cave in the mountains and came to Rome on the back of a donkey. After five months he walked out in disgust, relinquishing his titles. The next pope promptly locked him up, but Celestine escaped and went into hiding. Caught again, he died in a castle tower. Realization of the terrible power of the office, coupled with its subjection to the influence of worldly monarchs, cardinals, and bishops, had been too much for this simple man of God.

Historians commonly speak of the rise and fall of a papal monarchy, or of a papal attempt to establish a theocracy in Europe, but both obscure the fact that the highest leadership of the Church was dead wrong to play power politics. In doing so they too gave into the demonic temptation of worldly power. Histories and historians (including myself) waste far too much ink on the misdeeds and skullduggery of the powerful. The fact that we do is testimony to the human weakness for lurid tales of vile behavior.

God's Holy Spirit sustains the Church, despite her failings, in every age. The hopelessly wealthy papacy weathered one meltdown after another, but the Church was so much greater than the little papal court in the city of Rome. The common conception of the Church during this period was as the living body of Christ, entailing all the faithful, the whole community of all Christians in this world and the next. The vast majority of souls in Christendom, knew, saw, heard, and read nothing from or about the pope. Most people who visited Rome were not petitioners who wanted to see the pope but pilgrims wanting to pray at Rome's shrines, especially those of Peter and Paul. Most people considered St. Peter's intercession more effective than his successor's, whoever he happened to be. In spite of some of the popes, cardinals, bishops, and abbots, the Church thrived, all across Christendom. God regularly uses imperfect people, insufficient instruments, to do his work on earth. During a papal election, the Holy Spirit does not tell the cardinals to pick this or that character, especially in the cases where they turned out to be wanton criminals, but at the same time, God does not let things get totally out of hand. God keeps the Church on a long leash, so to speak, and just as her leaders are about to strangle themselves, the Spirit snatches them back from the deathly precipice they are dashing towards. The history of the West shows that no matter how bad things become for the community of Christian prayer, it will not fail or go under. The Church survives any and all crises, and she is never without one. Sometimes they are worse, sometimes not so terrible, but the Church's members are never without need for improvement. And whenever she comes through a particularly wrenching difficulty, she is usually the better for it, for a while.

A Christian Culture

In spite of the failings of the secular and ecclesiastical elite, the faithful of the West, and all of Christendom actually, produced a vibrant, beautiful Christian culture in the tenth to the fourteenth centuries. Groups and individuals worked in manifold ways to give faith in God unity and wholeness. "Culture" in English (i.e., the way groups of people do things), comes from the Latin *cultus*, which can refer to labor, training, refinement, and reverence. Human culture reflects all these things. In the first place, a given people's practice and object of worship reflects their understanding of reality and value. People show through their work, discipline, focus, and concentration what they truly revere. If they hold nothing of greater value than money and material possessions, with scarcely a thought given to extenuating circumstances, such as pollution, exploitation, greed, immodesty, injustice, death, and the afterlife, then their culture will show as much. If God is a mere personal perception, then they will not build their greatest monuments to his honor.

Christian culture in this period showed its spectacular energy in terms of quantity and extent. Beginning in the Greek East, the Roman Emperor in the ninth century sent two missionaries, Cyril and Methodius, to convert the Slavic peoples who had entered the Balkans two centuries earlier. The stupendous success of their mission can only be attributed to God's grace. The two missionaries brought the Gospel and the Greek Orthodox liturgy to the Serbs and others, and devised for them an alphabet, Cyrillic, based on Greek letters, and a written language, Old Church Slavonic, which served the Church in Eastern Europe for centuries to come. From the ninth to the eleventh centuries, dedicated missionaries brought Latin Christianity to Viking peoples from Scandinavia to the northern British Isles, Iceland, and Greenland. East of German-speaking regions, Poles, Bohemians (Czechs), Moravians, Hungarians, and Croats converted as well, in a missionary venture supported by both the Holy Roman Emperor and the Pope, and blessed by God. Bishops who went to serve among these people were loyal to Rome. During the same span of time, Byzantine missionaries carried the Slavic rite they had developed in the Balkans to Bulgaria, to Kiev, in what is now Ukraine, and further north into Russia. Clergy in these regions were answerable to the Patriarch of Constantinople. While Rome and Constantinople differed in terms of language and liturgy, their creed was essentially the same, but for one word about the Trinity. The pope, the patriarch, and their ranks of theologians regarded each other with more suspicion than brotherly love, but usually exercised a degree of restraint.

Nonetheless, a long history of squabbling, the rise of the Holy Roman Empire, the reduction of the Roman Empire in the Greek East, and the intense competition for souls in missionary efforts led the Latin West and the Greek East to go their separate ways. Both sides accused the other, rightly, of shameful arrogance and hard-heartedness. God's love, as embodied in the living Church, makes use of deeply flawed human instruments. Human foibles frequently strain the love of Christ, even between siblings in faith, leading to sad estrangement. The quarrel about the derivation of the Holy Spirit in the ninth century culminated in an eastern synod excommunicating the pope for about a dozen years. Two centuries later, a fit of papal high-handedness led to the excommunication of the eastern patriarch—and even the Roman Emperor. The split gave rise to hideous abuse when the Fourth Crusade, dispatched by Innocent III toward the Holy Land, instead unleashed its terror on Constantinople, crippling the Eastern Roman Empire in 1204. Eventually the Ottoman Turks would take Constantinople in 1453, finally bringing the Roman regime to an end. Freed from the Roman Emperors but subjected now to Muslim overlords, the Greek Orthodox Church followed her own historical stream, which may meet again, some day, with that of the orthodox Catholic Church in the third millennium, if God so wills it.

In the West, however, nothing exemplifies and testifies to vibrant, Christian culture like building. After the Viking, Saracen, and Magyar attacks subsided, an explosion of church building established cathedrals in bishops' main towns, parish churches in many others, and chapels and oratories across the countryside. By the mid-eleventh century, the city of Rome, with a population of about twenty-five thousand, boasted as many as two hundred churches. Under the Roman Empire, monumental building had been largely standardized in the Greco-Roman classical style, from Britain to the Holy Land. After the fall of the Empire, Roman basilicas and the related Romanesque style had persisted through the Germanic Age until the twelfth century, when a brand-new style began to bloom.

At the Abbey of St. Denis, near Paris, Abbot Suger oversaw working sheets of translucent stained glass into the stone walls, with delicate stone tracery, pointed arches, with vaulted ceilings to lighten the heavy, almost fortress-like quality of the Romanesque. Gothic architecture allows nature's outside light to create a mysterious, multi-colored world within. Stone masons make tall, sharp pinnacles bud with crockets, and windows burst into leaf. Fluted columns soar upwards, taking the eye and the soul with them. The vast majority of the great Gothic cathedrals of Europe were completed or at least begun by the fourteenth century, in France, England, the Low Countries, and Germany. Far too many to name, some of the most glorious examples are Notre Dame at Paris and the cathedrals at Amiens, Reims, Chartres, Wells, Lincoln, Salisbury, Cologne, Strasbourg, Regensburg, Prague, and Vienna. No matter where they were constructed, these entailed tremendous projects taken on voluntarily. Episcopal and civic authorities who began them knew they would probably not live to see their completion. They used local materials, wherever possible, and relied on local labor. No slaves or impressed workers were involved. In that way, they put the Roman

Empire to shame. While there was and is nothing wrong with the Roman and Romanesque style of building, Gothic reflects the welcoming of new life and light into the Christian faith.

Feudal Heights

Historians traditionally refer to this period as the High Middle Ages, and while the "High" is fully deserved, because of such cultural achievements, the "Middle" is off the mark and basically meaningless. As we have noted earlier, all people everywhere live in the middle—between the past and the future. Every age is the middle age. Terms like "Early," "High," and "Late" Middle Ages, while not without grounds, mainly sustain the prejudice that these centuries matter less in the story of the West than what came before or after. No one at the time, during the tenth to the early fourteenth centuries, thought that they were living suspended between more important periods. To insist on five hundred to a thousand years of Middle Ages is to grant tacitly that the bookends, so to speak, deserve greater attention. As we have seen, the Roman Empire never left the scene. In the Greek East, it lasted till 1453, and in the West it came back as dubiously "Holy," but still less centralized and oppressive than the original.

The "classical" eras of Greece and Rome are emphatically not the standard by which we should measure all cultures in the great story of the West. In Italy, however, a group of scholars in the fourteenth and fifteenth centuries articulated a dismissive, arrogant attitude that persists to this day: that the preceding thousand-odd years separating them and the last phase of the Roman Empire had been a dim, barbarous waste of time. Such scholars included the Latin poet laureate, Petrarch, Leonardo Bruni (whom we met earlier), called by some "the first modern historian," and the cohort of rarified intellectuals who followed in their wake. In addition to fondness for their own compositions, these men were elite lovers of a certain kind of Latin language and literature, namely those from the first century B.C. through the second century A.D. These Italian scholars, whom we now call "humanists," are largely responsible for the general periodization of Western history we still find standard today.

For those historians who tell the story of the West in terms of art, architecture, and technology, this terminology might make some sense. Achievement in Roman building—such as the aqueducts, the amphitheaters, and the great dome of the Pantheon—were unsurpassed for many centuries. But Roman technology was in other ways rather pathetic. Content to rely on masses of human labor, no one in the Roman Empire seems to have bothered to design a decent shoulder yoke for oxen and horses to maximize their pulling strength. A collar that tended to choke the beast of burden seemed to suffice. Roman cavalry never benefited from the simple stirrup, which the Frankish cavalry first exploited in the eighth century: The stirrup allows the rider to leverage his entire body weight in downward strikes with handheld weapons; from his greater height, such mounted fighters enjoyed a distinct advantage over infantrymen. The windmill, a brilliant advance in harnessing natural energy for productive purposes, came into use in France, England, and the Low Countries only in the twelfth century. Eyeglasses were developed in thirteenth-century Italy, and the magnetic compass came into use throughout the Mediterranean at about the same time. Gothic cathedrals relied on improvements in glasswork and window frames. Some group of clever individuals devised the mechanical clock in the early fourteenth century. In the realm of things, Rome was not the last word. Regarding people, it is true that the sizes of the Roman army remained unsurpassed until perhaps the reign of Louis XIV in France in the seventeenth century, but raw numbers of men at arms merely indicate the capacity to destroy.

The eleventh to the fourteenth centuries were feudal, not medieval. All political, legal, and financial bonds between people were essentially personal; bureaucracy had only just begun to make its case as a possible alternative. Government was never separated from the individuals who did the ruling. Order, therefore, was totally human, although the abstract constructs of Roman jurisprudence were starting to return. Everyone had a place in the world, and people were individual souls, not units of "society" – the word did not even appear in English usage until the sixteenth century – from the lowliest serf to the pope and the emperor. In an age without personal IDs and paperwork, everything depended on and happened through personal connections. Despite its limitations, we can see that it worked in that it endured such a long time and transformed only very slowly into something rather different.

The Feudal Age that grew out of the marriage of Roman and Germanic cultures, blessed by the Church, found its meaning and inspiration first and foremost in God, all the more because of the aristocrats' moral failings. Eleventh-, twelfth-, and thirteenth-century Christendom bustled with all kinds of worthy activity. Monasteries, real cultural centers in the holistic sense of the word, continued to serve for spiritual, artistic, agricultural, and industrial production. Thousands of houses sprang up across the face of Europe, founded by the Cluniacs, the Cistercians, and other orders that stemmed from St. Benedict's *Rule,* and by the Carthusians, who looked back to the hermitic traditions of the Middle East. The word "conversion" referred not so much to taking on a new religion – the overwhelming majority subscribed to orthodox, Catholic Christianity anyway – as to turning away from the secular life, taking the tonsure or the habit, and joining a monastery or a convent: becoming a "religious." People regarded monks as servants and soldiers of God, whose prayers helped to keep the world from going under. Monastic poverty, chastity, and obedience stood in stark contrast to the world's usual lust for money, enslavement to sensuality and sexuality, and self-destructive willfulness. The devil, the personification of evil, was very real to these people, as he had been to Jesus Christ, and to do God's work meant to fight the devil, both spiritually, in the reformation of one's own heart, and through a prayerful, devout life.

Most lords gave land to monastic houses and foundations, and most people wanted monks living nearby. Monasteries served as beacons of hope in a world, like unto ours, in constant need of consolation. The great monastic estates of the Holy Roman Empire, while not without the daily worries and nuisances of governance, tended to be peaceful, free of violent upheaval, and dedicated to the holistic, spiritual and secular well-being of their inhabitants. Abbots, abbesses, and bishops acted as stewards, not owners, of the monasteries' great and expanding landed wealth. They patronized and sustained art, music, literature, and the pursuit of knowledge and education in all forms, and God's wisdom suffused them with uplifting ideas and ideals.

Moving expressions of religious piety characterized the age. It was commonplace for people to go on pilgrimage to a local shrine. People joined confraternities, usually dedicated to a saint, for communal prayer, celebration of sacraments and festivals, community service, and mutual support. For most, holiness was a perfectly respectable goal in life, and not eccentric in most cases. For many, holiness became a set of rituals, prayers, services of worship, songs, and gestures, which gave life meaning in all its moments, good and bad. For others, holiness could also, in part, be purchased and brought home, in the form of a relic, book, carved figurine, or painting. Such behavior easily fell into superstition and invited unscrupulous abuse, but the faith, its creed and sacraments, was strong nonetheless and did not stumble into disrepute for the most part.

Population grew, thousands of villages seemed to sprout out of the soil, and scores became solid, busy little towns, most with only a few thousand inhabitants. Peasants cleared areas of forest for cultivation, drained fens and marshes, and made marginal lands fruitful. Towns purchased surplus agricultural products and readily absorbed young people, often runaway serfs, looking for a life away from the feudal manor or family farm. Walled urban centers usually governed themselves, largely independent of the local lord or bishop, and they hosted a wide variety of handcraft industries and served as centers for mercantile activity. Associations of merchants and craftsmen formed guilds that regulated commerce and exercised quality control. Northern Italy and the Low Countries led the pack in terms of urban density, with northern France, southern England, and the Hansa cities of northern Germany not far behind, but prosperity spread as well from Portugal to the Baltic coast, from Scotland to Sicily.

Business activity expanded and diversified. In central France, the counts of Champagne hosted wildly successful fairs, six every year, where traders brought and exchanged their goods – woolen cloth, spices, wine, and luxuries – from all across Europe. Merchant ventures became more complex and adventuresome, and financiers devised double-entry accounting (debit and credit), insurance, and joint-stock companies to share the risks. They did their best to loan money and invest it rationally, and they devised ways to charge interest (usury) in a Christian culture that absolutely condemned the practice. Banks grew in wealth and range of operations, exchanging currencies, issuing bills of exchange, giving "gifts" for deposits, and issuing bonds, not with interest but for higher sums than they had actually loaned. Priests, monks, and friars fulminated against usury in all guises, but bishops, popes, and kings did almost nothing against it. Indeed, they were some of the biggest clients.

The twelfth and thirteenth centuries also saw an expansion in education, to the extent that some historians speak of a "twelfth-century renaissance." It involved an enhanced interest in classical thought and learning, Aristotelian philosophy in particular, but only so far as it could be reconciled with Christian belief in the search for truth. In the first place, it involved higher study. In addition to the grammar schools at convents, monasteries, and cathedrals, groups of scholars teaching at a more advanced level gave lectures: in Latin rhetoric and civil law for those aspiring to be lawyers working for governments; in theology and canon law for those aiming for positions in the Church's administration; and in medicine for those wanting to assist the sick. The rediscovery and reproduction of Emperor Justinian's sixth-century compilations of Roman law gave legal scholars new impetus in their attempts to regularize and rationalize the old Germanic customs still in use after several centuries. Students studied texts by Hippocrates and Galen about medicine, and for mathematics, they learned Euclidean geometry and benefited from Arab advances in algebra and trigonometry. In philosophy, Muslim scholars working in multi-cultural Spain, such as Averroes (Ibn Rushd) of Córdoba, wrote a series of commentaries on Arabic translations of Aristotle's brilliant works, which had long been lost in the West. Scholars in Toledo translated both Averroes and Aristotle into Latin, and soon the great Greek philosopher's teachings inundated western intellectual circles. Another singular genius, St. Thomas Aquinas, managed to reconcile Aristotle with Christian Scripture and theological tradition. His *Summa Theologica* is an astounding masterpiece of scholarship devoted to the principle of unity in truth, that all elements of true knowledge belong together and do not mutually exclude one another.

The first universities of the twelfth and thirteenth centuries were what they all should still be today – communities of scholars and students in search of truth. Teenaged students, equipped with Latin, came from all over Europe to study with masters, and in keeping with the communitarian culture of the day, they formed their own guilds. The first *universitas* was basically a student union, formed to protect its members from exorbitant rents, over-priced, low-quality food, and incompetent instructors who were not worth their fees. Masters soon followed suit, establishing their own guilds that set standards in teaching, testing, and certifying success, in the form of granting licenses and degrees. Members of the town elite often sent their sons to study at universities, hoping that a good, professional education would secure good jobs for them in the growing institutions of Church and state government.

Emperors, kings, and bishops issued charters to maintain and regulate the universities under their jurisdiction. The first universities appeared in Bologna, Paris, and Oxford during the eleventh and twelfth centuries, and many more took root in the centuries to come. Colleges were founded, endowed, and built to house and feed masters and students alike. Despite the inevitable conflicts, the perennial tension between town-dwellers and university members, most people involved saw that these new institutions were on the whole a positive development. Leaders of principalities and the Church all wanted educated, competent men to run their expanding institutions. Bishops were in constant need of knowledgeable men to perform priestly service for God's Church on earth, and in 1224 Holy Roman Emperor Frederick II founded the first state university, in Naples, with an explicit charge to train and provide for service in the empire's administration. Prosperous merchants sent their sons, so that they could get ahead in various careers.

The most powerful religious movement of the era, however, was directed against the moral ambiguity of the new wealth and learning. St. Francis of Assisi embodied Christian culture as a matter of the heart, but he was a rebel against material prosperity and professional careerism. Born in 1182, the son of a wealthy merchant in the town of Assisi, St. Francis spent his youth in frivolities of the usual, moneyed sort, and then had a radical conversion experience. After a powerful vision, he rejected everything held sacred by business and society and devoted his life to reflect God's light and love to others.

St. Francis chose to embrace absolute poverty and took to the countryside, traveling barefoot, carrying only a broom to clean out neglected chapels and churches. He tended to lepers living on town outskirts, and preached God's love to anyone he met, with a dramatic flair that still wins hearts today. He went to Rome, met Pope Innocent III, and made a spectacle dancing for joy in front of him, but he received his blessing and support nonetheless. St. Francis traveled to Egypt to convert the Muslim sultan, and although he did not succeed in his goal, Francis' was a very different and much more appropriate example of how to run a crusade. For his pains, he received the stigmata, the wounds of the crucified Christ, in his own body. By his death in 1226, the number of his followers, known as friars, reached into the thousands. Pope Gregory IX canonized St. Francis only two years after his death. The Franciscan friars shunned property, endowments, money, houses, and formal education. St. Francis also founded an order for women, the "Poor Clares," but allowed them dwelling places for their basic safety. Friars and sisters chose their poverty and lived in simple humility for the greater glory of God. They spent their time with simple, ordinary people, in the countryside and the towns—those who need to know of God's love during the normal trials of daily life.

Another new order of friars from Spain, begun by St. Dominic, matched the Franciscans in their embrace of poverty, but not in their suspicious attitude toward education. Dominic, a young man from the kingdom of Castile, pursued a university education in theology in the late twelfth century. At the age of twenty-one, he sold all his possessions, even his precious books, after a famine struck his region in 1191, and gave the money to the hungry. In the early years of the thirteenth century, he traveled to southern France, and there experienced at first hand the Cathar heresy, a movement vehemently opposed to the Catholic Church.

The Cathars, Dominic realized, were not simply uninformed about orthodox Christianity—they were actually quite refined and articulate in presenting their anti-Trinitarian, dualistic philosophy, which taught that the material world and the human body were demonic, while the spirit and light were of God and therefore good. The Cathars preached against meat-eating, marriage, and having children. Reincarnation in a human body was the fate of the sinner, they said, which is why God could not have become man in Christ. Some more enthusiastic Cathars, it seems, promoted divorce, homosexuality, contraception, abortion, infanticide, and suicide. Their grave error was, in the name of purity, to deny the inherent good of all matter and the natural human family. Pope Innocent III declared a crusade against them in 1209, a crusade within Christendom, and an army of knights readily complied, with horrific results. Dominic quickly saw that papal thundering and knightly violence was not the way to deal with this challenge. Dominic and his friars therefore tried to outdo the Cathars in poverty, holiness, and argumentation. Their main purpose was to preach to the common people—to persuade them of the rightness of orthodox Christian teaching and the holiness of the Church's sacraments. St. Dominic also founded an order for women; the first Dominican nuns were noblewomen converts from Catharism, and their numbers grew rapidly from there.

The Franciscans and Dominicans were a clear sign from God that the Holy Spirit still lived and worked in and through his Church, no matter how corrupt and contorted she may have become in other ways. They embodied what the Church should be, a peaceful, peace-loving movement of human hearts and souls toward God. Friars wandered the countryside, exhorting people to repent of their sins and turn to God. They heard confessions, gave penances, and presided at burials. They lived by begging for alms. Loyal first to the pope, they were to support the general, evangelizing mission of the Church. Of course there were plenty of failures and compromises, numerous conflicts between them and the local clergy, and examples of hypocrisy and abuse, but people loved them on the whole and supported them in their efforts.

God wants Christianity to prosper, anywhere in the world, as long as its servants serve his love first of all. During the mid-thirteenth century, kings sent the new friars on missions to the Great Khan, the king of the Mongols who had just overrun Persian, Turkish, Russian, and Muslim lands and was threatening Christendom itself. The Great Khan was not interested in converting to Christianity, and seemed interested instead in allying with Christian kings against Muslim princes, but a decisive defeat of the Mongols in Egypt brought that poisonous project to nothing. Franciscan and Dominican missionaries traveled on into China and other parts of Asia, spreading God's word to all who would hear it and heed it. At the close of the thirteenth century, the Archbishop of Beijing oversaw six Catholic dioceses in and around the imperial city.

Life Lived in Common

In histories of the Feudal Age, the friars cut dashing figures, in part because of their elected poverty rather than in spite of it, and everything about the towns attracts a lot of attention from historians because of their dynamism and growth. But the fact is that only about 5 percent of the European population lived in urban areas. Christendom remained overwhelmingly rural, quiet, close to nature, and local. People of all societal orders – the clergy, the nobles, and the commons – lived in close proximity. The clergy led members of the other orders in worship and festivities. Priests, monks, and nuns educated, ministered to souls, distributed charity, administered institutions, and prayed on everyone's behalf. Lords lived in or near villages, and their houses crawled with people engaged in all the necessary tasks and services. The upper class was never hermetically sealed in its own neighborhood, behind tinted glass, or meeting each other exclusively in designated clubs and resorts. They traveled the same treacherous, unpaved roads as everyone else, though they certainly rode instead of walking. The sons and daughters of noblemen usually learned from private tutors in baronial households, and noblemen generally did not pursue a university education, which was unfortunately also closed to women. For the commons, about 95 percent of the population, convents and monasteries offered elementary instruction usually based on ability, not age. The system, if there was one, nursed talent rather than sought sameness. Small children and young adults could be found in the same Latin class. Members of the commons worked with their hands, in urban and rural areas, making a living for their families based on their own diligent labor. Few people used last names, and almost nobody celebrated birthdays. Virtually everyone was known, not as a solitary individual, but first and foremost as the member of a family and a community, secular or religious. One's face and reputation served as ID.

The commons was anything but a uniform social class, but all levels, including the serfs at the bottom, participated fully in all aspects of communal life. Peasant farmers cultivated their own lands and those of their lord, and they enjoyed a share of the harvest as well. Though they lacked the freedom to move their place of residence, they could travel with their lord's consent, and they also enjoyed the security of knowing they could not be expelled from the lands they occupied. Education, where available, was open to them, too. Abbot Suger, who was the son of a serf, studied at the same monastic school as the young prince who was to become King Louis VI of France. Serfs were always persons, not things, in ruling custom and law; unlike slaves, they could marry, have their own families, and pass their lands and possessions on to their children. While they could not sell their lands, neither could many lords do so. Stewardship of land was a life-long vocation. But still, the lowest rung of the hierarchy is a hard place to occupy, and many wanted out.

From the twelfth century especially, serfdom as a legal arrangement went into decline. The Church had always taught that it was a good, charitable deed for lords to grant freedom to their serfs, and more began doing so. As well, increased prosperity in the towns tempted serfs away from abusive lords. Towns granted the serf the right to remain after they stayed a year and a day. Some serfs who made money by selling agricultural surplus to a town offered their lords a lump sum in exchange for their freedom and paid rent instead of labor days. Lords wanting cash often accepted the offer. Still others who needed lands cleared, occupied, and tilled attracted serfs away from their masters by offering personal freedom, a cottage, a fixed annual rent, and no extra taxes and dues. Leases on farms were normally made for ninety-nine years at fixed rates, so as food prices rose during the thirteenth century, peasant farmers' rents fell in real terms, and they profited handsomely. Serfdom had spread all throughout feudal Europe in part due to deficient security; the custom retreated, especially in the West, with enhanced peace and greater general wealth.

Peasants were hardly a uniform group. Free and unfree, some families did well and acquired dozens of acres and thriving farms. Others could barely afford to remain in their tiny cottages and feed themselves. Communal living and the Christian religion held in common kept them together. Religion, the worship of God in communion with the saints and the people who loved him most passionately and exceptionally, added color, festivity, and meaning to peasant life on the land; it followed the rhythm of farm life in conjunction with nature's order. While the work of the average peasant family was hard and physically demanding, they usually had fifty to one hundred feast days and "holy days" off in a year: at Easter, Pentecost, Christmas, and more for venerating the Virgin and the saints. While there is always some job needing to be done on a farm, it is possible that they worked significantly less than the average Westerner does today. Peasants celebrated religious feasts with more than the essential liturgy and prayer, with music, dancing, and sport contests such as wrestling, jumping, racing, and rock throwing.

Year after year, peasants lived out the marriage of Germanic and Roman Christian cultures through all the seasons. The normal farming year usually began in September after the harvest was completed, rents paid, and surplus sold. Then peasants plowed and planted the winter crop of grains, such as rye and wheat. Feasts for All Saints and All Souls mingled with pagan All Hallows' Eve (Halloween). Villagers rang their church bells deep into the night and lit bonfires to ward off the malicious spirits, and there was much frolicking and mischievous behavior. November was the slaughter time for surplus animals, those not worth their winter fodder, and their meat was salted to last the winter. December darkened and grew cold for the Christmas festival, when lords hosted their peasants in the manor's great hall after Mass on the day of the Lord's birth, and the next twelve days were free as well. There was less outside work in the winter, and the long hours of darkness meant many hours together at the fireside, trying to stay warm and survive until the following spring, summer, and fall.

February and March were the months for the spring sowing of grains such as barley and oats, as well as legumes, peas, and beans. Lent and Easter, although movable feasts in the Church calendar, usually coincided with times when food supplies were running short anyway. Remaining grain stores were brewed into fresh beer, which dulled the pain of constricted stomachs on fasting days. Churches enshrouded the altar and crucifix in cloth, which were only removed at Easter, the feast of Christ's resurrection, the holiest day in the Christian year. Between Easter and Pentecost, a feast of the Holy Spirit, the May festival had to be celebrated as well, with pagan abandon in keeping with this festival's venerable enthusiasm for fertility. Parish priests always objected, usually to no effect, to peasants cavorting in the churchyard with lots of drinking, dancing, flirting, and late-night carousing. After Pentecost came the longest days of the year, Midsummer, and the festival of St. John the Baptist on June 24, with more celebrating similar to May Day. Work continued and increased, from shearing the sheep and weeding and fertilizing the fields and gardens with manure, to harvesting hay in July for the coming winter and the grain crop in August. At the conclusion of the harvest, the peasants could celebrate at another supper in the lord's hall, and the cycle would begin again in September.

Everywhere the population was young. Persons aged forty and above were in the distinct minority. Princes and bishops, husbands, wives, and mothers were frequently in their early years of adulthood. Youth carries with it terrific energy and resilience, but its own set of excesses as well. Many of the innumerable wars would not have taken place if young knights, bursting with strength and exuberance, had not desperately wanted to clash with an opponent, whether they had just cause or not. The young tend to live life more intensely than the old, and life in the Feudal Age never suffered from a bored certainty of ease and enduring lethargy. In the villages and in towns, conflicts often turned into fights, their violence intensified by alcohol and the fact that every man carried a knife in his belt. The murder rate in the thirteenth century was high, but scarcely higher than in a number of twenty-first century American cities.

The Burden of Living

Every century carries its triumphs, temptations, and inevitable pains. In the tenth to the fourteenth centuries, as for preceding millennia, suffering had few artificial alleviants. Many but not all knew that an effective pain reliever came from boiled willow bark, the natural version of our aspirin. Alcoholic beverages were the main treatments for pain, but the negative effects of excessive, continuous use can lead to further, greater misery. Given the preponderance of beer or wine in the daily diet, alcoholism and its ravages must have been pandemic. Surgery was routinely lethal and usually reserved as a last resort. Bacterial and viral infections ravaged the young, the old, and all in between. People turned to prayer, whether private or communal, in churches and homes or outdoors on pilgrimages, as well as all kinds of devotions, begging for God's mercy and for the intercession of his mother and the saints. While we have many records of prayers answered, the proportion of disappointments is anyone's guess. Life in general was uncertain, for everyone, and death always lurked around the corner.

Nutrition, however, was adequate; most people consumed what health experts today say we should eat – mainly whole grains (in those days, in the form of bread, gruel, and beer), vegetables, fruits when available, sometimes meat and cheese in small quantities, and rarely oils, fats, and sweets. The wealthy ingested an excess of meat and fat. The problem was that most people did not get enough regularly. Feast and famine were the norm for the general population, and disease always hits the malnourished harder. Inclement weather often resulted in marginal, bad, or disastrous harvests. As production and consumption of food was overwhelmingly local, whole regions suffered terrible deprivation if the weather patterns turned against them. And they had virtually no protection against crop-ravaging rusts and diseases, to say nothing of swarms of locusts and grasshoppers, infrequent as these pests were.

Most people lived in simple dwellings with one or two rooms around a hearth, with space or shelter for animals attached. No one had any private space to speak of, except perhaps hermits or contemplatives in individual caves and cells. Even in castles, families slept together in the same bed, for warmth and because it was simply the norm. Cold drafts permeated cloisters, common people's huts, and noblemen's castles alike, and diseases and infections readily leapt about. The fact that roughly half of all babies died before reaching two years of age kept the average family size to two to three children per couple—what contraception and abortion accomplish in our day. Death, not divorce, was what cut marriage short and broke up families, and necessity demanded second and third marriages. Almost no one made the mistake of going through life assuming they would not lose their loved ones. Only a very small number of fortunate parents escaped the torment of losing a child.

People in general during the Feudal Age hoped for salvation, eternal life with God. Simple people tend to have a simple faith. They pled for God's mercy, especially when they needed it, and they prayed for their loved ones, both living and deceased. The more they loved God, the more they asked for his forgiveness when they did wrong. They believed in God's unchanging, heavenly order as revealed by Christ, and they generally accepted their lives as they came. They could easily relate to the stories in the Bible, which for centuries were told to audiences of mainly farmers and shepherds. Rural life for 95 percent of the population might seem like the picture of stability—quiet, slow, and peaceful—but living so close to nature exposes one to constant change and vicissitude. In an unplanned, uncontrolled world, one is generally more aware of God's mysterious workings in and through nature. The human side of the world also brought on an endless series of upheavals, as it does today.

The edifice of the Church, while so present, important, and powerful in people's lives, suffered terribly under the burden of its own increasing wealth. Simony and pluralism plagued the Church, especially at the higher levels. Simony is the business of selling church offices, usually involving the popes, monarchs, and other lords appointing bishops, abbots, abbesses, archdeacons, and other authorities according to who paid the biggest bribe. This practice denied the Church the true lovers of God she so needed and deserved. Just as damaging was pluralism, where one cleric held multiple offices and benefices, pocketed the rewards, and left the work to be done by poor deputies. A similar version of this corruption is rife today in corporate echelons and at all levels of government, wherever people are granted jobs with handsome salaries because of their connections and supposed prestige, but in reality with their needing to do little or nothing for them.

Corruption, the lowering of standards, and the generous allowance given to sin, all assaulted God's Church everywhere. It almost seems as if every religious order over time waters down the lofty, rigorous standards of the founder, usually for the sake of comfort, convenience, and the ability to enjoy the wealth that flowed to it. Within a generation after their establishment, the Dominicans and the Franciscans were roped into serving the Inquisition. Much against the wishes of St. Francis, Franciscans made use of houses and properties, even if the order did not specifically own them. The Dominicans quickly built majestic churches and colleges to aid their educational mission. St. Bernard of Clairvaux angrily attacked the Benedictines, especially the Cluniacs, for their wealth and sumptuous forms of worship, which he claimed were just meant to encourage ever greater donations and bequests, but his own reformed order, the Cistercians, is a case in point.

The Cistercians sought to maintain hardship in monastic life, adhering to the letter of St. Benedict's *Rule,* and rejecting later emendations and exceptions. They built their houses in wastelands, forests, mountains, and heaths, and they shunned all luxuries. For liturgies, their vestments were of simple linen and no finery. Metals in their church vessels were copper and iron, not precious metals. Even their copied texts lacked illumination and decoration. For the Cistercians, the ascetic path was the best way to Christ, and many agreed. By the end of St. Bernard's life in the mid-twelfth century, Cistercian houses numbered three hundred. But the holier a Cistercian house was, the more people came to it, the more it grew, and the more people gave it gifts. Buildings expanded in size and number. Soon lay brothers took over the physical work, allowing the monks less strenuous lives. St. Benedict's *Rule*, so simple and unadorned, always has to struggle against the fruit of its own success. Monasticism, although dedicated to heaven, is very much part of the imperfect world in which Christianity lives.

We can see this misdirected religiosity, the love of God misplaced, among the laity as well as the clergy. Laymen lavished lands and money on the monasteries, engaging the monks' prayers in order to obtain a better deal in the afterlife. Kings left foundations to say thousands of Masses for their besmirched souls. Europe was awash in fake relics, encouraged by avid consumers in a thriving market for holy objects. The clergy played along merrily. Pope Innocent III to his credit banned all new cults of saint veneration unless the papacy first certified the relic as genuine. He also declared that all priests and monks should refrain from war, hunting, attending taverns, simony, pluralism, the taking of concubines, and fancy dress of all kinds. Innocent III was young—thirty-seven at his elevation—and full of reforming, regulating, crusading zeal, but many of the abuses he railed against went on as before, and for long afterwards.

The Feudal Age showed the same general level of human strife and discord to counterbalance the unity bestowed by its Christian culture. Humanity's weak tendency to fall into self-love only leads people to struggle against circumstances, to be discontented with authority and responsibilities, whether God's or anyone else's. Common people in the towns and countryside yearned for peace and security, but chafed against the new law codes, courts of justice, and learned officials in the service of princes. Coroner's records and manorial court rolls give the impression that every village suffered from personal and familial conflicts and vendettas. The quarrels of monarchs, princes, and lords made mincemeat of lofty, heartfelt feudal oaths of loyalty and fealty, especially when mutually shared vassals were forced to choose their primary allegiance in acts of blood. There appears to be little point in speaking of improvement and consolidation in government when the fourteenth century played host to the Hundred Years' War, a series of conflicts among the nobles that tore the French kingdom to shreds and inflicted decades of terrible suffering on her peasants and townsmen.

God showered the centuries of the Feudal Age with life, in the forms of a milder climate than in the centuries before and a burgeoning population, as well as with human genius for agricultural, technological, intellectual, and cultural improvements. He gave his Church saints to encourage others to dedicate their lives to his love, whether in the familial or religious context. And people, in their freedom, savaged his gifts and rejected him, as they had rejected his son over a millennium beforehand. When justice came to the living, it was terrible. The Black Death, a horrendous wave of lethal contagion, swept over Europe from the south to the north, from 1347 to 1350, killing about one-third of the population. Which disease or diseases were at work is still subject to debate. Whether it was bubonic or pneumonic plague or anthrax, all three, or something else is beside the point. Where we in our day look for microbes and germs, people at the time saw God's judgment in the mysterious pestilence. Many souls collapsed in the face of the horror, forgot family and friends in need, and turned to wild partying, resigning themselves to the belief that nothing meant anything or made a difference anyway. The braver and more selfless steeled themselves and helped others until their own end. Some ninety percent of clergy and religious in the towns died; if they did not care for the suffering, who would?

The plague was a nightmare, and many thought the sins of their age roundly deserved it. A great debate among historians is whether the Black Death ushered in the Italian Renaissance and brought the so-called Middle Ages to an end, making way for the modern period. In a Christian telling of the story, however, the periodization is misleading and irrelevant to the real matter at hand. The true cause, the real reason, we leave to God, knowing that his justice is absolute. What came after, however, shows how God can turn evil into good.

7

A Tear in the Heart

Know this, my dear brothers: everyone should be quick to hear, slow to speak, slow to wrath, for the wrath of a man does not accomplish the righteousness of God. Therefore, put away all filth and evil excess and humbly welcome the word that has been planted in you and is able to save your souls. Be doers of the word and not hearers only, deluding yourselves.... If anyone thinks he is religious and does not bridle his tongue but deceives his heart, his religion is vain. (James 1:19–22, 26)

The three centuries, 1350–1650, saw dramatic recovery from the Black Death's devastation, a time of new unity and divisions, fantastic discoveries, and horrific reminders of what happens when man loves lesser things, including his own intellect, over the creator of all existence. This era in the West begins with yet another renaissance. The main proponents of this one, however, unlike the renaissances of the ninth and twelfth centuries, considered themselves and their literary, artistic, and intellectual achievements with even greater pride. Where a sense of pessimism characterized the twelfth-century renaissance – scholars, philosophers, and poets bewailed a decrepit, unloving, exhausted world – the Italian Renaissance of the fourteenth to the sixteenth centuries, through its emphasis on man, sometimes promoted an optimistic confidence in mankind that in some cases diverted people's attention, gratitude, and love for God.

This time around, as in prior renaissances, the renewed attention to the Greco-Roman past brought anything but a utopia of the wise and reasonable. During the sixteenth-century Protestant Reformation, western Christendom slashed itself in the heart, in its most basic beliefs and sacred practices, first with one great, deep gash, followed by many more fissures stemming from it. The princes used the great debates over God's truth to further their own, worldly ambitions. As the sixteenth and seventeenth centuries progressed, countless souls died and killed others in senseless conflicts. Western humanity appeared to savage itself through war in God's name, the most tragic of all possible rationalizations. And yet, despite murderous human folly, God allowed for great vitality in the West. Families and communities prospered in terms of number and productivity, and the Church extended her branches over whole continents where she had never spread her message before.

Historians typically refer to this era as "Late Medieval" and "Early Modern," which furthers the leading teleological myth of the field: that high civilization, first conceived by a few Greeks and in part enacted by the Roman elite, subsided for about a thousand years and slowly came back, surging forward in the eighteenth and nineteenth centuries, and finally culminating in the glorious cornucopia we have in the world today. The "Early Modern" designation for the sixteenth and seventeenth centuries is justified in terms of economic and military structural changes, i.e., money and violence: landlords' enclosure of common pastures, the rise of cash-based regimes and empires, pan-European inflation, burgeoning international trade, and a "military revolution" due to artillery and firearms. But the fourteenth to the seventeenth centuries were anything but modern in terms of domestic technology, culture, attitude, and belief. For the people who lived in them, the connections with the Feudal and Germanic Ages were much more pronounced, albeit with important differences. Whether the cultural novelties of this period deserve the name of "modern" is for the reader to decide.

As the fourteenth century came to a close, Christendom righted itself from the disaster of the Black Death. Hard-working farming families brought the population back, and the ranks of the clergy and towns, having taken an appalling hit, gradually refilled their ranks. The nobility behaved itself somewhat better, even permitting a few decades of rest in the horrible Hundred Years' War in France, preferring nostalgic knightly tournaments to mutual slaughter on the battlefield and the torching of villages in the name of some king's honor.

The papacy in the fourteenth century, however, set off an awful farce, known as the Great Schism. After losing a vicious fight with the King of France over taxation, the pope in Rome, accompanied by some of the cardinals, moved the papal court to Avignon, a town still in the Holy Roman Empire but just across the Rhone River from the kingdom of France, and there it remained for seventy years. But in 1377 the pope eventually decided to return to Rome, to the shrines of Peter and Paul where he belonged, in no small part because of the exquisite, holy scolding of a simple, illiterate Italian girl known to posterity as St. Catherine of Sienna. Not all cardinals approved of the move, and one year later the papacy tore itself into two. For thirty years, two men laid claim to being the pope of Latin Christendom, one in Rome and the other in Avignon. As part of their struggle, they excommunicated each other and their followers and taxed all who would pay. Then, to make matters worse, after a well-intended general council in 1410, there were three papal claimants! But no farce as risible as this goes on forever. In 1417, at the Council of Constance, one of the most spectacular extended parties in Western history, the assembled leaders of the Church and the principalities agreed to sack all three popes and pick a new one for the good of Christendom. In their exuberance, however, they burned alive a reasonable reformer, Jan Hus of Bohemia, whom they dismissed as a dangerous heretic.

One might think that such a demeaning series of events would have set off a grand rebellion against the papacy, such as the Protestant Reformation, but nothing of that magnitude occurred for another hundred years, some three to four generations later. The truth of the matter is that it was entirely possible at the same time to love and worship God as a member of his Church and to hate or distrust the pope. The vast majority of people lived and loved locally. The bishop of Rome was an unknown, almost irrelevant personage for people of that day. In Christian love for God, no one matters more than Christ. In the mid-fifteenth century, a humble monk who lived in Cleves by the Rhine, Thomas à Kempis, wrote a short, gloriously uplifting little book, *The Imitation of Christ,* which became a spiritual classic as fast as copyists and printers could reproduce it. Thomas was neither scholar nor artist, but a simple man who loved God with all his being. That love gave him a clear view of what was essential. He understood and communicated to others the truth that being a Christian demands doing as Christ did. Imitating Jesus' virtues was not a project born of pride but the way of wisdom.

Humanism and the Italian Renaissance

The greatest achievements of the Italian Renaissance were either inspired by love of God or directed toward that purpose. In the fifteenth century, the towns of Italy hosted yet another revival of Greco-Roman learning and culture, adapted to serve the Christian mission, and this renaissance would surge through the sixteenth and seventeenth centuries, west to Spain and north to France, Germany, and England. Great artistic geniuses, people who used their God-given talents – such as Giotto, Masaccio, Donatello, Botticelli, Leonardo da Vinci, Raphael, and Michelangelo Buonarroti – have made the Italian Renaissance the most famous of all, and the main showplace and patron of artwork during this period was the Church itself. Renaissance artists, if they can be said to have had a common project, strove to adapt Greco-Roman styles, motifs, and techniques to further the Christian Gospel message. In doing so, they beautified the natural fusion of Jerusalem, Athens, and Rome: Judaic faith and Greco-Roman philosophy and aesthetics, brought together under the mantel of Christ's glorious revelation and sacrifice.

In conjunction with the art, an intellectual movement later generations called "humanism" pulsated in civic and religious circles. At the simplest level, humanism was a scholarly method. Renaissance humanists promoted working with the most original and reliable manuscripts available to get back to the purest version of Latin and Greek texts. In their enthusiasm for the truth, many humanists airily dismissed the commentaries written by university scholars from the preceding couple of centuries. Some in their arrogance consigned the work of St. Thomas Aquinas to the rubbish pile. Leonardo Bruni, as discussed in the Introduction, wrote off the whole preceding millennium. Many Renaissance humanists wrote about the inherent glory of humanity, which lies in the dignity and freedom of every individual—the ability for each of us to choose a higher morality and attain it through education and training. Historians debate renaissance humanism's philosophical, spiritual, and political tenets, but the education and formation humanists promoted was overwhelmingly, almost exclusively Christian.

Humanism, which was born of Christianity and only makes sense within it, points to the only real form of human progress. While utopia is impossible and temptation and sin are omnipresent, we do have the freedom to elevate our souls and selves, only if we make the right choice and sacrifices. The Incarnation, God's becoming man, is the real inspiration of Italian Renaissance humanism, through which he showed us the truth about life, love, and reason, on both sides of eternity. Honoring God in word, deed, and art was a charitable act, serving humanity as well. This humanism worked toward the further Christianization of an already Christian culture, but, as ever, one in constant need of conversion, evangelization, and clear warnings against the evil pitfalls of false loves.

Over time, however, the almost exclusive attention some humanists paid to Greco-Roman texts naturally led to a revival of pre-Christian, polytheistic or atheistic values, attitudes, and beliefs. The poster child of this small group is Niccolò Machiavelli, with his chilling tour-de-force, *The Prince,* a little book he wrote and published in the sixteenth century in order to regain favor with reigning princes of Florence. Machiavelli's treatise on politics is a written expression of love for worldly power, not for people or their creator. *The Prince* became the father of amoral social and political sciences, because it looks at the human being as a kind of mechanism: if treated this way, it will behave that way; if it hears and sees this, it will respond like that. Machiavelli's treatment of power politics decidedly divides fact from value. While he does not promote savage violence, he expresses no concern about its evil quality. When he discusses the possibility of one prince murdering scores of his perceived rivals, for example, all that matters is whether such a move would help to solidify a prince's power over his principality. While Machiavelli pays lip service to ecclesiastical principalities, saying that the Holy Spirit protects and sustains them, Christian truth about life, goodness, beauty, right, and wrong has no role in his discussion of the workings and maintenance of worldly power. Such are the intellectual roots of the social sciences today.

Machiavelli, a product of Renaissance humanism, was an aberration among Renaissance humanists. He horrified people already in his day, and his name rapidly became synonymous with a lying, scheming, amoral individual, a "Machiavel." The overwhelming majority of humanists were devout Christians. From Petrarch, the "father of humanism" in the fourteenth century, to Erasmus of Rotterdam, the greatest "prince of the humanists" in the sixteenth, most humanists saw the Christian faith as the answer to the social, political, economic, and all other problems of their day, not as the problem. Humanist admiration for ancient Greek and Roman texts readily comingled with Christian belief. While Petrarch strove to imitate Roman Latin style and wrote adoring letters to Cicero and other long-dead Roman literary figures, he also attacked Aristotle's belief in the mortality of the soul, praised the contemplative life of Christian mystics, and upheld the Church's traditional teaching about the faith, much as he derided the papacy in Avignon. Erasmus of Rotterdam, whose vast learning spanned ancient Greek literature as well as Latin, was a genius devoted to Christian pedagogy. While he mercilessly mocked all forms of misbehavior, immorality, hypocrisy, and superstition in his own day, his writings firmly show that a simple, pure faith in Christ's gospel had the power to correct all sin, from the murderous pride of princes to the eager dupes who avidly sought salvation in fake relics and questionable religious practices.

From the nineteenth century on, many "modern" scholars, seeing themselves as heirs to this glorious period, have written themselves back into the history of the Italian Renaissance and its counterparts elsewhere in Christendom. Some see Renaissance humanism as a political program, or one promoting individualism or secularism, and there is certainly some evidence in support of these theories. But humanists of this sort comprised a small minority of a tiny elite. The Renaissance graced churches and public spaces with beautiful art based on Christian and Classical themes, the latter often celebrating the virtues associated with Christianity. Reflective people during this period, as in the ninth and twelfth centuries, looked more to the past for answers to their questions rather than to a future no one can really know.

While some Renaissance humanists sought to distinguish their own "modern" or contemporary age from the dark, medieval millennium that came before, it is not the case that all knowledge of the Classical past had vanished until Renaissance scholars brought it back to light. Many monastic libraries were well stocked with used copies of Plato, Aristotle, Cicero, Virgil, and Horace. The writings of earlier intellectual and spiritual leaders such as St. Bernard of Clairvaux (1090–1153) demonstrate wide knowledge of ancient Greek and Roman authors, from the well-known to the rather obscure; the range of learning of Dante Alighieri (1265–1321), as evidenced in his epic poem *Divine Comedy*, was simply astounding. Greco-Roman texts "rediscovered" during the Renaissance were often misplaced or uncatalogued copies from the ninth century, and such discoveries happen today, even in well-visited institutions like the Vatican library and archives.

The Old World and the New

Beginning in the fifteenth century, God permitted the mental and physical borders of the West to expand. Western Europe was fully settled and organized into kingdoms and principalities, with the Church, organized by canon law, unifying all parts. God, the great dramatist, has little interest in tidy pictures. He flung the West overseas, at first to the south and east, but then, and most drastically, across the western hemisphere. In doing so he challenged Western minds to open themselves to his wondrous diversity, and through his son, to seek unity therein. To the old world he gave gifts of new life and wealth—and, as always, the freedom to use both for good and evil.

The real, truly astounding discoveries in the Renaissance involved lands and peoples previously unknown to Europeans, and the ability to spread word about them through print. Here the divine gift of human resourcefulness rose to meet God's challenge to proclaim his word to the whole world, and, as ever, human weakness for sin gladly rode alongside. In the fifteenth and sixteenth centuries, Christian missionaries traveled in the same ships as the mariners, and both risked life and limb to fulfill their vocations in life. Sailors hoped to return with their holds filled with precious goods from foreign lands, including spices (for cooking, cosmetics, perfume, cloth dyeing, medical uses, and aromatherapies), while many missionaries chose to stay overseas and give of themselves to their new flocks. Through Portuguese and Spanish explorations in the south and west oceans, in Africa, India, southeast Asia, Central, South, and North America, and the Caribbean Islands, many religious preached, blessed, and baptized, merchants traded, and soldiers protected. At the same time, however, members of the same groups manipulated, proselytized, and abused; greedily and unethically maximized profits;

and inflicted obscene violence and carnage in the name of some distant king who most likely knew nothing of their crimes until long after they were committed.

Stories about all of them, good and bad, spread quickly over Christendom by means of Johann Gutenberg's movable type printing press. Word of these exotic new lands and souls jarred European mentalities, raising all sorts of questions about God's will for them and the rest of the world, however large and diverse it may be. That the planet was round had been almost common knowledge in educated circles for about three centuries, but now cheap paper pamphlets, replete with pictures, could show everyone just how extensive, wondrous, and mysterious it actually was. Printing presses, unfettered by copyright law, poured forth Bibles, devotional works, theological treatises, how-to booklets, and sensationalized news pamphlets across the West to a growing number of readers eager for more. Even as prices for printed works plunged, the number of cities with working presses surpassed two hundred by 1500.

While almost everyone in towns and countryside lived and worked as they had for centuries, those who lived longer than others noticed real signs of material growth and change for the better. A few village elders in sixteenth-century England were asked what had altered during their lifetimes. Some answered that pewter spoons had replaced wooden ones, and others said that there were more chimneys and paned glass windows around. Great cities like Florence, Rome, Venice, Paris, London, Amsterdam, and Madrid grew in size and importance. Mercantile activity rose with the growing population, and surging inflation, driven in part by the influx of gold and silver from Central and South America, burdened the real wages of simple workers.

Kings increasingly took over the power to tax and levied their exactions on the populace, at everyone's expense. Many members of the nobility lost the influence and independence that their ancestors had enjoyed (and abused) during the Feudal Age. The advantage of the new arrangement was a decrease in internecine warfare, but royal taxation was no lighter than what came before, and the king's justice, the royal law courts, while arguably more professional, were probably just as corrupt and on the whole, almost certainly slower. France, England, and Spain consolidated somewhat, behind their respective monarchs, while Italy and the Holy Roman Empire remained as decentralized as before.

The main disadvantage with richer, more powerful kings was naturally larger, more destructive armies. Warfare remained one of Christendom's foremost perennial plagues, and it seemed to grow in intensity and vileness as the West grew in numbers and wealth.

From the fifteenth to the seventeenth centuries, the people who worshiped the one God traversed the world more than ever before. For centuries, Muslim traders had plied the waters of the Indian Ocean and Asiatic seas, and Christians outdid even them. The areas of the world where people gave witness to the one God increased exponentially, but, unfortunately, the newer Christian lands were usually extensions of rapidly growing overseas empires, territories where lawlessness and cruelty reigned as long as base profit recommended it. The West crossed the Atlantic, proclaiming everywhere that God is the Lord, although the attempt to administer his justice quite often fell flat or degenerated into wanton abuse. The spread of the Christian gospel was and is good in God's eyes, but the grasping talons of empire scar the beautiful face of the earth he gave to humanity. And even back in the old world, in Christendom itself, Christians during this period tore their Church and each other to shreds instead of pursuing peace and unity.

War brings much evil, and it stifled the spiritual and artistic glory of the Italian Renaissance. Its gradual wane coincides with a French invasion of northern Italy in 1494 and counter-strikes over the following decades by the great dynasties ruling Spain and the Holy Roman Empire. Italy's reduction to a stomping ground for princes' worldly ambitions inspired Machiavelli, if his views could be considered inspirations. In the Empire, France, England, and Scandinavia, Renaissance humanism became associated with a protest movement against the only thing holding Christendom together at all – the body of Christ, the Church.

Luther's Reformation

All devout Christians in all eras of human history strive for honesty, purity of faith, and rightness of worship out of love for and obligation to God. The constant temptation, however, is to disagree with one another about what that faith and rightness are and how they are best achieved, and then to go separate ways—usually in little groupings, each according to its wishes. In that case we do not please God but only our jealous, prideful selves. Division has been the ugly side of the Christian story ever since Jesus returned to heaven; there has been no lack of schisms and heresies, to say nothing of acrid disagreement in general. The struggle for Christian unity will never end, because Jesus bid all his followers to be one in love.

In the Feudal Age, rich and powerful popes and bishops, in close alliances with the princely relatives, tried to stamp out independent-minded groups through violence, and they largely succeeded. The Church in the West stayed together, united with Rome, through the fifteenth century despite the charade of the Great Schism in the first decades, as we noted earlier. The rest of the century saw the same abuses—simony, pluralism, incompetence, and corruption—combined with a new menace, the cash-bought indulgence. Citing Christ's injunction to go and forgive sins, indulgence preachers hawked printed pages, available for cash, to those who wanted to draw on the Church's infinite credit line of graces and spend less time in the purifying fires of purgatory. Friends and relatives bought them for one another, and local municipal officials, bishops, and princes, in regions where indulgences were proffered, got a share of the loot. When Pope Leo X in 1517 authorized another round of indulgences to cover the costs of rebuilding St. Peter's basilica in Rome, the papacy got more than it bargained for.

The sixteenth century is a sad chapter in the history of the West. It saw a perfect storm in the Church – a uniquely unhappy coincidence of passionately reform-minded Renaissance humanism, new printing technology, and characters like the Augustinian monk named Martin Luther. This very intelligent and dyspeptic man had an established career as a university theologian, and in 1517 he proudly displayed ninety-five theses against the Church's use and abuse of indulgences. At that time he confirmed and did not attack the papacy, the hierarchy of bishops, the apostolic succession, the sacraments, the creed, the councils, or Scripture. Over the next two years, other theologians confronted Luther with counter-questions about the Church's divine mission and the divinely ordained authority of popes, bishops, and councils. Luther, given to fulmination rather than cool, probing discussion, responded with a flat denial of that authority.

By 1519, Luther came to the conclusion that Scripture, the Holy Bible, was the sole source of authority, rather than any specific person or persons. Religious authority, he proclaimed, was equally shared among all those who had faith in the saving power of Jesus Christ. The priesthood, for Luther, automatically included all believers. The Church's traditions in teaching and worship meant nothing to Luther if they lacked specific scriptural support. Salvation was available to Christians by faith alone in God's word alone. The dynamic, according to Luther, was beautifully simple. One hears the Gospel read or preached; it enters the ear, and if accepted, goes to the heart, changing the human being into a saint. Obligations and behavioral requirements were useless for attaining favor and eternal life with God, but Christians would comply with them anyway if they just had faith.

With those simple, straightforward assertions, out went the Church as it stood, however much Luther took pains to deny it. He was nothing if not a gifted demolitionist. The first to go, for him, was the papacy. In numerous, furious writings, he portrayed that venerable institution as the Antichrist, the whore of Babylon, and an Italian boondoggle against the German people that siphoned away hard-earned German coinage. The clergy and all the monasteries went with it, simply because, for Luther, being a priest was merely a matter of having faith; the oaths involved in ordination meant nothing. The sacrament of ordination, Luther stated, lacking specific scriptural support, was a man-made invention. With ordination went another sacrament, confession, which Luther unsurprisingly found particularly burdensome – narcissists loathe the idea that they could be or do wrong. While Luther saw sufficient evidence to retain the other five sacraments, he unwittingly provided the justification for other reformers to take them out as well. Finally, his denial of the authority of Church councils undermined the shared, common creed, and orthodoxy itself. If there is no mediating authority, working over and through time, in conjunction with the individual, the Bible, and God, then anyone can read just about anything into the Bible that he or she wants to find. Luther denied warnings that such beliefs were implicit in his theology, but history has proven him wrong.

Luther based his absolute certainty on his great learning, a sense of outrage, and ignorance. He concerned himself almost exclusively with Scripture and virtually never with the Church and her history, apart from scandals for condemnation. He had a general kind of theory that the popes had taken the Church hostage and corrupted her thoroughly, but when and how this happened remained rather vague for Luther for many years. In 1536 he baldly admitted, "At the beginning I was totally innocent of historical knowledge. I attacked the papacy *a priori*, as one says, meaning on the basis of the Holy Scriptures." He was unbothered by the fact that Scripture has very little to say about the papacy and so could not serve as the basis for attacking it. Instead Luther conflated the Catholic hierarchy with the Pharisees who persecuted Jesus.

One may reasonably conclude that, in Luther's view, God does not and cannot reveal himself through human history, at least after the composition and compilation of the Holy Bible. But knowing a bit about history might have tempered Luther's sweeping arguments. The four Gospels were written down in the latter half of the first century, and even after they were, Christians leave no record of perceiving them as superior to the Church's living tradition of oral teaching. St. Irenaeus, Bishop of Lyons in the late second century, declared that he had learned the faith in Greece from St. Polycarp, who as a young man had learned directly from St. John the Evangelist. Clement, the third bishop of Rome, Irenaeus said, still had the apostles' words ringing in his ears and their actions in his eyes. The Church preceded and predated the Holy Bible, making it what it is, using it in liturgies to recall the words and deeds of Christ; indeed there was no fixed Canon of Scripture until 382. Instruction in the faith was an oral tradition in the first centuries A.D. The "apostolic succession" was a necessary, practical reality, not a later fabrication of power-hungry popes. Luther declared popes and bishops just so many demons and devils incarnate, and he called on German princes to take a reformation of the Church into their own hands. Had he learned more political history of the preceding millennium, he might not have been so ready to turn from the devils he perceived to the devils he did not know.

But whatever his limitations, no one in all of Christendom fulminated better than Luther. Without a trace of shame or irony, Luther stated that his great reforming insight, that salvation came through faith alone, had come to him in the outhouse, as he struggled against constipation. With vigorous argumentation, ranting, and crude language, Luther's printed pamphlet polemics washed over the whole of Germany, cheap and readily available, read in public gatherings by enthusiastic adherents. Historians have established that well more than half of all printed works circulating in the Holy Roman Empire around 1520 derived from Luther's angry pen. With alarming rapidity, princes and municipalities pounced on monasteries, convents, and other ecclesiastical foundations, confiscated their assets, and put the spoils to their own use. More than a few bishops joined the party, taking the chance to marry their mistresses, legitimize their progeny, and pass on the diocese as a heritable foundation, in effect a private principality. Luther himself accepted as a gift the monastic house in Wittenberg where he had lived as an Augustinian monk, which served as a roomy chateau for his wife, a former nun, and their six kids.

Luther's central and most appealing message, that we achieve salvation through faith in Christ alone, gave masses of people a sense of spiritual liberation. There is no denying that grace is a free gift from Christ to those who believe in him and his gospel. Luther was right to condemn the outright sale of indulgences and various forms of cash-devouring devotions as so many futile attempts to manipulate God and eternity, but he went too far in denying the freedom of the human will. For Luther, the weak, hapless, sin-ridden human being is tied to two teams of horses— one the devil's, the other God's—and obviously we are powerless to do anything about it but to turn our hearts, minds, and souls to Christ and have faith in his saving grace. Luther's world was chock full of devils. He said he heard them making bothersome noises in his monastery, and in later years he claimed to see them from time to time. All who opposed him he eventually declared to be members of that awful coven. Even poor Aristotle, Luther wrote, was closely akin to the devil himself. By 1520, Luther came to believe that the whole Church had fallen under the sway of the Antichrist. No one knew the real truth but himself.

Luther claimed to speak and write with the authority of the Holy Spirit, because he had faith in Christ, regardless of the fact that he made mistakes. He never considered himself a mere reformer but an "evangelist." He was unbothered by the reality that, despite his insistence on the primacy of scripture, his favorite phrase, "salvation by faith *alone*," does not appear in the Bible as such, and the Letter of St. James, with its emphasis on deeds and actions, specifically denies the idea. Paul does say, "we consider that a person is justified by faith apart from works of law" (Romans 3:28), and by "law" he meant the Torah. Salvation by faith and grace is a hallmark of St. Paul's letters, but nowhere does the great apostle declare faith's essential exclusivity in the matter of attaining salvation, especially if it is separated from charity, the love that is Christ. Luther's writings gave many the impression that their own, personal version of faith and salvation was all that mattered, because they read Scripture and opened themselves to God's inspiration.

This was actually the last thing that Luther wanted, even though he showed the way by his own example. After Luther opened the floodgates of reform, he spent much of the rest of his life trying to hold back the surge—in vain.

More Protestantisms

The early 1520s showed Protestantism's true colors: it is first and foremost a protest against Catholic orthodoxy, and no single idea or ideal—not even the Holy Bible— really holds it together beyond that. Many enterprising, compelling preachers jumped on Luther's bandwagon, co-opted his slogans such as *salvation by faith alone, the priesthood of all believers*, and *no authority outside of Scripture*, and took the protest movement in directions Luther never intended and utterly detested. Some prohibited all practices that could not be found in the Bible. Ulrich Zwingli swung the wrecking ball against fasting, veneration of the saints, decorations and singing in church, pilgrimages, purgatory, and, most importantly, the real presence of Christ in the Eucharist. Sacraments fell one after another. Anabaptist groups reserved baptism only for mature adults and refused to swear oaths of any kind, effectively separating themselves from the society and government of their day. Other non-conformists denied the Trinity, dismissing it as a man-made invention, simply because the precise word does not appear in Scripture; there went the common creed. In 1525 masses of peasants revolted against their lords, proclaiming Scripture as the source of all authority, spiritual and secular, since, in their reading of the Bible, it said not a word about their taxes and obligations.

These developments horrified Luther, who lashed out in all directions. Earlier his reformation had pleased him so much that he was certain even the Jews would convert to Christianity (as he understood it). Later, when that did not happen, and he heard of some disgruntled Christians adopting Judaism, he turned his spiteful pen against the Jews. The peasants in 1525 fared no better; in response to their revolt, Luther exhorted the princes to slaughter and burn them all, being so many devils against God's heavenly order. Luther similarly demonized Zwingli and other reform leaders, just as he did his Catholic opponents, and he proved himself incapable of establishing an orderly, reformed Church out of the ruins of Catholicism. It did not take long for his followers to realize that the man was almost incapable of giving clear, implementable answers to their questions; the institution of the Lutheran Church was left to Philip Melancthon, one of Luther's most able devotees.

The Christian religion is as much a matter of the heart and soul as of the mind, to be lived as much as pondered, a business of the whole body, not just the mouth. In Luther's German translation of the New Testament, he pointedly dismissed the Letter of James as "an epistle of straw," because, quite frankly, it warned its readers against people like himself. James warned against the lashing tongue. Wisdom, he said, is only found in people who live in humility, peace, and tranquil constancy. Beware, he warned, of those who judge and speak evil of others. Lest we be judged, we should not even complain about our fellows. All trials, said James, were tests of faith, to be borne with perseverance, which brings blessedness. Those who suffer temptation should realize that their own desires, not God, are responsible for it. Religion, according to James, requires correct action and behavior in addition to faith. *Faith of itself, if it does not have works, is dead.* (James 2:16) Where Luther insisted that salvation occurred by faith alone, James insists on the opposite: *See how a person is justified by works and not by faith alone.* (James 2:24) No wonder Luther could not abide this text.

Luther was a born revolutionary, and his contribution to Christianity, despite its many strengths, is a perfect recipe for disunity, which has reigned among Christian communities ever since. When people speak of the sixteenth century as the "early modern" period, they tacitly admit that much of the modern era's revolutionary anger and fervor reflects the character and mindset of Luther himself. In 2000, popular polls revealed vast numbers of people who considered the lapsed monk the most important person of the last millennium.

Where Luther protested, John Calvin instituted. After receiving an education in Paris and Orléans, paid for by Church benefices, Calvin abandoned Catholicism for a reformation after his own design, although it clearly derives from Luther's basic ideas and Zwingli's revisions. In 1536, Calvin went to Geneva, a town that had recently driven out its bishop and freed itself from the ruling regional duke. There the young, brilliant lawyer helped to establish a functional, authoritarian Protestant government where the Church and the state worked together as one fused entity. He designed a law code that regulates life in accordance with his reformed theology and stern puritanical standards of behavior. Churches were to remain closed outside of scheduled services, lest people should pray in them, leading them to superstitious practices, such as praying for the souls of the departed. All sorts of fun-loving behavior were strictly forbidden and punished. Attendance at frequent, lengthy sermons was compulsory and monitored. The elders of the Church served as a moral police force, enforcing discipline in the streets. Where Luther could offer little more than protest, Calvin offered Protestants a template for turning towns into theocracies.

Like Luther, Calvin, a gifted writer and rhetorician, also put together a catechism, a text for teaching people the basic tenets of Protestant Christianity. His catechism had a special emphasis on predestination, whereby God has decided from all eternity who shall be saved and who shall be damned, irrespective of the life one chooses to lead. There is no free will, and no one can know God's will. Calvin's God is absolutely all-powerful, he is purely just, and nothing can influence him. He can consign to eternal fire the holiest, saintliest, most innocent young girl, and, for Calvin, that would be the epitome of justice. By that measure, one could argue that Calvin's God hates humanity more than he loves it, choosing, in his infinite wisdom, to create his most perfect, wonderful creature in order to damn it, given a few exceptions (such as Calvin and his followers). In a telling debate with Cardinal Sadoleto, who frankly admitted that the Church was in a woeful state and badly needed reform to reduce corruption, but who questioned the need for a new schism, Calvin took him to task on his theology of salvation: "I was amazed when I read your assertion that love is the first and chief cause of our salvation. O, Sadoleto, who could ever have expected such a saying from you?"

After a rocky start in Geneva, the city's leadership fell into line, and Calvin reigned supreme, the theocrat above the limitations of office; by the 1550s, zealous Protestants who had been exiled from their homelands came to Geneva for sanctuary. Not all, however, were equally welcome. A humanist and medical doctor, Michael Servetus, who had published works denying the Trinity and attacking the practice of infant baptism, fled persecution in France and came to Geneva, where Calvin had him convicted of heresy and burned at the stake. Calvin's church model spread to communities in France, the Low Countries, Scotland, England, areas of the Holy Roman Empire, Hungary, and Poland. In all areas it took on different shapes according to the people, community, and reigning church-state authority.

The coming of Protestantism in England matched neither Luther's nor Calvin's designs. A succession of Tudor monarchs – Henry VIII, Edward VI, Mary I, and Elizabeth I – pulled the Church in England this way and that, first away from Rome, then a bit toward Lutheranism, then over to Calvinism, then back to Catholicism, before settling into something that draws on elements of all three. Each shift was violent, oppressive, and basically unnecessary, and the poor people tried to make do with each shift of the royal wind. In each change of tack, the government stole what assets it could get its hands on and ran roughshod over those who refused to obey. Scores of beautiful old Gothic churches lost their stained-glass windows, paintings, and sculpted figures and liturgical treasures. All monastic estates, entailing about one quarter of England's landed wealth, were liquidated to fill the Crown's war coffers, and the ensuing campaigns against France were totally useless. By 1603, the end of Elizabeth's long, repressive reign, the Catholics who remained had been driven underground and stigmatized as traitors. The Church of England, run by the Crown, was a singular amalgam of beliefs, practices, and structures from Calvinism, Lutheranism, and Catholicism. Lutherans and Calvinists across the Channel denied that the Church of England was one of them.

From the first part of the sixteenth century, Lutheranism, Calvinism, Anglicanism, Anabaptism, and various forms of Christian non-conformism spread across the West, and more groupings and variations would spring up in the centuries to come: Mennonites, Quakers, Methodists, and Unitarians, just to name a few of the more prominent. The process continues today. The Anglican Communion, now a world-wide association of churches, is undergoing new separations over such matters as openly homosexual bishops. In the US alone, there are anywhere from 700 to 1000 separate Protestant denominations, depending on who is counting. The only things all these self-proclaimed churches have in common are their insistence on freedom from taxation and their conviction that Catholics are wrong. In the twenty-first century, Christ can mean anything to anyone.

Where is God in the history of the Reformation? Did he instill his truth into Luther? Did he send a plague of chaotic heretics to punish the Catholic Church for her many sins? Does he even *want* one holy, catholic, apostolic Church? Or does the Reformation show us that even if there is a God, he does not care what we think about him? Is there actually only free will, so that we can all think and do as we please? Are sincerity and passion all that matter? According to the present narrative of the West, however, God certainly wants us to be one, to find unity among diverse communities that love him above all, but human pride and hard-heartedness make the project very, very difficult. The irony of Luther's great rebellion is that he and his fellow reformers arrogated to themselves more power over the Christian religion than any of the popes whom they accused of such appalling tyranny. No pope in the previous 1000 years dared to alter the Nicene Creed, scrap any of the seven sacraments, do away with bishops, or devise a new liturgy.

The Catholic "Counter-Reformation"?

The leadership of the Catholic Church in the sixteenth century watched the Protestant Reformation with a mixture of horror, guilt, and self-satisfaction. Some said it was God's punishment of the Church for her endless addiction to abuse and corruption. Pope Hadrian VI readily admitted in a public statement in 1523, "We know for years there have been many abominable offenses in spiritual matters and violations of the Commandments committed at this Holy See, yes, that everything has in fact been perverted." A reform of the curia, the papal court, "the origin of all the evil" according to Hadrian, was a necessary starting point. Some Catholic apologists, however, pointed out that the nature of heresy is disagreement, disorder, and disarray, and Protestantism amply proved itself as such. The best reaction, such men stated or implied, is to stand solid and strong. The Church reeled and suffered terribly, as principalities and whole kingdoms ended their spiritual communion with the rest of the Latin West. Something had to be done, and the crisis demanded a proper, unified response.

Charles V, who had no sympathy for Luther's cause and was eager to see Catholicism meet the Protestant challenge, prevailed on hesitant, defensive popes to hold a general council of the Church. The Council of Trent met off and on for eighteen years (1545–1563), delayed at intervals due to interruptions of war, plague, and political crises. It restated all traditional doctrine in contemporary terms, reiterated injunctions against simony and pluralism, and called for greater discipline and clerical celibacy. It made provisions for better education and training of priests, such as the establishment of a seminary in every diocese, so that priests could compete with the Protestants in preaching about God's word and will. It curbed the sale of indulgences, but insisted on a priest's power to forgive sins and the pope's power to reduce the penalty for sins confessed and forgiven.

Historians often speak of a "Counter-Reformation," but the Catholic Church did not form itself into anything she had not been before. While the Council tried to work against old abuses and took measures to counter Protestantism's gains, the Church reformed none of her stances on anything essential. Her orthodoxy and sacraments remained just as they are. Other historians refer to this period as "the Catholic Reformation," but this is a contradiction in terms. The Reformation, as she appears in history, is a Protestant phenomenon.

The Council of Trent was merely part of a general movement within the Church, inspired by Protestantism, whereby she became more self-consciously Catholic, in her theology, liturgies, institutions, and traditions. While condemning Luther's idea of salvation by faith alone, the council acknowledged the absolute necessity of God's grace in salvation, reaffirming the freedom of the human will to accept or reject it. As in the thirteenth century, new orders, such as the Jesuits, sprang up from the faithful and directed their energies toward the battle for people's hearts, minds, and souls. Many of these enthusiastic, well-educated religious trained aspiring priests in the newly established diocesan seminaries. The Church did not become perfect by any stretch of the imagination, but after Trent there was hardly a doubt that Catholicism and various Protestantisms were different. By the end of the sixteenth century, historians estimate that about half of all people who had accepted Protestantism had turned back to the Catholic Church.

This account of the Reformation and the reaction it provoked has focused on the progenitors and leaders, but what did it mean to the common soul? The whole business as it was lived was not as glorious as its proponents described it in their writings. The heavens did not open and shed rays of saving light down on churches and religious communities new or old. Typically, if the Reformation came to a small town or village, it meant that some person brought Luther or Calvin's message about Christ's promise of salvation, accompanied by a firm attack on the old way of worship. Reformers all across Europe, despite all their differences, shared among themselves and conveyed to others the perception that all had been thus far hoodwinked, that the Church was an empty shell, a bad, worm-ridden apple—in short, a lie. The Reformation preacher would recommend taking it back for more effective use. Away with the Latin Mass, and all services shall be in the local language. Away with the special legal privileges of the clergy – at the time such persons could only be tried in ecclesiastical courts that gave out lighter sentences to its members. Away with indulgences and the special taxes to the papal court in Rome. Destroy the local convent and take back the wealth they had falsely amassed. Luther's men let churches stand with a few changes, but followers of Zwingli, Calvin, and others recommended shooting out the windows, white-washing the walls, and destroying paintings, sculptures, organs, altars, and tabernacles.

Who would have welcomed this message? Naturally much depended on the probity of the local clergy. If the resident priests had been scoundrels, abusing their rights, neglecting their duties, debauching the young, and fleecing the old, one can readily imagine a receptive audience. But if all was more or less well in the community, and people looked to their priests with more respect and gratitude than spite, then receptivity to Reformation slogans was at a lower level. The niceties of theological argument are lost on most people, who simply want to live their lives as they can. Later in the sixteenth century, catechists of both Lutheran and Calvinist churches despaired at the lamentable results of their theological surveys. In Heidelberg, one of the Holy Roman Empire's chief centers of Calvinist learning, a visitation in the 1590s revealed that scarcely one third of all heads of household could explain salvation according to Calvin's teaching, and many could not recite the Our Father. We can only imagine how bad the situation must have been in the villages of the region. In Lutheran areas, people routinely thought God would let them into heaven if they had regularly gone to church, done their charitable works, and believed in him however the preacher described it. When asked to explain how faith alone saves, and no good works make any difference, although one does them anyway, many drew a blank. No wonder Luther grew more bitter in his later years.

Indeed, simple people of the age usually accommodated religious differences, especially when different, rival churches were near, though resentful neighbors. They preferred peaceful co-existence on the whole, despite their thorough displeasure with the other religion, which amounts to real tolerance, literally suffering and enduring the undesired other, instead of resorting to violence. In the twenty-first century, many people understand tolerance as an automatic, uncritical acceptance and celebration of all differences, just because they happen to be different. Sixteenth- and seventeenth-century tolerance meant suffering.

In the early modern period, while some authorities forced Christian minorities to emigrate, others settled for letting them merely leave the city, town, or village limits to go worship outdoors, or in an inconspicuous building. Clandestine churches abounded in towns despite formal regulations against them. People often crossed Catholic-Protestant barriers: they took part in various festivals, meetings, and processions; they sent their children for apprenticeships with different families; and some intermarried, to the usual dismay of religious authorities. And in a few places, such as St. Martin's parish in Biberach, the church itself was remodeled to accommodate Catholic and Lutheran worship, alternating every one to two hours on Sundays. Just living with such differences is the wiser way to go. If Jesus did not recommend vengeance against those who killed him, would he approve of oppression or death for those with different Christian theologies?

The high-powered, vitriolic theological debates that raged during the sixteenth century concerned mainly the elite, learned few. Protestantism itself, with its strong emphasis on reading Scripture, had a limited chance of success among a population of largely illiterate people. For that same reason, the Reformation found its nesting grounds mainly in towns, which also had more people concerned with cash flow and monetary profits than in rural areas. What were the chief concerns of simple peasant farmers in this fuss beyond their own village and parish? The Peasant War of 1525 showed what could happen when men with a revolutionary political agenda co-opted religious rhetoric; the military elite slaughtered indiscriminately all those who, with insufficient power and violence, made the mistake of trying to overcome them.

In general, simple people were not asked what they thought of the Reformation. Indeed, changes most often came from the top down, and people usually followed along in tow. In England particularly, changes imposed on the Church emanated from the monarch and his or her parliament. People simply had to endure them. In Germany, too, when the local prince or town mayor and corporation decided that the

Reformation was good for them, then it was supposed to be good for everyone else as well. In this era, as in so many others, cultural changes were things people just had to accept. The incidence of popular uprising shows that at times they did not, especially when religious zeal turned into brutality toward persons and property. Individuals who stood against reforms and changes sometimes paid with their lives. Martyrs came from all sides of the sixteenth-century Christian spectrum, some accepting their death sentences with a gladness that smacks of lunacy, many others, however, with the quiet resolve that comes from a firm, interior decision of the soul to worship God as he or she loves best, come what may. Deserved or not, they all need the Lord's mercy.

The real tragedy of the Reformation era was not martyrdom, the accepted sacrifice of self, but that all parties had leaders who were ready and willing to fight for their cause, physically. Martyrdom is one matter, when members of rival versions of Christianity readily showed their willingness to die for their beloved beliefs in the face of oppression. It is another matter, however, to kill. Smeared blood stained and soiled the hands of all who embraced raw power in order to promote their spiritual cause.

Wars of Religion?

The risen Christ is still crucified. Those who experienced him first, immediately after the Resurrection, noted the presence of his wounds. Expiation for humanity's sin demanded his crucifixion, and our continued addiction to sin injures him throughout time. When people abuse one another in the name of true devotion to God, they hurt him all the more. Killing in the name of Jesus Christ tortures the God all should love first and foremost, now and forever.

The coming of the Reformation was fully in line with human history, in the West in particular. Total unity of thought and teaching in the body of Christ and in Christendom has never been attained, from the very beginning to this day. The human soul longs for higher meaning and true peace, but the pride and vanity in the mind and the heart can lead to resistance against Christ's time-honored Church. All involved agreed that the stakes could not be higher; all sought salvation in right teaching and feared damnation as recompense for error. The greatest problems came from the unnecessary anger of people, who, rather than leave the matter to God, took judgment into their own hands and used violence to clarify the issue in their own minds.

The standard historical narrative of this sixteenth and seventeenth centuries moves effortlessly from the Reformation and Catholic reaction to the so-called "Wars of Religion," which ravaged France for much of the later sixteenth century, the Holy Roman Empire for thirty years in the seventeenth, and the Low Countries for eighty years. While religion and religious strife certainly played a role in these conflicts or added fuel to the fire, one errs in thinking that armies and mobs slaughtered each other for two centuries primarily over theological distinctions. People during this time were just as human as we are today, with their own particular group of blind-spots and failings. If we ever make the mistake of dismissing them as a bunch of overly zealous fools or religious maniacs, we should not fail to recall that the twentieth-century Cold War nearly saw the nuclear incineration of the world due to the ideological struggle between Marxist socialism and capitalist democracy, especially during the Cuban Missile Crisis of 1962. The governments of countries that fell to Marxism, such as Russia, China, and parts of Asia, have a horrific record of killing tens of millions for disagreeing with Karl Marx's ahistorical, impracticable philosophy. People in the sixteenth and seventeenth centuries were mild by comparison.

Things were just as complex then as they are now. Each person has a history, usually unwritten, and there are as many histories as there were people living at the time. When Calvinism spread throughout France in the sixteenth century, the French monarchy operated on the philosophy that only one king, one law, and one faith could hold the large, diverse kingdom together. Kings, thanks to some zealous Renaissance humanist lawyers, made increasing claims to rule over and above the law, as had Roman emperors before them. Calvinism, in its damnation of the Catholic Church, effectively denied the reigning order of the kingdom. The Church managed family law, wills and testaments, all education, and social and charitable welfare institutions; the King's justice relied as much on it as on the power of his sword in his law courts and the military. Where Calvinists could always claim they were seeking spiritual purity and God's desired order on earth, others could insist that they were insidious traitors out to destroy the kingdom, in the firm and false belief that everyone else was simply reprobate and hell-bound.

The Wars of Religion in France had as much to do with the struggle for control of the royal throne as with religion. The wars erupted in the 1560s owing to the death of a king, Henry II, the subsequent accession of two child-kings, Francis II and Charles IX, and intense competition between two powerful noble families, the Bourbons and the Guises, for influence over Francis and the French royal apparatus. Bourbons and Guises already loathed each other, but the prevalence of Calvinism among the Bourbon princes made the divide seem infernal. The Queen Mother, Catherine de Médicis, sought to protect her royal progeny, maintain the integrity and power of the monarchy, and keep rival noble factions from fighting. Across the kingdom, Calvinist aristocrats sided with local Calvinist communities in desiring local freedom from control of the Catholic monarchy. Catholics saw them as wanting to ruin the realm. The disaster merely waited for its moment.

Catherine de Médicis was in favor of tolerating Calvinists for the sake of peace, by giving them the right to meet and hold services, but when violence began between rival aristocratic factions, she had to work to stop it. After years of wanton bloodshed, Catherine arranged a marriage in 1572 for the sake of peace, between her Catholic daughter and a leading Calvinist, Bourbon prince Henry of Navarre. During the celebration, an assassination attempt against another Calvinist prince led to perhaps the nadir of the whole conflict. During the St. Bartholomew's Day Massacre, Catholics in Paris butchered 3,000 of their Calvinist neighbors, and 20,000 more met the same fate throughout France in the days that followed. The horror went on from there until the 1590s, when Henry of Navarre defeated his enemies, converted to Catholicism to placate the vast majority of Frenchmen, inherited the throne, and issued the Edict of Nantes, a decree of tolerance for Calvinists that also tried to keep the realm in one piece. Suspicion and hatred remained as wounds old and new festered, but at least the civil war in France was over. In Paris and other places, the desire for life and peace led to co-existence and acceptance on a practical level.

Also beginning in the 1560s, a similarly complicated and destructive war in the Low Countries, what are now the Netherlands and Belgium, began as the result of religious rioting between Calvinists and Catholics. The Habsburg overlords of the region, who had their power bases in Spain and Austria, then tried to reform the Church and strengthen the authority of the regime, but oppressive measures backfired and increased the turbulence. Unrest became open revolt, especially in the northern Dutch provinces, in reaction to the atrocities of the Spanish armies sent to re-establish order by the sword. The war for Dutch religious and political independence raged off and on for eighty years, until 1648, when the Dutch finally won recognition of their sovereignty from the Spanish monarchy and the Holy Roman Empire. This was the central, destabilizing conflict in the sixteenth and seventeenth centuries, but we should not portray it as a war between Calvinists and Catholics. The rebellious United Provinces of the Netherlands were as religiously diverse at the end as at the beginning of the conflict, their population representing Calvinists, Lutherans, and Catholics in almost equal proportions, with small minorities of non-conformist sects and Jews. Calvinist thought and the desire for revenge and profit helped perpetuate the war. While Calvinists dominated the Dutch government, they were more interested in peace and tolerance at home while they fought against the Habsburgs on the borders and on the high seas.

By far the most contorted, convoluted conflict of all is the Thirty Years' War, 1618–1648, which essentially turned the Holy Roman Empire into a battlefield for all Christendom's rivals and enemies. As in France and the Low Countries, a vicious quarrel over religion and the rights and privileges of churches, this time in Bohemia (now the Czech Republic), broke into open rebellion against the ruling king, who for centuries had been a prince of the Habsburg dynasty. A German Calvinist prince, one of the seven electors of the Empire, Frederick V of the Palatinate, jumped into the fray, making himself the new king of Bohemia with the help of the rebellious Bohemian elite. The Habsburgs went to war, and soon a Spanish army joined the fight. Over the years, soldiers from Scotland, England, Denmark, Sweden, Poland, Hungary, Italy, Spain, France, and the Low Countries fought it out in the poor empire. Catholic powers fought Catholic powers, Lutherans Lutherans, and Calvinists against both. Unsupplied, poorly paid armies roved about Germany, devouring peasants' food supplies, spreading destruction, dearth, malnourishment, famine, and lethal disease in their wake. When the futile, insane violence finally ended in 1648, the empire on the whole had lost one third of its population. Achievements were few: the Dutch broke away from the empire, as did the Swiss; Calvinists received official sanction for their religion; and France advanced her eastern border closer to the River Rhine. The empire remained a diffuse organization of hundreds of estates, left with the task of restoring what had been decimated in yet another stupid war.

The British Isles had their turn in the mid-seventeenth century. The English Civil War and Revolution fit the loose mold of other "wars of religion," in the sense that, upon examination, we see they weren't really so. As with others, they began with a religious rebellion—in Scotland, this time, over the issuance of a new, theologically Anglican prayer book for the Calvinist Presbyterian Church in that kingdom. The book came from their king, Charles I, who also reigned as King of England and claimed to be King of Ireland and France and other regions as well. Charles ruled from England, but his parliament would not finance a war in Scotland for a book and a cause they did not approve. Too many suspected Charles was a crypto-Catholic, and even more objected to his tendency to rule like the King of France, claiming to be above and beyond the rule of law, in the tradition of Roman emperors. Charles, for his part, suspected that many of his more important and vocal subjects wanted to dismantle his monarchy and establish a republic, like the perennially rebellious Dutch just across the English Channel. War turned mistrust into anger and rage, and soon Charles faced rebellions in all three kingdoms. He eventually lost the wars, and his head in 1649, and his kingdoms were left with a large army to feed, pay, and suffer, led by a self-righteous warlord named Oliver Cromwell. After a decade of constitutional flailing, the English decided enough was enough, and welcomed back Charles' son, King Charles II, to rule over the old monarchy that was humbled but nonetheless restored.

In all ages of history, people find reasons to fight one another—within the family, with neighbors, between communities, and among allies as well as enemies. We quarrel and fight and make war because we can, and we are too often too weak to resist the temptation of anger, which is almost a prerequisite for wrongdoing. The world, God's great gift to us, is the way it is in history because we have made it so. It is ludicrous to claim or imply that the sixteenth and seventeenth centuries would have been free of war had it not been for the coming of Protestantism and the Catholic reaction against it. In that sense, calling them "wars of religion" is mistaken. All ages, all communities, and all souls suffer from war, interior and exterior. We, not the extenuating circumstances, are to blame.

God called all nations, through Jesus Christ, to join him in love. God allowed for both the Reformation and the Catholic reaction insofar as he moves people's hearts to want to know, love, and worship him to the best of their ability, to honor and glorify him as he deserves. Our weakness, however, our failings shaped the unhappy history of the era. While God whispers to us, quietly inviting us to find true freedom in subjecting our prideful selves to his divine will and plan, it is we who darken our hearts with anger and turn our thoughts to violence. Pride lurks behind both anger and violence, and they always lead to more evil. This is as true in the sixteenth and seventeenth centuries as in any other since the coming of Christ.

In these two centuries, the West continued to expand, grow, and intensify, despite palpable human error. Christianity suffused Western Civilization, notably in the evangelical fervor of all groups competing for the title in the Nicene Creed: "one, holy, catholic and apostolic." As the economy expanded through greater trade, and the literacy rate rose, churches and governments both worked to clarify and consolidate the religious beliefs of their people, even if that often meant turning them against their neighbors. Beyond the confines of Europe—actually all across the globe—European seaborne travelers spread the Christian faith, their languages, cultures, and institutions, for good and for evil.

In Mexico, in 1531, a decade after the Spanish *conquistador*, Hernán Cortés, and his local Indian allies overthrew the Aztec Empire, a local man, a simple peasant named Juan Diego, who had converted to Christianity some years before, experienced something truly remarkable and inexplicable. After a number of mysterious encounters with a young woman who spoke his language, an image of that lady appeared on his *tilma,* a cloak made of cactus fibers. The image matches traditional depictions of the Virgin Mary, and to this day, no scientist researching it has been able to explain the chemical composition of the image or how it came to be part of the fabric that should have disintegrated long ago. Millions of conversions to the Christian faith came as a result of these quiet events. Before and during that time period, however, 90 percent of the indigenous population succumbed to smallpox and other diseases initially and unwittingly introduced to the Americas by Spaniards and other Europeans. Thereafter, the contagion raged on its own. Do we dare to say that this annihilation was part of God's will? The dimensions of the tragedy make the thought all the more intimidating. Does God choose the death of each person, even as he gives the gift of life? If God creates each person and calls them back to himself, then the answer is

Yes, however much it pains us to hear it. Perhaps the preferred answer is "we don't know." At any rate, the proper attitude toward God's plan for history is humility and awe. And life did not end in the western hemisphere but began anew. As one group of cultures receded, a new one arose.

God always shows his people that the way forward in time, in spite of all difficulties, is through love, no matter how bad things have become. While the presence and activity of Christian missionaries in the Americas, Africa, and parts of Asia do not excuse the horrors inflicted by imperialist conquerors, slave traders, ruthless merchants, and lethal disease, the faith in God preached by the missionaries is a source of light for the dark, age-old, painful, human patterns of evil behavior and interaction. Hope counters despair. God's drama for humanity remains the same across time, and the next notable tragedy specifically, that of the eighteenth and nineteenth centuries, is that more and more people began to blame him, our creator, for misery of our own making.

8

Christendom Repudiated

Vanity of vanities! ... All things are vanity!

One generation passes and another comes, but the world forever stays....

All speech is labored; there is nothing man can say.

The eye is not satisfied with seeing, nor is the ear filled with hearing.

What has been, that will be; what has been done, that will be done.

Nothing is new under the sun.

Even the thing of which we say, "See, this is new!" has already existed in the ages that preceded us. There is no remembrance of the men of old; nor of those to come will there be any remembrance among those who come after them. (Ecclesiastes 1:2–11)

The last three or four hundred years, for many historians, comprise the so-called modern era. For the overwhelming majority of history buffs today, the modern era is the time when things finally get really interesting and more directly relevant to our lives. We can relate more easily to the American Revolution than to the Thirty Years' War. The great events of the eighteenth century – the Enlightenment and the Scientific, Industrial, American, and French Revolutions – are not distant memories but recent events, relative to the history of humanity in the West. This book, too, gives greater attention to the last three or four centuries than to the others for that reason: rightly or wrongly, they are at the forefront of the West's prevailing common memory.

Conceived as a coherent, self-contained era, modernity embraces the new, not the old. This modernity fostered explosive growth in knowledge, technology, population, and production. Beginning in the seventeenth century, so the story goes, leading thinkers turned away from silly old paradigms and embraced new paths toward the right understanding of a host of phenomena. People everywhere benefited from new scientific discoveries, and living standards improved across the board. Indeed, work and living became easier, and researchers and explorers made great progress in clearing away the world of ignorance. The story culminates in ourselves, in a time where there have never been so many people, so much information, and such tremendous material wealth, not only in the West but in the whole world. Knowledge and material affluence empowers, and power saves and redeems humanity. Is this not the view of the mainstream?

A Christian history of roughly the same period, relying on the same set of available historical evidence, has a rather different take on modernity. As Ecclesiastes reminds us, there is nothing really new under the sun. God's revealed truths are the same as they ever were. Humanity is the same as it ever was. Modernity is just another scene in the same, timeless human drama, played across the millennia.

Beginning in the seventeenth century, according to this Christian history, the thinkers of the Scientific Revolution found ways to explain nature in physical, mathematical terms, and, at the same time, they developed ways to understand nature without reference to or reverence for God, even when this was not their primary intent. The temptation to enjoy the world and its fruits without God fed off a perfectly understandable revulsion toward the so-called wars of religion and their bitter, lingering memory. How could such a tragedy have occurred? For some, God had punished Christians for their many sins, but for others, the Church, the living Christian faith itself, was responsible for inciting and exacerbating the violence.

The eighteenth-century Enlightenment began an attempt, which goes on to this day, to devise a new faith—one based on morality and virtue, but cleansed of unreasonable, silly Christian myth. Enlightenment thinkers sought to reform states and societies by freeing them from the churches that had supposedly held them in the thrall of ignorance for too long. Thinkers and writers tried to find ways to enhance human freedom without the Church. Salvation, they said, each individual could find not in faith but in reason alone: there is no problem that human reason cannot solve or overcome.

Many people listened to this message and chose to make it their own. Bloody revolutions and pointless wars, however, revealed its limits and only increased disillusionment and desperation. But the temptation to cast away God altogether grew in strength. Continued developments in nineteenth-century thought, and unprecedented slaughter and material surfeit in the twentieth, have built the idol, the temple, or the regime of secularism that increasingly dominates the West in our day. In this project there is nothing new. The Psalms bewail the blasphemers who deny that God is there, hears, and judges. The eternal temptation for humanity is to love things lesser than God, be it money, force, technology, nature, or even human reason. To make idols of these necessarily leads to greater error, and harming one's neighbor.

But no one should entertain serious doubts. Christianity will not go under. The children of the faith will always be on hand – whether in large number or few – to give testimony to God's redeeming love, all throughout the world, now and forever. Christians will use their human reason, itself a scientifically inexplicable miracle, to glorify God and serve others out of grateful obligation to the creator. God promised not to abandon his people, no matter how badly they fail, as long as they recognize their error, turn away from it, and beg for his mercy out of the love that is ultimately his.

New Worlds in Earth and Heaven?
The Scientific Revolution

The joke about the Scientific Revolution is that many historians deny it happened at all. Indeed, especially since the English Revolution in the seventeenth century, the crushing wheel of war that wiped out the monarchy only to restore it about a decade later, the word "revolution" has acquired an extra layer of meaning. Its simplest usage, which describes circular or rotating motion, is now no longer adequate. In the modern era, almost any significant change, violent and otherwise, can claim revolutionary status. These days, in addition to great political transformations, as in the case of America, France, Russia, and China, we have the industrial, the sexual, the green, and many other revolutions, down to hemlines and shaving technology. The banality of the term reflects our culture's addiction to constant, fundamental change.

But the Scientific Revolution, whether or not it deserves the name, was very real and lives on today stronger than ever. The term merely points to the indisputable fact that over the course of about a century and a half, a tiny number of individuals in Europe, such as Nicolaus Copernicus, Tycho Brahe, Johannes Kepler, Galileo Galilei, and Isaac Newton, put together a vision of the universe that was not personal, spiritual, and philosophical, but mechanical, material, and mathematical. It makes no difference that countless people did not know about them in their own day. Their contributions to knowledge, however seemingly small, imperfect, and insignificant in their day, took on towering importance in the modern era. No one of them can claim full credit. Each drew on what the others had done before; progress towards this transformation was neither constant nor complete.

Copernicus, a Polish priest in the mid-sixteenth century, known today as the inaugurator of the "Copernican Revolution," drew up a plan for the solar system with the sun, not the earth, in the center, but he was not the first to do so. He also theorized, incorrectly, that the orbits of the planets were circular. While his mathematical formulae for predicting their position in the sky were far simpler than those of the ancient Greek thinker Ptolemy, who had located the earth in the center, Copernicus' calculations were actually less accurate. Tycho Brahe, a Danish nobleman who died in 1601, observed better than he theorized. Desperate to prove Copernicus wrong and show that the earth did not revolve around any other body, he gathered mounds of astronomical data from his observatory, and he did in fact show that planets did not move in circular orbits. His younger German assistant, however, Johannes Kepler, used Brahe's data to prove Copernicus right, albeit only in part. While the sun did reside in the center of the solar system (his master had been mistaken), his calculations showed that the planets' orbits were elliptical, not circular. Despite the great mathematical breakthrough, Kepler, try as he might, could not explain why the planets had orbits in the first place, or why they stayed in such fixed paths at all.

Everyone knows about Galileo. Using his telescopes, he observed and recorded the lunar landscape, sunspots, moons around Jupiter, and the Milky Way as an assortment of various stars, not as some special celestial substance. Galileo adopted Copernicus' system using Kepler's mathematics, and he went further. He claimed that mathematics was a better means to read the "book of nature" than all of philosophy and theology. When presented with counter-arguments based on Scripture, he stated the obvious: that the Bible was not to be taken literally except in matters of faith.

For a while Galileo had important supporters, such as Cardinal Barberini (later Pope Urban VIII). Urban VIII allowed Galileo to publish a book about the heliocentric solar system, but in a fair, balanced dialogue with the older, geocentric system, according to Aristotle and Ptolemy. Galileo's book, published in 1632, portrayed the supporters of geocentrism as little more than fools. Urban did nothing to protect Galileo from his own irascibility. While his resulting condemnation before the Inquisition was unjust, today we know that Galileo did not get everything right—among other things, our sun does not hang motionless in the universe. Galileo's increasing blindness did more to stop his writing than his nine-year house arrest. He completed and published (in the Netherlands) an important book about his earlier work on material strengths and the physics of motion, which contributed to a real intellectual revolution.

Three men from the British Isles—Francis Bacon, a lawyer, Robert Boyle, a chemist, and Isaac Newton—showed what the Scientific Revolution was really all about. Bacon, a contemporary of Galileo, argued in favor of a method for scientific research that relies solely on empirical observation. All older textual "authorities" were to be scrapped, he declared, because philosophy and deductive reasoning failed to explain the complexities of nature. Humanity's improvement, he believed, depended on the application of this radical, mental, and methodological transformation. Only empirical observations counted, Bacon declared, and all reasoning had to derive from them: induction over deduction. By such means, new knowledge and technical advances could triumph over nature. Eventually, he predicted, people would learn to travel undersea and through the sky; nature, and man himself, could be remade. If humanity concentrated on technical progress, and not textual revelations of old, then material conditions, government, and life itself would improve, potentially without limit. Such knowledge brings real power. Humanity, through science and technology, could help itself to salvation.

Robert Boyle, following in Bacon's vein, experimented and observed constantly, and his lasting achievement is his discovery of the inverse relationship between gas volume and pressure, which he was able to discern after detailed experimentation. Boyle generally hesitated theorizing about causes and usually did not develop a mathematical means to quantify observed phenomena. As with all "laws" of science, the law that bears his name describes how things behave, but not what makes them behave the way they do. Boyle loved his work. He compared his laboratory experimental work with worship, in the service of truth in nature's temple; he even declared it an appropriate Sunday pastime.

Boyle championed the view that everything in nature functions as a mechanism—that the natural world itself is comparable to "a great piece of clockwork." Neither alive nor intelligent in itself, nature works and is intelligible, as constructed by God, the greatest craftsman of all. Boyle saw "two grand principles" at work in nature—matter and motion—but he did not subscribe to a radical materialism, denying the existence of the immaterial spirit or other unknown forces. He and the other members of the Royal Society of London, a group of elite gentlemen engaged in science research in the later seventeenth century, believed in demons, witches, and other spirits, although there was great disagreement about their role in the mechanical universe, and the right method to measure it. Nonetheless, the Society's motto, *Nullius in verba* (literally "On the words of no one"; in effect, "Take no one's word for it"), highlights the importance placed on individual experiment and observation over merely citing a textual authority. The writing was on the wall.

Sir Isaac Newton, a reclusive Cambridge professor working a generation after Galileo, was the real revolutionary who did more to mathematize and mechanize the human understanding of the cosmos than anyone who came before. Building on the work of others, this stupendous genius finally found the way to explain the planets' orbits; gravity, a force, although mysterious in nature, he could calculate in mathematical terms. Following Galileo's work on inertia, Newton developed formulae for the "laws" of force and motion, which applied equally to heavenly and earthly bodies. These laws Newton believed to be unbreakable. He also invented the calculus (at the same time Gottfried Leibniz did so) and made path-breaking advances in the science of optics—the study of light and its many marvelous properties. Like everyone else, he had his blind spots, wasting research time and effort in alchemy and the occult. Following Bacon and Boyle, however, Newton based his work on empiricism, and his mathematics fully supported mechanical theories about the natural world. But he too was not a materialist—in his view, gravity, electricity, magnetism, and other "active powers" remained immaterial.

Other major figures in the Scientific Revolution thought otherwise. René Descartes, the seventeenth-century French mathematician and philosopher, attributed seemingly every observable phenomenon to the mechanical activity of tiny, invisible particles. Magnetism, he said, was due to screw-shaped particles twisting and grinding past each other in circuitous patterns. Our reflexes pull us back from hot fires, he theorized, because at that moment too many invisible heat particles leap onto the skin, disturb its fabric, and tense the nerve strings to a certain gland in the brain, releasing the bodily particles that induce the movements and responses of alarm and retraction. For him, digestion was a highly complex process of particle sifting, through heat, the coarser particles going down and out the back end and the rest going everywhere else in the body. The human body, in Descartes' view, was a "statue, an earthen machine." But the mind was something very different.

Descartes, writing in the mid-seventeenth century, having fought in and survived the Thirty Years' War, thought that humanity was ready for a new philosophy, all the others hitherto being inadequate. Like Bacon, Descartes began his search for truth not with any older textual authorities, such as Plato, Aristotle, and their twelfth- and thirteenth-century commentators, to say nothing of the Bible, but with radical skepticism. What could he know for certain? Nothing, except that he thought. "I think," he concluded, "therefore I am." The human mind, for Descartes, was not limited to space, as in the case of the human body. While the body was a machine, built of matter, the mind was a spiritual entity, tapped into God who created it. By completely separating mind and matter, Descartes tried to render nature physical, mechanical, and mathematical, but not to let God and the world of spirits leave the picture completely. Descartes believed that God creates every human "rational soul" and bestows it gratuitously on every human being. But despite this acknowledgment of immaterial reality, Descartes could scarcely escape his own mechanistic philosophy. The immortal soul, he actually believed, resided in the humble pineal gland, located in the center of the brain. He did not believe that the body actually resides within the soul, as its living, physical manifestation—as its form—so he was left with positing that the immaterial soul has a physical location in the mortal bodily mechanism—the famous ghost in the machine.

The Scientific Revolution is of paramount importance in the standard story about how Western lifestyles became as amazingly rich and comfortable as they now are, but the fact of the matter is that very few indeed knew anything about it until the eighteenth century. A minuscule number of stargazers, mathematicians, and experimenters thought they were doing and thinking new things; they strove to cast off the past and forge ahead on the never-ending search for knowledge. Galileo's struggle against Church authorities was a tempest in a teapot. Church leaders and most people were much more concerned about the Thirty Years' War in the 1630s. Only in the centuries to come did Galileo's case acquire the epic significance people give it today, as a purportedly classic instance of Catholic backwardness frustrating forward-looking truth and progress. Newton's works, written in Latin, circulated only among the most educated elite, who had a fighting chance of understanding them, and a dim inkling about what they would mean to the future. Be that as it may, the Scientific Revolution dethroned ancient cosmology and natural philosophy: a portent of things to come.

The sixteenth- and seventeenth-century Scientific Revolution provided glowing examples of God's gift of intellectual genius to certain, few individuals. Some, like Newton, worked in quiet, to advance knowledge of nature in mathematical terms. Others, like Galileo, made a great, noisy show of his discoveries, alienating perhaps as many as he persuaded. None of these men were atheists wanting to bring about a world without God, even if some people accused them of this. They actually all sought to find God's truth—his law and order in nature. This attitude was fully in keeping with the age; pamphlets from the early seventeenth century display the Trinity as the triangularly shaped human heart. This is not to say that all scientific revolutionaries were by any means orthodox in their Christianity. Newton, for example, thought the idea of the Trinity to be rubbish and took pains to demonstrate, through scholarly research and argument, that the dogma lacked scriptural support. All involved, however, actively undermined the notion that biblical texts had authority in all matters, and many promoted the idea that God, while the most brilliant and creative craftsman ever to exist, was distant, non-participatory, and therefore of questionable relevance for people on a daily basis.

Like the Renaissance scholars who came before, the scientific revolutionaries adored the ancients—or, at least, their imagined versions of them—but all alike detested Aristotelian physics. Copernicus asserted that several ancient Greek natural philosophers subscribed to heliocentrism, which subsequent, medieval stupidity, exacerbated by reading Aristotle, clouded and corrupted. Andreas Vesalius, an empirical researcher of anatomy from the Low Countries, thought he was merely getting back to discoveries made by Galen, a Greek physician in the second century A.D. Descartes' supporters called him "the *New* Aristotle." While some scientific researchers claimed that that they were forging into new intellectual territory, others argued they were merely looking backward. Both were equally right and wrong. Scientific knowledge truly is nothing new; it is merely human recognition of what already *is*. All discoveries in nature are only new to the discoverer. The omniscient mind of the Creator already knows all that is. The novelty, however, comes in the way people work out nature's mysteries and wrest control of them for our purposes.

Beyond the stargazers, more people, particularly among the elite, began to embrace mathematical, reasoned, empirical thinking and limit the influence of their respective churches, perhaps as the lingering result of the festering wound the religious wars had left in divided Christendom. Warring princes and states in the later seventeenth and early eighteenth centuries justified their destructive pastime more in terms of reason of state or imperial ambition than in terms of benefiting this or that version of Christianity. The War of Jenkins' Ear between Britain and Spain (it actually did involve a sea captain's severed lobe); the war of Austrian Succession, which pulled in most of Europe; and the Seven Years' War between Britain and France: all are sufficiently explicable in terms of political, mercantile, and financial interests. Religious attitudes and sentiments usually come to the fore in all wars, but no one would classify armed conflicts in this period as "wars of religion." Legal trials for witchcraft and fiery executions of convicted witches also subsided notably—a happy result of a more empirical attitude toward the occult. By the end of the seventeenth century, judges faced with such cases dismissed them as just so much nonsense. The Salem witch trials in New England during the early 1690s were the exception to the rule.

The overwhelming majority of Westerners in the later seventeenth and eighteenth centuries lived as they had before, on farms, in villages clustered around their local church. Their Christian faith gave order to time and bestowed meaning on their lives. Peasants had no knowledge or appreciation of Newton's formulae or Galileo's arguments. War in Europe retreated somewhat, as armies professionalized and tended to confine their slaughter to the battlefield. Plagues and pests remained a problem, but not as severe as before, on the whole, allowing families to bear and nourish their children and endure fewer losses. Building increased in the towns and countryside, and a particular example of growing wealth was renovations in local churches everywhere, particularly in central Europe.

In Catholic areas especially, a new, exuberant style of religious architecture and decoration, the baroque, moved beyond the Gothic and Romanesque styles of the preceding millennium. Building on the intense decoration of the Gothic, the baroque embraced more color and motion. Baroque renovation brightened church interiors through rounded, clear-glass windows, softened the pointed arches, and decorated lavishly with gilded woodwork and stucco painted in pastel colors. Carved figures of saints and martyrs gesture dramatically, wrapped in swirling, golden robes, their faces wearing passionate expressions. And legions of chubby, winged infants, usually cast in white plaster, hover about the church, invoking the delight that all babies bring. A further development, the rococo, only intensified the baroque, aiming to awe the viewer with the drama of God's splendid majesty, even if in some cases overawing with the lavishness of the décor. These exultant, sensual, and thoroughly unembarrassed buildings played host to the likes of Johann Sebastian Bach, Franz Joseph Haydn, and Wolfgang Amadeus Mozart, some of the greatest Western composers who ever lived, and whose works move and inspire people's hearts, minds, and souls to this day.

Nor did Christianity retreat at the government level. The regimes of European states, whether great absolutist monarchies like France or Spain, smaller principalities as found in Italy and Germany, parliamentary monarchies such as England, or republics like those of the Netherlands and Venice, all expressly adhered to one or another version of the Christian faith. Their laws espoused official tolerance only in varying degrees. If the scientific revolutionaries set off a cultural revolution and undermined faith in God in their own day, there is scant sign of it. What came after the Scientific Revolution, however, reminds us of the human tendency to celebrate its achievements, and itself, for the wrong reason.

The Eighteenth-Century Enlightenment: Writers, Wits, and, Renegades

Only God, the constant creator of light and life, enlightens. His suns and stars make the day and cast myriad pinpoints of light throughout the infinite dark of the universe. Man is actually incapable of lighting or enlightening himself. That his intelligence and industry allow him to master fire, electricity, and the like is testimony to the uniqueness of his gift. But before we pride ourselves on our rationality, we need to remember that the animal world has a number of exotic creatures who make light with their own bodies or need none or very little to see. Even without the light of reason, their phosphorescence exceeds our capacity to create light. Moreover, through human reason we can blind ourselves. The men and women who led the self-proclaimed Enlightenment in the eighteenth century claimed to enlighten themselves, and, they hoped, everyone else, and the results were precisely what one would expect, given human imperfection and history. Enlightenment writers, wits, and thinkers took many of the ideas and attitudes of the Renaissance and Scientific Revolution to new heights—or at least extremes.

The West, Enlightened types proclaimed, was in desperate need of reform, perhaps because so little had changed in the past one or two thousand years. The vast majority of people, three quarters or more, were peasants, farming the land with their hands, assisted by tools and animals. They lived in villages that had been occupied for many centuries, following an annual calendar of work and festivals in accordance with nature and their Church. Some peasants were destitute, a few were rather well-to-do, and many more just got by. Most people wore basically all the clothing they owned, until it fell from their backs. The poor literally wore rags. All found their identity in their families, and legal status in their local community. Individualism was not a word of ordinary use, and people did not celebrate birthdays, preferring the name-days of saints. Feudal obligations, such as days of unpaid work for the local lord or to repair the local roads, survived in varying degrees. In England and France, they were gone for the most part, but in Prussia (northeastern Germany), Poland, Austria, Hungary, and other areas of eastern Europe, many were still in force. In Russia, peasants, mostly serfs, were in effect slaves, closer to Diocletian's *coloni* than to their contemporaries in

France. Everywhere, the farm, occupied and worked by a family, was the basis of the economy. All were subject to the vagaries of weather and disease. Few could read or write beyond the demands of the family business.

The aristocracy lived off the land and peasant labor as before. They were no longer as violent directly against each other as in previous centuries, but dominating professional armies allowed them to increase their total death toll. The aristocracy was also still every bit as expensive in their self-glorifying profligacy. They had increased in number in countries like France, where legal noble status, with its highly prized exemption from most taxation, went to royal bureaucrats as well as titled, noble families. Some aristocrats held only their special legal status, lacking money to match it, while others were wildly rich in every kind of material wealth available. The clergy was also usually tax-exempt, but the vast majority of parish priests were poor, humble individuals, as they were supposed to be, serving their local flocks of souls. Cardinals, bishops, abbots, and others in the upper echelons, however, often swam in wealth, and all too often shirked the duties and responsibilities associated with their spiritual office. It appears to be a timeless state of affairs, because concentrations of wealth always come with the same set of temptations. But at least in the countryside, rich and poor lived together and intermingled, albeit never on equal terms. The rich did not live in walled neighborhoods or gated communities where they only fraternized with each other. That was to come later.

Villages and towns in the eighteenth century were larger and growing faster than ever. The widespread planting of fodder crops and new crops such as the potato increased the food supply for man and beast, and the population of Europe as a whole rose from about 110 million in 1700 to 190 million by the end of the century. Towns burgeoned as young people left the countryside to seek work, independence, and potentially greater income in urban areas. By 1800, the number of European cities with populations of 10,000 and higher reached 360, as opposed to 150 in 1500. The proportion of the total population living in towns and cities rose from 5 to 9 percent. London and Paris soon rivaled the size of ancient Rome in its heyday. The urban elite, making their money mainly in trade, finance, and commercial ventures, built elegant townhouses and staffed them with servants to minister to their needs. Only a small minority of town-dwellers enjoyed noble status; the urban populace in general had little connection to the land and the people living on it. Money—acquiring it and spending it—shaped their lives more than anything else. In some cases, they were richer than members of the nobility. The urban elite gladly aped the pretensions of the aristocracy and dreamed of sharing in their power, influence, and prestige.

The Enlightenment was an intellectual reform movement, more trendy and literary than substantive, propelled by fiction writers, irreverent wits, cultural critics, and passionate reformers. The Enlightenment appealed most to a diverse minority of people: some wealthy, some educated, many who were generally disgruntled with the current state of affairs, and those who wanted to dismiss the past. Historians commonly refer to these influential Enlightenment writers as *philosophes*; very few were philosophers in the traditional sense, heavy-hitting intellectuals who aspired to devise a rational system to answer life's great questions. Instead, *philosophes* questioned, challenged, entertained, and attacked. Despite its flippancies, however, the Enlightenment had enormous ramifications for the West.

The movement never resulted in a specific ideology or belief system, but there are a number of common attitudes that pervade the writings associated with it, none more important than anti-Catholicism. If all self-declared supporters of the Enlightenment agreed on anything, it is that the Catholic Church, superstitious, fanatical, and priest-ridden, should give up its lands and its special legal status, and submit its educational and social institutions to the authority of the reigning government. All monasteries and convents should close for their irrelevance and uselessness. The prevailing attitude of the Enlightenment was that Catholicism was worn out, immature, inherently hypocritical, hostile to progress, and, above all, unreasonable. Worst of all, it bore responsibility for the preceding century's violence and fanaticism. Among *philosophes*, Protestant churches fared a little better merely for their not being Catholic.

Other Enlightenment ideas have resonance with us today. To begin with, for most people today, the universe and all nature is little more than materials in motion, according to universally applicable laws, such as those articulated by Newton, Galileo, Boyle, and others. Mathematics suffices to explain the empirical world, and the fount of all knowledge is human reason. Humanity as such, as described by John Locke, does not have either a special nature, a character, or anything like an essence.

All people are born blank slates, or simple sponges, and the environment where they live makes them who they are. Government and society are human creations, and their problems are structural rather than based on any inherent shortcomings of human beings. The correct application of human reason, the *philosophes* thought, can solve their problems and make humanity better than it was. They put their uncritical confidence – one could also say love – in human reason. Many agree with these views today, and historians generally follow suit. It is normal to tell the story of the last three or four centuries as the march of progress, of growing wealth, improving health, and retreating poverty, ignorance, and misery. A Christian history of the West challenges this point of view.

The most important foundation of Enlightenment belief was found in deism, a kind of cult or mythology of reason. Deism lacked and denied any associated institutions and theology, beyond the idea that God, the Creator, existed and created nature, through which we humans can discern his reasonable precepts. Deism needed neither priests nor divinely revealed texts. It promoted virtues as discerned and articulated by reason, the most important being tolerance of all reasonable points of view (except for the orthodox Christian one, which was automatically unsupportable). Eighteenth-century deist adherents showed sympathetic interest in then-exotic, non-Western religions, such as Islam, Hinduism, and Confucianism, and highly inventive deist scholars managed to turn ancient Egyptian polytheism into a religious system of reason. With no overarching dogmatic systems and communal religious structures in place, there was nothing to stop people from taking fragments of scientific-sounding beliefs and cobbling them together to fulfill their own individual desires. Such an approach is alive and well today in commercially viable spiritualities that share a very similar set of tenets.

Enlightenment *philosophes* wanted real, palpable reforms in government and society above all. Many viewed England as a model, in particular with its constitutional, parliamentary monarchy, which kept the monarch under the rule of the law; its relatively unregulated economy, which saw more initiatives and higher profits in the eighteenth century; and its ostensible religious toleration, perhaps because of, and not in spite of, its hypocritical ban on Roman Catholicism. In addition to wanting the Church out of politics and under the heel of the state, all *philosophes* argued for official toleration for all Christians, Jews, and thinkers such as themselves, regardless of what they said and wrote.

Many promoted legal reform, such as a ban on capital punishment and the use of torture in interrogations, innovations championed by Cesare Beccaria. The Baron de Montesquieu wanted government divided into different branches, such as the legislative, the executive, and the judicial. He argued that law should vary according to local circumstances; it should have nothing to do with God and his revelation. No group of laws had universal application, according to Montesquieu—not even the Ten Commandments. Christian theology and philosophy, he asserted, have a pernicious effect on law and legal institutions: "The speculative sciences render men savage." *Philosophes* claimed that monks and nuns who lead the contemplative life rejected society and the state; they were as subversive as they were useless. Such anti-Catholicism was unfortunately widespread.

Some *philosophes* were genuine philosophers in their own right, but still just as hostile to Christianity. Adam Smith, a Scottish professor of philosophy at the University of Glasgow, wrote *The Wealth of Nations,* laying the foundations of modern capitalist, dehumanized economic thought. For Smith, free unregulated markets operate like rational, self-regulating mechanisms, explicable in mathematical terms. Market prices, he said, "gravitate" toward the natural price, which basically covers the cost of the product and no more. Smith wrote of the "invisible hand," making an indirect allusion to a Godlike force, but Smith's economics bears little resemblance to faith in the God of Israel. Workers, for Smith, vanish into a commodity called labor. David Hume, another Scottish thinker, developed a philosophy of skepticism that went much further than Descartes, effectively removing all traces of divinity from the human mind. Hume argued that we think and live in response to sensory impressions, nothing more. He denied the possibility of miracles, because they lacked empirical evidence.

Finally, Jean-Jacques Rousseau, a philosopher of tremendous importance in the modern era, first made his name in an essay contest in 1749, on the question, "Whether the progress of the sciences and the arts has contributed to corrupting or purifying morals?" (This question is just as relevant in the twenty-first century as it was in the eighteenth.) Rousseau responded, "[M]an is naturally good and… it is by institutions alone that men have become wicked." In his prize-winning essay, and in the other writings that followed, Rousseau fabricated a vision of man fully at odds with that of the Catholic Church and Christianity in general. Christianity, he asserted, was responsible for returning Europe to barbarism after the fall of the Roman Empire, and it held all in a thrall of ignorance for about a millennium until the Renaissance era. The Church's sacraments and teaching authority he dismissed as "priestcraft." Rousseau also wrote landmark theoretical works about human nature, child-rearing, and proper, popular government. His writings about government and society are extremely confusing; in some passages he sounds like a champion of individual freedom, in others a proponent for popular tyranny. Rousseau alienated most of his fellow *philosophes* and remained a marginal figure during his lifetime, but his influence ballooned after his death, during the French Revolution.

But the greatest *philosophe* of all was Voltaire, a brilliant, acerbic wit, who lambasted Christianity and the Catholic Church for decades in his essays, plays, novels, poetry, and letters, with one hilarious jibe after another. Voltaire in the Enlightenment was not unlike Luther in the Reformation. Both were hostile or at least dismissive toward history. (Voltaire once referred to historical details as "the vermin that destroy books.") Both assumed leadership roles, but where Luther tried to hold all others back, Voltaire's example egged everyone on, in his day and ever since. All anti-Catholic entertainers today owe a debt to the great Voltaire and follow in his footsteps, whether they know and recognize it or not. Voltaire scandalized through withering sarcasm and merciless lampoon. Nothing was sacred to him. Nothing in his day escaped his brutal wit.

Voltaire lived according to his own creed. For his scandalous remarks, French royal authorities locked him up for about a year in the Bastille, an old medieval fortress in Paris, and thereafter he went in exile to England, where he relished the country's greater political freedoms, contributions to science, and official anti-Catholicism. When he returned to France, he nestled into an open *ménage à trois* with an enlightened noble couple for nearly fifteen years, during which time he read and wrote prolifically, popularizing Newton's achievements. After his female patron died, he visited Frederick the Great, the King of Prussia, but Voltaire's scalding tongue and pen soon saw him expelled from the court and the kingdom. Voltaire settled in Geneva, near France, where he wrote his masterpiece, the novel *Candide,* an uproariously funny satire of eighteenth-century Europe, its princes, governments, churches, overseas empires, culture, intellectuals, and philosophers. It roasts the fashionable philosophy of optimism and asks the great question, "In what can we have hope in this world of misery?" As usual, Voltaire offers no answer, apart from a few lines at the end, in which he tells us to mind our own business and work in our garden. Voltaire lived into his eighties, became a Freemason, and died in 1778. Since that time, no one in the West has made scoffing more delightful and seductive.

Voltaire and the *philosophes*, despite the fact that their views represented only the small enlightened minority in their day, gave rise to the modern mindset: practical, empirical, materialist, literate, confident, and doubtful of all pretenses of authority, nobility, and holiness. There is no room therein for loving God. Paris publishers illustrate the *philosophes'* influence: of all books published in Paris in the seventeenth century, one half concerned religion; 10 percent did in the 1780s. The writings of some *philosophes,* like Voltaire, made them rich and famous. The historical narratives by David Hume and Edward Gibbon (see Chapter 5), works by Montesquieu and Rousseau earned them high regard during their lives. Wealthy Parisian ladies brought the more popular writers and thinkers together in their salons, where notable men and women exchanged ideas, gossip, and barbs. There were many other enlightened writers, however, who lived in poverty, their screeds becoming ever more bitter, extreme, and scandalous, blaming society for their lack of recognition. Looking for profits, printers produced reams of seedy pamphlets and texts. As people showed a willingness to buy literature of any kind as long as it attacked something once held sacred, the tabloid press grew, and the Enlightenment ushered in pornographic literature, the forerunner of today's multi-media, multiple billion dollar pornography industry.

Taken as a group, precious few of any of the *philosophes* make for good role models in life. Voltaire's sexual libertinism speaks for itself. Rousseau is another case in point: the man who wrote lengthy advice about how to raise children never married his humble mistress, and he consigned the five children she bore him to the foundling hospitals, where the death rates ran about 90 percent. Rousseau met and befriended a number of the more famous *philosophes,* but his pride, vanity, and paranoia usually turned the relationships into bitter enmities. Rousseau was a powerful thinker but tended not to give credit where it was due; he diligently perused Montesquieu's *Spirit of the Laws* and took careful notes, later using many of these ideas in his own work, though he did not admit it. The most famous *philosophes* tended to live as they preached: unmarried with varying levels of promiscuity, and childless, at least when it came to acknowledging and caring for offspring. Their dedication to reason did not seem to include much room for the natural family.

The so-called "enlightened monarchs" of the eighteenth century likewise exhibited widely varying qualities of governmental skill and personal morality. King Frederick II of Prussia, despite his flute playing and high regard for art, literature, and the music of Johann Sebastian Bach, invaded neighboring Silesia with his mighty army in the 1740s, taking it away from the Austrian Habsburg dynasty, for no real reason apart from greed. He successfully held on to Silesia during the Seven Years' War in the 1750s and '60s, which apparently left the once prosperous province a ruin. King Frederick II declared himself "first servant of the state," rationalized the bureaucracy, and instituted official toleration for all Christians (including Catholics) and Jews. He also said he would welcome members of all faiths as long as they were honest and productive, which made him sounds like a *philosophe,* but it was all done for the sake of war and aggrandizement. He later seized the western portions of the Kingdom of Poland and turned Prussia into a contiguous, modern state with one of the most fearsome militaries in Europe. Voltaire rightly excoriated him for his savagery. Though married, Frederick II paid his wife only about one formal visit per year, and they bore no children.

Holy Roman Emperor Joseph II of Austria perhaps best deserves the title of "enlightened monarch." During his quarter-century reign (1765– 1790), he granted religious toleration to most if not all Christians and Jews, and, although a Catholic himself, he dissolved 600 monasteries and convents and brought the Catholic bishops in his lands to heel. He reduced local taxes, streamlined judicial courts, and invested in roads and canals to encourage domestic commerce. He abolished serfdom, granted more legal rights to peasants and greater access to primary education, and tried to roll back the privileges of the nobility, particularly in Hungary. In the last years of his reign, he dared to tax the landed assets of the nobility, in the interest of having all pay for the maintenance of the state, not just the peasants. In this project, the nobility stymied his efforts. His diffuse empire, which encompassed many different peoples, landscapes, cultures, languages, and creeds, did not become a modern, bureaucratic state. While his success was more limited than Frederick II's, Joseph II had much less blood on his hands. After two childless marriages, he left his empire to his brother, and humbly arranged for his epitaph to read, "Here lies Joseph II, who failed in all he undertook." While certainly not a failure overall, his reign revealed the difficulty of instituting the reform ideas of the Enlightenment.

Empress Catherine the Great of Russia, who ruled from 1762 to 1796, avidly read enlightened writers and kept a copy of Montesquieu's *Spirit of the Laws* on her bedside table, but she ruled over Russia as an absolute monarch. This German princess had had her idiot husband, Peter III, murdered shortly after his accession to the throne, and her hold on power was always somewhat tenuous thereafter. Vast, sprawling Russia offered her few towns, and only a tiny minority of educated people who could establish and run a modern state's bureaucracy. Nonetheless, she took some steps to reorganize local government, careful not to alienate the local nobility, drew up a formal charter of noble privileges, and promoted internal industries, trade, and exports. With gusto she made war against the Ottoman Turks for the sake of securing Russian access to the Black and Mediterranean Seas, and against the Poles, who dared to resist her annexation of Poland's eastern provinces. Stories about her exotic sex life are so wild as to deserve a certain amount of skepticism, but there is no doubt that she had a long line of male lovers, who received handsome awards of land and serfs when she had had enough of their services. The coming of the French Revolution in 1789 confirmed her reserved stance toward the Enlightenment's anti-monarchical, pro-republican political reforms.

Obviously, from a Christian standpoint, much of what the *philosophes* claimed, cried out, or insinuated is quite contestable, if not outright false. The whole notion that the Catholic Church is inimical to science and learning is off the mark. While events such as the Galileo affair are a blemish, we should not forget that Copernicus was a Catholic priest, whose writings in favor of heliocentrism earned not punishment but praise after they were aired before the pope and some cardinals. Copernicus remained true to his Catholic vocation during the headiest years of the Protestant Reformation, and Pope Gregory XIII used his research to reform the calendar later in the sixteenth century. Members of the Jesuit order alone have an excellent record of achievement in early scientific research. Their missionaries to the southern hemisphere dutifully charted star constellations unseen in the northern. Others, through ingenuity and curiosity, observed Jupiter's colored bands, the rings of Saturn, and the Andromeda nebula. Jesuit theoreticians wrote about the cause of tidal ebb and flow, light's wave-like properties, blood circulation in human beings, seismology, and the potential for human flight. Jesuit mathematicians made a list of contributions and achievements of similar significance. A Benedictine monk, Ulrich Schiegg, a mathematician, astronomer, and priest, staged Germany's first hot-air balloon flight in 1784 at Ottobeuren, a monastery founded in the eighth century, an estate of the Holy Roman Emperor, which had survived the Peasant Rebellion in the early sixteenth century and the Thirty Years' War in the seventeenth. In 1802, however, it lost its lands and was completely dissolved, according to the new destructive spirit of a revolutionary age.

The Coming of the French Revolution

God moves in mysterious ways. He accompanies us in daily life and intervenes in great moments of history. He keeps the great human story from falling into total chaos, absurdity, and gibberish. His hand is visible in the French Revolution, a crisis that shook the West to its core, and, one can argue, is still being played out today. From 1789 to 1815, he laid low the mighty and raised up the lowly, on both sides of the political chasm. Kings failed in their pastoral duty to guide and protect their flock, but the revolutionaries, for their part, fared worse. God protected his Church while many people, in their freedom, sought to destroy her. The faithful came through, as always, despite the terrible loss and suffering. The French Revolution shows what God allows humanity to do to itself when it makes itself the absolute judge of good and evil. It shows that human revolutions are hollow, for all their self-righteous noise and terrible violence, and that too many suffer for the supposedly greater good for the greatest number. And yet, despite the horror, the return of peace and reconciliation shows what love and self-giving can do when they are given a chance.

Compelling, exciting narratives of these dramatic events abound, and there are still more works of scholarship that analyze all aspects of the French Revolution. People will always marvel at it, because, like all great historical events, it is, for us, a moving target, hidden in the ever-darkening fog of time; its true meaning can only be found in mystery. Scholars searching for a historical mechanism to explain it, some set of worldly, historical laws, have come, made their case, won recognition, and fallen by the wayside with the advent of the next set of theories. And so it will go. The West still grapples with the French Revolution. When asked about its ultimate historical significance, the mid twentieth-century Chinese Premier Zhou Enlai replied, "It is too soon to tell." And yet, though its consequences are far-reaching, this great crisis is a blip in history compared to the coming of Christ. The French Revolution, its rights and wrongs, successes and failures, subjects the Enlightenment to history's bright light of truth.

Some historians have tried to explain the tortuously complicated events of the revolution in terms of the main characters' shared ideals and ideas. The guiding ideology behind the major reforms, so this argument goes, is one of individualism and universalism—and anti-Catholicism. The revolutionaries wanted to reconstitute the French state not around communities, estates, and the Church, each with its traditional rights and privileges, but based on the individual and his (*not* her) universal rights, inherent in his manhood and citizenship. Such a view, the revolutionaries believed, was universally applicable throughout the West and the whole world. While certainly true, this interpretation of the Revolution is only part of the picture. According to Mona Ozouf, one of the foremost historians of the period, the revolutionaries had further aims in mind— to remove God from the center of human affairs, and indeed of all existence, and replace him with man. The modern, secular, liberal view of the world will forever look back to the French Revolution for inspiration and example, regardless of the body count.

How did it happen in the first place? At the simplest level, the French monarchy mortgaged the country's future by borrowing money to fight the Seven Years' War and supporting the revolt of the British colonies in North America in the later 1770s. By the 1780s, fully one half of the royal budget was spent on paying interest on loans. War does not pay. Expenditure for the king's glittering court at Versailles amounted to a 3 percent line item. A vast amount of money went to paying pensions for well-to-do, well-connected people. King Louis XVI, a well-meaning, peaceable, but somewhat dim-witted soul, bid a number of finance ministers to solve the problem, but all attempts to tap the wealth of the nobility and higher clergy through taxation failed. The elite would not give up their ancient privileges, unless the crown would relinquish some of its own. The "Old Regime," the French absolutist monarchy, was no longer financially sustainable, and it proved incapable of reforming itself. The Enlightenment had given the elite every reason not to believe the Old Regime was worth the trouble.

Facing yet another political impasse in 1788, King Louis agreed to call the Estates General, a special meeting of representatives of the whole realm – it had not met since 1614 – to address and resolve the kingdom's problems. Over the winter, the king asked all communities to articulate and submit their grievances to the king, and almost all complied. These documents show a chorus of complaint about the state of France—the corruption, inequities, inefficiencies, and obsolete, obnoxious, and abused privileges. Nearly all express the opinion that if the king knew what was amiss, he would be able to solve the problem. Some proclaimed him "the new Augustus" who would usher in a new golden age. Across France, if revolution was in the air, the end of the monarchy was not.

Unsurprisingly, however, when the Estates General came together, it mainly represented the elite: the highest clergy, the greatest nobles, and the so-called Third Estate, the urban wealthy, who were supposed to represent all the peasants. The mood was confused and embittered. The assembly rapidly decayed into a quarrel about voting procedures, until the Third Estate members, joined by a few reform-minded clergy and nobles, walked out in protest. They gathered in a tennis court, declared themselves the National Assembly, and gave themselves the task of drawing up a constitution for France, because they allegedly represented the French people better than anyone else. Some warned King Louis he had a revolution on his hands, but he did not shut down the assembly. To the contrary, after hesitating, he asked the remaining representatives of the clergy and nobility to join them.

Despite these tensions, all might have ended well had it not been for the violence. The storming of the Bastille on July 14, 1789, which left about one hundred dead, was a symptom of the wider problem. A popular militia, naming itself the National Guard, formed in Paris and declared itself protector of the Assembly. With royal troops converging on Paris and its environs, people feared the possibility of a crackdown. Riots similar to the one against the Bastille broke out in towns across France, aggravated by hunger due to food scarcities, high prices, and low wages. Mobs of peasants invaded aristocratic homes, plundered food reserves, and burned records, accounts, and documents, all in protest against the few feudal obligations that remained in force.

On August 4, the Assembly voted to end all privileges—of rich and poor, clergy, nobility, and commons alike. With that resolution, they swept the Old Regime off the table, but not into the trash bin; it would come back to haunt them later in terrifying ways. From 1789 to 1791, the Assembly drew up a constitutional monarchy, enshrining enlightenment values into its foundational law, which guaranteed the rights of men as individuals. All estates, guilds, corporations, and unions were summarily disbanded. The right to vote was given mainly with landholders, and the king was left only with a temporary veto. All of France was reorganized into eighty-three *départements* of roughly equal size, regardless of the resident population and its local, regional history and identity, and the metric system, a wonderfully simple and rational means of empirical measurement, was officially adopted. Then, to honor the debts of the Old Regime, the assembly seized all the lands of the Church and forced the clergy to become civil servants of the state. As before, Louis sent mixed signals; he must have been hopelessly confused. In June 1791, he and his family tried to flee the country but were caught in the act. When he signed the new constitution, no one really believed he would abide by it for long. Few knew his intentions or trusted him, and war made everything worse.

In April 1792, the new government of France declared war on Austria – the Habsburgs ruled the Austrian Netherlands (now Belgium) to the northeast. Both supporters and detractors of the Assembly seemed to have supported the move. The king, as far as anyone can tell, may have thought the war would rally his people behind him. Frustrated revolutionaries who thought the new constitution had not gone far enough hoped that victory would embolden their reforming cause, while conservatives and reactionaries thought a sound defeat would give them the chance to turn back the calendar to 1789 and restore the Old Regime. Initially, the war went badly. Austrian and Prussian armies entered France, Paris sank into hysteria and violence, and ruthless radicals pounced. Siding with the Paris mobs, a group called the Jacobins did away with the new constitutional monarchy and declared France a democratic republic. When the tide of war turned in their favor, they performed the most extreme, revolutionary act, executing the king and his queen in 1793. Now there was nothing they would not dare to do. Europe recoiled in horror, and the French government declared war against most of her neighbors, promising to bring revolution to their oppressed peoples, with individual rights universally applied. The revolutionary mission was born of blood.

The French revolutionary republic aspired to reorganize politics according to moral principles and individual human rights, but they ended up denying them in the most appalling way. The new government readily adopted an authoritarianism that made the Old Regime look mild by comparison, and they backed it with insane savagery. In the Old Regime, the king had in fact been above the law, but below God and answerable to him for the sake of his people. Nothing stood higher than the new arbiters of power, however. The republic established a Reign of Terror to guarantee full compliance with the new republican virtues of their government. Anyone who disagreed with or departed from the program in any way was liable to summary execution. The guillotine was the new symbol of rational justice. Where under the Old Regime, nobles had their heads cut off by the sword, and commoners were dispatched by hanging, drawing, and quartering, now all citizens could equally enjoy the mechanism's impersonal, efficient justice (when it did not malfunction).

The revolutionary government mobilized the country for war on an unprecedented scale and shut down the Catholic Church. To drive the point home, they scrapped the Church's Gregorian calendar and reordered time, issuing a new, 365-day calendar, based on that of ancient Egypt, with twelve months (their names related to the seasons) of thirty days each, with holidays on every tenth, plus five at the end. They called it more rational. The first year began not with the birth of Christ but the establishment of the republic. They expelled all priests, monks, and nuns from the schools, reducing the number of young people in secondary schools by 80 percent. They demolished and sold off many churches, leaving some to serve as storehouses for grain or weaponry. They converted the Cathedral of Notre Dame in Paris into a Greco-Roman "Temple of Reason," and they planned to do the same in other cities. In Strasbourg, over the cathedral's crossing dome, they placed a gigantic red Phrygian cap (the revolutionary headwear reminiscent of freedmen of the pagan Roman Empire). Near Paris, they orchestrated grand, theatrical festivals to encourage support for the republic and its new government-run Cult of the Supreme Being. In 1794, they installed

Rousseau's remains across from Voltaire's in the *Panthéon*, a former Catholic church converted into a Roman-style mausoleum. Thousands of clergymen, male and female, were rounded up and killed, and thousands more were imprisoned on charges of extremism.

All this anti-Catholic fervor thrilled enlightened revolutionaries but revolted much of the rest of the population, who treasured their faith and wanted to protect their local church. France had never been a particularly strong center for Protestant fervor and had largely remained Catholic, so anti-Catholicism largely overlaps with anti-Christianity. In the Vendée, a western region of France, devout Christians—peasants and townsmen led by nobles—had had enough in 1793 and declared for their Church, claiming justly that the revolutionary government had removed their religious liberty and their freedom of thought as stipulated in the French constitution. First they refused military service for the regime in Paris on the grounds of conscientious objection. Then violence broke out, and the revolutionaries responded with dreadful force. The accounts of the atrocities churn the stomach. A quarter million died in the Vendée.

If there was one thing all proponents of the Enlightenment loathed, it was persecution in the name of religion. Rousseau, however, had argued for the need for a national cult, based on a tolerance everyone had to accept; for those who did not, Rousseau recommended capital punishment. The French Revolutionaries followed suit. The slaughter in the Vendée tears away the proud, hypocritical veil of Enlightenment toleration and revolutionary moral righteousness. For the revolutionaries, the blood in the Vendée was a necessary, calculable sacrifice for the survival and legitimacy of their secular, rationalist regime. In truth, they were no better than the warlords who came before, however "modern" one wishes to portray them.

After officially killing 40,000, mostly peasants and urban poor, in Paris and around France, the revolutionary Reign of Terror collapsed in on itself. The Terror's greatest exponent, Maximilien Robespierre, who clearly derived many of his ideas from Rousseau, lost his own head in July 1794, after he threatened other members of the government once too often. For one who spoke much of virtue, Robespierre apparently saw no value in self-restraint. But his regime did a few good things in the interest of individualism and universalism, such as ending slavery in French overseas colonies and granting full legal rights to black men. The orgy of killing went on, now unofficially. Robespierre's tyrannical republic had put together a gargantuan army of 700,000 and flung itself to the east, against the Austrian and the Prussian armies and anyone who lay in its path. This army, espousing a modern, unholy gospel of individualism and universalism, crushed and looted the German principalities neighboring France in the name of liberty, equality, and fraternity. In 1794, a "White Terror" followed Robespierre's "Red Terror," a fit of vengeance directed against the main proponents of the latter. The word "terrorism" derives from this era.

Eventually a measure of calm returned to France in 1795, with the formation of yet another new government, called the Directory, based on ancient Spartan and Athenian precedents. The Directory lifted the ban on Catholicism and sought to return traditional peace and order to France's towns and localities, without sacrificing the revolution's major legal changes and property transfers. It also wisely made peace agreements with Spain and Prussia. The Directory repressed radical democrats and defeated royalists, and it relied on its army to enforce its will in France while the war against Britain and Austria ground on. Faced with more riots in Paris in October 1795, the Directory sent a young, relatively inexperienced general named Napoleon Bonaparte to gun them down. Napoleon readily complied, and when he finished, over one thousand people lay dead in the streets. This did not bode well for the future.

Napoleon, The Revolution in Person

The French Revolution culminated in Napoleon, in all ways good and bad. This diminutive narcissist from Corsica makes an unlikely hero, unless one is in love with the Enlightenment and modernity. Napoleon worshipped himself, as is clear from his writings. He had some of his most moving visions of his own great destiny during the heat of battle, but despite his many talents, he never amounted to more than a common bandit and butcher. Napoleon often declared that he would uphold the goals of the French Revolution, and he dutifully exported individualism and universalism across the face of Europe, by means of artillery fire and the sword. He plundered without remorse and aggrandized himself and his family in high office to the point of absurdity. While his many military victories are impressive in themselves, the fact of the matter is that he was done for as soon as all his enemies had decided to bury their differences and combine against him. Napoleon was certainly not as bad as Robespierre, but they both owed their careers to the same revolutionary disaster.

Napoleon came from the island of Corsica, and he never would have had a career as a commanding officer in the French army if not for the revolution's abrogation of noble privilege, which opened all high military offices to deserving candidates regardless of birth. He had supported the Jacobins and the revolutionary republic but never assumed a prominent position in its shifting ranks. His service to the Directory in October 1795 won him a higher commission, and he led a successful campaign into northern Italy, forcing Austria to accept peace in 1797. His next campaign, to Egypt, to interrupt British trade with India, was a fiasco, but he portrayed it as a grand success, even as he left his troops behind, high and dry in the desert, diseased, and unsupplied. After returning to Paris in 1799, he planned and executed a coup against the Directory, setting up a government by three consuls—a good, old-fashioned, ancient Roman triumvirate—but it lasted only about a month before Napoleon made himself First Consul, in effect a dictator, who proclaimed that the revolution was safe in his hands. While he incorporated representatives of both pro- and anti-revolutionary positions into his government, his secret police crushed opposition wherever it reared its head.

Napoleon amassed and exercised more authority than any king of the Old Regime. He secured peace within France and spread murder and mayhem abroad, all in the name of liberation. In 1801 he made peace with the Roman Catholic Church, conferring on that religion a kind of official status, but without assets or real freedom. Clergy remained state servants. The move was popular enough; in 1802 a national plebiscite extended Napoleon's rule for the duration of his life. In 1804, the dictator issued the Napoleonic Code, a legal document that once again endeavored to enshrine the revolution into law. Birth bestowed no legal privileges, individual property rights were protected, and no workers' unions were allowed. Consistent with tradition, however, fathers held legal authority over their families, but women received some inheritance rights. Napoleon outdid himself in 1804, when, in the Cathedral of Notre Dame in Paris, he crowned himself Emperor of the French; he had brought in the pope to observe but not officiate. Napoleon had himself represented in paintings in the style of Roman Emperor Diocletian, who referred to himself as Lord. Then the slaughter really took off.

Emperor Napoleon, using the revolution's military machine, unleashed his armies on the whole of Europe, defeating his enemies one after another. He put the thousand-year-old Holy Roman Empire to death, seized the Low Countries, and conquered much of northern and central Italy. When Pope Pius VII resisted, Napoleon held him captive for five years. He made kings of his Corsican relatives and married an Austrian Habsburg princess to start a new dynasty of Bonapartes. His glory was laughably short, and limited. He never defeated Britain, his invasion of Spain sank into a quagmire, and his Grand Army that invaded Russia in 1812 met an icy death. Still, his self-esteem was undamaged. In an unguarded moment in 1813, he said to the Austrian chancellor Prince Metternich, "I grew up in military camps. I know nothing but the battlefield. A man like me craps on the lives of a million people."

But in 1813, for the first time, Britain, Russia, Austria, and Prussia allied together, and Napoleon was done for. Utterly defeated in 1814, he abdicated and went into exile. After a brief, pathetic comeback in 1815, he spent the rest of his days parading about a foggy little island in the southern Atlantic, lording over its cold ground and the few devoted courtiers who joined him in oblivion. Military historians have praised to the skies his battlefield victories, but what end did they serve? Wherever he had brought and delivered the French Revolution, it was through force of arms, and at the cost of murder and thievery. And his supposed liberation of Europe was all rolled back in the peace concluded at the Congress of Vienna in 1815. The debate about Napoleon's status as a great man will never end, but not because it has much to do with him. Those who love him do not love the God who became man and died for our sins, or, if they say they do, they love France and its revolutionary, republican heritage first. Napoleon was a far cry from Christ, but as we shall see, not as bad as other warlords who came later.

The French Revolution is now part of human history and memory, and as such it remains a force in Western politics. The French Revolution gave modernity political configurations of "left" vs. "right," and gave institutional and legal expression to secularism, one that seeks not only to divide Church and State, but to drive Christianity and especially Catholicism out of the public sphere and into the private. In 1815, the Congress of Vienna picked up Europe's broken pieces, rolled back France to within her pre-revolutionary borders, and undid Napoleonic constitutional and legal reforms wherever he had imposed them all across

Europe. Yet the cat was already long out of the bag. Even in Catholic principalities such as Bavaria, the state had shut down monasteries and convents and stolen Church properties in order to pay for a larger army. The state was on the march, having used its coercive and military power to quell all opposition, from within and without, whether secular or religious. The French Revolution, for all its hopes in founding a new, man-made republic of rational, natural virtues, one liberated from its Christian trappings and burdensome past, showed that humanity is incapable of real moral progress in goodness without God's help.

The secularizing, de-Christianizing force of the Scientific Revolution, the Enlightenment, and the French Revolution lives on in the West today, more powerful than ever before. The Capitol of the United States of America, completed in the mid-nineteenth century, symbolizes it perfectly. In the center, between the House of Representatives and the Senate, sits a massive and beautiful neo-classical dome, an architectural structure normally used for temples, churches, and chapels. On the inside, suspended between the onlookers far below and the cupola just above, is a painting of George Washington, in full frontal view, as iconic as images of Emperor Diocletian. The President, dressed in royal purple, with a rainbow reminiscent of the Old Testament under his feet, sits with his arms extended, not very unlike Jesus Christ in Leonardo da Vinci's *Last Supper*. Around the circular periphery, a female personification of war drives away kings and tyrants; figures representing science, mechanics, and commerce on land and sea point to a fruitful, prosperous future of material well-being. The message is clear: the power of a U.S. President brings peace and prosperity. Who needs God in that happy picture?

9

The Perils of Wealth

*"How hard it is for those who have wealth to enter the kingdom of
God!" The disciples were amazed at his words. So Jesus again said
to them in reply, "Children, how hard it is to enter the kingdom
of God! It is easier for a camel to pass through [the] eye of [a]
needle than for one who is rich to enter the kingdom of God."*
(Mark 10:23–25)

*"No one can serve two masters. He will either hate the one and
love the other, or be devoted to the one and despise the other. You
cannot serve God and mammon." (Matthew 6:24)*

Money fueled the Enlightenment and the pride that accompanies
luxurious living. The Enlightenment as a general cultural
movement among the lands and peoples of the West away
from God and his Church was barely traceable until the end of the
eighteenth century, and then only in certain, prosperous urban areas.
A wave of wealth creation in the eighteenth century, tied to growing
overseas mercantile empires and new discoveries in industrial technology,
led to the emergence of new areas for cultural life outside of the parish
church: theaters, libraries, assembly halls, coffeehouses, bookshops, and
social clubs proliferated, along with secular societies such as Masonic
lodges and literary and philosophical groups. Whole towns like Bath and
Tunbridge Wells built spaces to accommodate people attracted to such
centers for urbane entertainments of a civil society. But to enjoy most

of these, one needed money, literacy, and a certain level of education. This bourgeois society in England was open to people of various social backgrounds — it was not closed to an aristocracy based on birth — but wealth was a requirement.

In all parts of the West, those who read the writers of the Enlightenment were of the higher orders of society, the so-called upper and upper-middle classes. The towns of the Dutch Republic showed similar levels of requisite prosperity for the Enlightenment's cultural patterns, as did Paris, of course, and a few other cities in France. In these places the urban elites developed pastimes of their own, separate from those of a traditional, landed society, where lords and peasants mingled during regular religious festivals. All across Europe, however, the simple, farming majority had little exposure to or interest in the Enlightenment. Urban professionals, the educated elite, led it. Doctors, lawyers, government office-holders, technocrats, and some clergymen and noblemen provided the leading voices in this small but important choir. Most members of the long-standing nobility, most merchants great and small, and even more modest craftsmen and wage laborers had little in common with *philosophes* and their supporters. In Portugal, Spain, Italy, the Holy Roman Empire, and the lands of the Austrian Empire, the Enlightenment was dimmer still. The French Revolution and the plague of Napoleon's armies made it everyone's business.

God did not retreat in the nineteenth century, but ingenious scoffers invented elaborate arguments for why we can do fine without him and his Church. The era after the French Revolution, when many people turned away from faith in God, gave rise to an assortment of ideologies that seduced those seeking to answer life's great questions. Romanticism in literature, music, art, and philosophy; powerful revolutionary ideas championed by thinkers such as Charles Darwin, Sigmund Freud, and Friedrich Nietzsche; and political ideologies such as liberalism, socialism, and communism sought to break humanity away from its old Christian understanding. Following in the spirit of the Scientific Revolution and the Enlightenment, these sowed the seeds for the future de-Christianization of Western culture and civilization. In the mid-nineteenth century, a British writer, George Jacob Holyoake, who endured public prosecution for blasphemy, invented a term to refer to his beliefs: secularism. The only reason this individual deserves mention here is that current, Western, mainstream culture consciously looks back to him but ignores his context.

A Century of Progress?

In keeping with the spirit of the Scientific Revolution, the Enlightenment, and the French Revolution, the watchword of the nineteenth-century West was "progress." Progress entailed raw growth, multiplication, and increase, in numerically measurable ways. It stood for advancement, for general improvement; the application of reason and empirical research, it was believed, should always make things better rather than worse. Many people believed it was nature's way, and God's way, that Western Europeans (including Americans) should make the whole world a more civilized, prosperous, and livable place, even as they resorted to the tools of imperial domination and oppression. The growth of Western power and wealth coincides perfectly with decline of Christian faith among the elite, or a reduction of faith to moralism.

Progress entailed expansion in trade that led to wealth creation. Fifteenth-century overseas ventures had rapidly given rise to mercantile empires, the greatest being Spain's in the sixteenth century. Europe's primary import shifted from spices from the East to silver and gold from the Western hemisphere (although the spice trade remained strong). In the seventeenth and eighteenth centuries, however, the bulk of business shifted again, away from spices and bullion to African slaves, tobacco, and sugar (an important ingredient for rum and chocolate, and already at the time the favorite additive for tea and coffee). France and Britain outstripped Spain, the Netherlands, and Portugal in pursuit of wealth through trade, bolstered by overseas colonies and fearsome navies.

All these imperial powers tried to keep the others at bay, and blood flowed for the sake of pure greed. The whole system of cash crops, such as sugar, which was fantastically profitable to investors, ran on the sweating, bloodied backs of African slaves. Mother countries only allowed their colonies to trade with them directly, not with any other imperial power, still less with their immediate neighbors, an arrangement which was a boon to smuggling and piracy, and actually inimical to growth within the colonies. Dutch, British, French, Spanish, and Portuguese imperial navies and foreign legions fought each other all over the globe for greater access to resources and markets. Taxes on trade paid for the wars meant to increase their revenue base.

Overseas empires aside, the West saw continued, almost explosive growth in its homelands during the nineteenth century. The overall population grew from 190 million in 1800 to 260 million in only fifty years. By 1900, it reached 400 million, with 20 percent of the world's total living in only a fraction of its land area. In the earlier stages, agricultural improvements produced more food to feed more mouths, reducing deaths due to malnourishment and attendant illnesses. Later, however, increased prosperity from industrialization raised real wages, enhancing workers' ability, however marginally, to feed themselves and their families.

The *Industrial Revolution*, beginning in the eighteenth century and still going on throughout the world today, accelerated noticeably in the nineteenth century. The term refers to a gradual transformation in work and production, a slow shift from human and animal power, living labor sources, to hydraulic and mineral power used to drive machines. With steam engines, it was no longer necessary to build a factory next to a river or stream to run the water wheel. Products produced and available on the market increased in number and variety, and increasingly, people made them en masse rather than one at a time. The Western economy itself shifted, very slowly and quite irregularly, from simple subsistence to a consumer base. The family, on the land the primary unit of production, started to become what it is more or less today, the prime center for consumption. Marketing took on new ways and means, such as newspaper advertising, to encourage greater consumption of more products of questionable necessity. Fashions and consumption trends, a usual pastime for the rich, reached further down the social scale as product prices fell and the consuming groups grew in size. When coal mining, iron smelting, and the steam engine came together in the railroad, people began to change their attitudes to time, distance, travel, work, leisure, living, and family. Time measurement had to be regularized. The seasons, so central to agrarian life, retreated in relevance.

The effects of the Industrial Revolution, then and now, are immense. Means of production, work and its conditions, place and mode of living, and attitudes toward material consumption moved, for millions, from the normative, humble rural existence of the past to today's opulent suburban society. The path, however, has been anything but easy.

Already in the eighteenth century, the business of making cloth and clothes began to move from women working in their cottages to men in mills, above all in Britain, where industrialism first took root and made its greatest impression in the early stages. Throughout the nineteenth century, people moved from countryside farms to cramped, shoddy, slum housing in towns and cities, while the urban elite, the non-noble business owners, merchants, and financiers, built fine homes in desirable, separate neighborhoods. Cities began to sprawl and segregate according to class. By 1850, perhaps a quarter of Europe's population lived in cities. Industrial laborers, living on low wages and subject to the boom-and-bust vagaries of the consumer market, lost whatever community support and protection had been part of living and working on the land. Cholera outbreaks, which were much more lethal for populations living in close quarters, snuffed out lives in the tens of thousands. Soaring crime and urban riots often resulted from desperation and squalor in the cities, and, in response, urban leaders set up police forces, paid for by local taxation, to protect property and persons.

On the whole, in the early nineteenth century, far fewer got richer while the poor suffered in new or at least different ways. Children working in mine shafts and dangerous factories had no legal protection until the 1830s, when Britain finally passed a law to end the horrific abuse, limiting children under thirteen to nine hours of work with two hours of schooling per day. Women received unsustainably low wages, usually for unskilled tasks. While many young women gladly left the country and headed to the cities to earn for themselves and their families back in the village, the usual expectation, theirs and others', was that they would marry and spend the rest of their days with domestic responsibilities. In a similar vein, men were expected to earn enough wages to supply the needs of their families. When they failed to earn, or squandered their wages in cheap gin and urban amusements, women and children suffered most from it. Women who had to work to make ends meet had to turn care of their children over to others. On the whole, industrialism led to parents spending less time with their children. Squalid, anonymous cities, not the more communitarian countryside, became the seed-bed for extreme social, cultural, and political movements.

Progress, in terms of economic growth, was apparent across the world. In the vast stretches of North America, industrial growth was slower but still noticeable, mainly concentrated in an increasing number of sizeable cities. Especially toward the end of the nineteenth century, the total population swelled rapidly, largely due to immigration. Outside the cities in the United States, land cultivation, livestock, and building saw constant expansion across the continent from east to west. In Latin

America, there were still fewer cities, and industrial growth was slower yet. With smaller populations mainly settled in coastal and fertile areas, southern and central American economies, totally dominated by urban elites, concentrated on supplying European industrial economies with raw materials. Almost the entire world, with the exception of Japan and the interior of China, came under the sway of some Western, European country in the nineteenth century. European exploration and conquest of Africa reached a fever pitch in the last decades before 1900. Even countries that had shown little interest in overseas empire, such as Germany and Italy, carved out their portions—mainly for prestige's sake where economic gain was lacking. Cecil Rhodes, the British diamond magnate who brought much of southern, central Africa under his control, famously remarked, "Expansion is everything."

An increase in wealth is a blessing from God, but it always comes with the same set of temptations. How we respond to them determines the costs, in human terms, of the venture. The main problem with money is that people, whether they have too much or too little, tend to squander it, falling in love with the act of material acquisition itself. Buying turns into an addiction, so even those who have too much money often will do anything to get more. Money is a limitless, artificial commodity of sorts, because it has no inherent worth; it is merely a medium for exchange, a sign for a general agreement about work and product value. While people can also waste food, in its consumption there is a point at which the body can take no more. And with alcohol and drugs, the consumer eventually collapses from the strain. Money itself usually imposes no such bodily burden.

The West's percolating monetary wealth in the nineteenth century followed paths well traveled. Much of it ended up in fewer hands, whose owners tended to use it for their own needs, comfort, amusement, and delight. Those who needed it the most received the least. Government authorities, as always reliant on taxation, spent vast sums on armaments, which are neither productive nor useful, except in case of attack. For the monied, city living distinctly improved. Great cities, where the ruling elite concentrates, beautified themselves for the people who mattered. Paris cleared away slums and installed sewers, clean water supplies, street lighting, broad boulevards, garden parks, river walks, open plazas, museums, monuments, concert halls, and opera houses. The reigning aesthetic recalled the cultural grandeur of Greece and imperial Rome.

To this day, millions of people from all over the world go to admire the beauty and splendor of such urban architectural projects. Public works removed squalor in their areas and shifted it to others, usually those nearest the factories' smoke, soot, and waste by-products. No one believed in progress more than the members of the so-called "middle class" or *bourgeoisie*, those who held the lion's share of monetary assets.

General progress in nineteenth-century material well-being cannot be denied, and cultural change accompanied it, although the nature of its quality is debatable. Reacting strongly to the French Revolution, writers, artists, composers, and intellectuals contributed to a new artistic movement called Romanticism. Against the hyper-rationalism of the Enlightenment, romantic writers, composers, and artists gushed with raw emotion, projecting revolutionary passion and fervor into other, non-political walks of life. Lord Byron, William Wordsworth, Samuel Taylor Coleridge, Victor Hugo, and Johann Wolfgang von Goethe are just a few noteworthy names among romantic writers who conveyed powerful transports of emotion, leading variously to transcendent peace, humiliation and penance, passionate love and death, and even redemptive suicide for love's sake. Romantic composers such as Ludwig van Beethoven (in his later works), Franz Schubert, Friedrich Chopin, Richard Wagner, and Giuseppe Verdi brought classical music out of the church and aristocratic court and into public, urban middle-class venues, glorifying human emotionalism and its ability to make for grand drama. Artists and architects revived Europe's "medieval" artistic heritage in the neo-Gothic style, which often celebrated a romanticized memory of those distant centuries. In the nineteenth century, neo-Gothic art featured a primeval mysticism frequently devoid of theological content.

As a cultural movement, Romanticism was even more lacking in commonalities than the Enlightenment, except for a general revulsion toward the latter's exaggerated rationalism and a shared emphasis on feelings and their siblings: passion, inner knowledge, dreams, mysticism, and yearning for transcendence. Romantics were not nearly as anti-Christian as Enlightenment *philosophes,* but their artistic and literary work reflects a waning interest in Christ, God, the Church, and scriptural truth. The Catholic Church, which lost most of her property in the years before and after the French Revolution, could no longer support the arts as she had in the Italian Renaissance. The main patrons of Romanticism were members of the urban middle classes.

Romanticism finds its philosophical roots in three atypical
Enlightenment writers whose thought leaves little room for God in
the world or for divinely ordained standards of morality. Jean-Jacques
Rousseau, in his famous novel *Émile,* argued that a child's upbringing
should be as natural and unbound by rules as possible. Rousseau often
blamed human failings on "society," which, he said, should be freer
and closer to nature; otherwise it distorts and oppresses. But society is
nothing more than a wide forum, a community of human beings living
according to their loves, good and bad. To blame society for individual
human suffering also removes personal responsibility—something at
which, as we saw earlier, Rousseau personally excelled.

Immanuel Kant, the punctilious Prussian philosopher who never left
his native city of Königsberg, critiqued reason and divided it into two
forms: "pure reason" appropriate for math and science, and "practical
reason," the realm of morality, where we discern God's call to goodness.
Kant disagreed with the belief, shared by John Locke and David Hume,
that humans are passive receptors of sensory impressions. Instead, Kant
emphasized an individual's ability to perceive, to understand actively the
world as best he can, responding to an inner "categorical imperative,"
a moral voice, conscience, which urges each of us to follow the Golden
Rule: do unto others as we would have done unto us. While Kant took
God, morality, free will, and personal creativity seriously, one could
argue that his philosophy allots infallibility to the individual conscience.
Johann Gottlieb Fichte, a contemporary, took this idea even further:
the "I," the ego, does not merely contribute to shaping the world—it
basically determines itself and the world around it. Fichte, one could
argue, was ready to dispense with objectivity for the sake of subjectivity.
But is existence really the way it is because you or I see it that way?

One influential early nineteenth-century thinker, Georg Wilhelm
Friedrich Hegel, a Prussian university professor, denied neither human
reason nor God, but came to alarming conclusions about both. God, in
Hegel's view, was "absolute spirit," which reigned over history absolutely.
God, Hegel thought, had little to do with Christianity, a religion Hegel
found lacking in happiness and hostile to freedom and beauty. Hegel
himself was hostile to history and argued that it does not deserve study
for its own sake, because, as he put it, "the only lesson history teaches is
that history teaches no lessons." Obviously there is no room for divine
revelation in this philosophy, and Hegel's spirit is certainly not holy or

loving. Using individuals as tools, the absolute spirit shapes history as it sees fit, so war is both unavoidable and justifiable. History moves along a trajectory set by the spirit, and Hegel saw the Prussian state, with its constitutional monarchy and massive army, as the summit of human development. Hegel's writings exemplify misplaced love. He denies God his mystery and his love as a divine person; God becomes just another reigning idea.

Hegel's followers include Karl Marx. Marx, in the spirit of Voltaire, Rousseau, and Hegel, redrew all of history into a single, insufferable story of hatred—in Marx's case, hatred between "classes" and oppression by those who controlled the means of production. The French Revolution, in his story, was merely the latest chapter in this story of woe, and the Church is nothing but a device of the rich to stupefy the poor from rebelling against their misery. Against the alienation, inequities, and exploitation of the industrial revolution, Marx advocated violent uprising of the industrial working class—the proletariat—against the business class, the bourgeoisie. After the massacre, which he regarded as inevitable, he foresaw a future without wars, states, or private property, a perfect utopia of proletarians, led by communist party members who had studied his works, all sharing according to their needs. For some reason, people working the land did not figure into his grand vision. In Marx's view, love is a bourgeois delusion, the family is an instrument of oppression, and hope is only a matter of material goods, to be had by all at the cost of violence. The same goes for freedom.

While progress in secular philosophy left much to be desired in the nineteenth century, improvement in general education and scientific knowledge was truly revolutionary in the best sense of the term, on the whole a real gift to humanity. In 1850, about half the European population had at least basic literacy skills, the greater proportion found in countries with more cities and more industrial economies, such as Britain, France, Germany, and the Low Countries. By the end of the century, because of state-mandated primary schooling, these countries achieved about 85 percent literacy, and Europe's south and east rose toward nearly 50 percent, subject to great variation, being far higher in towns and cities and significantly lower in the rural areas.

Beginning in the 1870s, real scientific breakthroughs led to major victories in humanity's timeless struggle against disease. The laboratories of Louis Pasteur in France and Robert Koch in Germany revealed pathogens, tiny micro-organisms, responsible for a host of lethal, epidemic diseases, such as the plague, syphilis, dysentery, pneumonia, tetanus, cholera, typhoid, and tuberculosis, and they sought to develop treatments to guard against them. Although vaccination has ancient roots in China and had been practiced, with limited success, in India and the Ottoman Empire for centuries, the therapy was still rather new in Europe. Smallpox vaccinations became fairly common in the eighteenth century, and Pasteur's work led to successful vaccination against anthrax and rabies. The germ theory of disease was new, and one of the most triumphant achievements of Western science. Some of youth's awful murderers, thanks be to God, began to falter. In other branches of science, engineering and chemistry led to new kinds of products for the continuing industrial revolution: steel, paints, rubber, petroleum-based lubricants and fuel, chemicals, electricity, and the internal combustion engine, all of which contributed to humanity's power to dominate and exploit nature, and render the living conditions more comfortable, according to our preferences.

All these genuine achievements seemed to confirm, for some, a new ideology, founded in human pride, called "positivism," famously articulated by Auguste Comte earlier in the nineteenth century. Comte said that human understanding had progressed, in an astoundingly lop-sided chronology, from the "theological" phase (everything up to the Enlightenment), where people believe in spiritual beings and attribute natural phenomena to their action, to the "metaphysical" phase (the French Revolution to Napoleon), where people understand nature in terms of abstract principles, such as reason, to the final phase, the "scientific" or the "positive," in his own day. Comte is another prime example of a thinker who believes that his era represents the apex against which he may define all prior history. Positivism declares that knowledge can only be empirical, and that nature can only be explained in empirical terms. For Comte, observable facts were the only basis for truth. Problems in society, he argued, could be solved without bothering with human rights or God. Not without reason, some consider Comte the father of sociology and anthropology. Comte suffered mental instability. Toward the end of his life, he styled himself a prophet and positioned positivism as the new "Religion of Humanity." While his faith came to nothing, Comte's view of human understanding is the default position for millions of Westerners today, particularly among those who are inimical to God and religion.

Cutting-edge science, however, quickly lost absolute devotion to empiricism as the nineteenth-century gave way to the twentieth. Some prominent scientists and mathematicians, such as Henri Poincaré, urged researchers to acknowledge the limits of their sensory-based, empirical observations and view their theories as approximating hypotheses rather than final truths. There are aspects of reality beyond what human senses can perceive, and technological development helped to reveal some. At the end of the century, Wilhelm Röntgen discovered X-rays, and other researchers soon linked them to radioactivity and uranium. Around 1900, physicists began to speak authoritatively about the components of the hitherto seemingly invisible, indivisible atom—first the electron, with many more to come. Max Planck developed a quantum theory of energy, and Albert Einstein, in 1905, began to publish his writings about relativity and the time-space continuum. Isaac Newton's tidy universe frayed. About twenty years later, Werner Heisenberg formulated the "uncertainty principle," in effect arguing against the old idea of simple cause-and-effect relations between particles. Many of the supposedly predictable phenomena in nature, he said, act not according to laws, but in accordance with statistical probability.

Other researchers and thinkers did much to undermine certainties of varying antiquity, particularly those related to still popular, Christian beliefs. Some nineteenth-century biblical scholars argued that Scripture was nothing more than a body of written myth stemming from poor, hungry, oppressed Palestinian people, merely expressing their deepest desires in exotic, primitive ways. Charles Lyell, a geological researcher, undermined the idea that the earth stood as it was first created, arguing that the surface of the earth had changed greatly over the past millions of years. Lyell's research threw biblical dating of the age of the planet, which suggested a planet only several thousand years old, out the window. In the field of biology, a number of people articulated theories about gradual evolutionary change, but no one did more to advance it than Charles Darwin and Alfred Wallace. These two researchers, working in separate parts of the world, knew and discussed each other's work through letters, and both conclusively demolished the idea that each species of animals was fixed, their bodies never changing across generations. Darwin and Wallace argued that natural selection, essentially a random but viciously competitive process of life, mutation, and death, explained life on earth as it was in their day. But Darwin, a real revolutionary, took the idea further.

Darwin, and Wallace to a lesser degree, applied evolutionary biology to humans. Darwin showed how the human body derived from the ape, and he claimed that the human mind had no special qualities, not even reason, being much closer in kind to an ape's than a fish's. Belief in any kind of spirit, for Darwin, was the hallmark of primitive species. Having located human beings in the tree of evolution, Darwin failed to acknowledge any real distinctiveness for what it means to be human. While Wallace agreed with much of Darwin's theory of natural selection, even as it applied to humans, he resisted denying the existence of a spiritual realm, belief in which one finds among all peoples throughout the world. Wallace also questioned Darwin's theory with regard to atrophy: if humans were once tree-born monkeys, why did we lose our fur and tail, even as we acquired, through accidental mutation, other recognizably human qualities? Darwin, for his part, chided Wallace for not going far enough, for not daring to attack head-on the traditional, Christian forces of ignorance.

The irony is that the scholarly, scientific, *bourgeois* sophistication of Wallace's and Darwin's ideas led to barbaric, dehumanizing attitudes towards mankind, the one human family. Darwin wrote how "civilized races... encroach on and replace" savage people, the "lower races." Herbert Spencer, who coined the phrase "the survival of the fittest," emphasized that the struggle to survive was also waged, quite naturally, between human beings. Casting away the Christian idea of spiritual equality before God, Spencer frankly endorsed the idea that some races were more evolved, advanced, or developed than others, and the strong should survive, while the weak, whether at home or abroad, should die. For Spencer and other Social Darwinists, it was nature's way. The survival of the fittest was a sign of progress. Bizarre new sciences arose, such as phrenology, which related skull shape to character traits, anthropometry, which determined race according to skull size, and finally eugenics, which promoted human progress through selective breeding. People used them to establish the supremacy of white over dark, of rich over poor, in fact the replacement of the latter by the former in each case. A president of Stanford University in the early twentieth century, David Starr Jordan, believed "the germs of pauperism and crime" were heritable biological traits, and that the states should prevent "feeble-minded" folk from having children. In 1914, Margaret Sanger founded the National Birth Control League, as much for the cause of eugenics as for the emancipation of women.

The nineteenth century had more listeners to such ideas than in earlier centuries, not only because more people were wealthier and literate, but because, especially in the cities, more lived in a milieu of daily anonymity and alienation. As cities burgeoned in size and number, a greater proportion of the population grew up divorced from nature and lived in entirely man-made surroundings, never experiencing smaller, rural communities. Are not city dwellers more likely to fall into the trap of living for themselves, without bothering to help their neighbors? Many living in a fully constructed world fall into the utopian, Enlightenment temptation of thinking they can remake the world and its people to suit themselves (obviously the best sort).

To be sure, no one should romanticize the village, its slowness, its banality, the kind of entrapment that comes from situations where everyone knows everyone and what everyone's ancestors did decades ago. At the same time, in smaller communities, no one is unknown, and everyone has a place and a story of his own, shared with others. Granted, this can lead to abuse, as in the case of the witchcraft accusations thrown at poor, older, single women whom no one in the village liked or wanted to defend. Conflict was inescapable, but even in this, in smaller communities people matter more to others.

Roman writers eighteen centuries earlier complained about their metropolis' noise, dust, filth, and brutality. Where no one matters to anyone, except in their relations to money and power, the individual loses inherent worth. Furthermore, we cannot forget the alienating effects of industrial labor and consumption. Workers did not keep and sell what they produced. People did not buy as much from the maker as from the retailer. Things produced en masse lack the stamp of personality. This is just as true in our own day. While a personal quality is unnecessary for hairpins, it is vital for violins, violas, and celli; after a century of effort, all those produced in factories sound half-alive or just dead. Only those made from a man or a woman's hand are worth listening to.

The nineteenth-century belief in progress and its anonymous, urban culture also gave rise to two thinkers of lesser influence in their own day, but of towering importance in the twentieth century: Friedrich Nietzsche and Sigmund Freud. Nietzsche studied Greco-Roman literature and had a short academic career, truncated by serious mental problems. He wrote prolifically, however, not as much about his field as about contemporary matters, from an angry, anti-Christian perspective.

Nietzsche concerned himself with metaphysics, history, politics, ethics, religion, music, and other topics, and he viciously attacked his own middle-class and civic culture, blaming both Christianity and Judaism for Europe's problems. They had made people soft, sheep-like, a mere herd, unlike the real men of the past, such as Julius Caesar, and more recently, Napoleon.

Nietzsche tried to put together a new philosophy for a new, modern age, one that tried to rise above and beyond rationalism, logic, standard versions of truth, good, evil, and humanity. Naturally, all he could come up with was nihilism, belief in nothing. Nothing mattered but the will— the will to power, especially. Life is nothing but a battle, and nothing was true, good, or beautiful unless one wills it to be, regardless of whether it involves slaughter, abuse, and oppression. Totally giving in to one's will was the only way, Nietzsche said, for humanity to transcend its pathetic self, to become a race of supermen. Nietzsche coined many aphorisms, such as "God is dead," but failed to build a coherent philosophy, beyond base nihilism. His books did not attract much attention until shortly before the end of his life in 1900, and the most radical ones remained unpublished for some years. A man who visited him in the later 1890s met a madman, naked but for a sheet thrown over his shoulders, proclaiming himself the new Christ. Nietzsche best exemplifies the truism that those who try to recreate humanity by rejecting and denying it only doom themselves to wallow beneath.

Sigmund Freud, a Viennese medical doctor, read his Nietzsche and developed a version of psychology consonant with it. Freud turned the human mind into a universe unto itself, effectively constructing a psychology of perfect loneliness. Each one of us is unto him- or herself, and unsurprisingly, we are not at peace. Like a pressure cooker, the "ego," basically our consciousness, keeps down the seething forces of the "id," our inner, subconscious selves, with all its conflicting drives, desires, and wills. The "super-ego," society and its repressive, confining expectations for behavior, adds the heat, which can bring the human pot to the boiling or bursting point. Human psychological disorders, Freud theorized, came from excessive societal pressures and the patient's inability to let off steam, so to speak.

In his analysis, Freud, a grandchild of the Enlightenment, made up a new confessional, but with no moral compass and certainly no Catholic priest. His psycho-analytic therapy claims to interpret the patient's dreams and free-flowing commentary to locate the source of the trouble, which usually comes down to sex and its attendant passions and frustrations. If the patient agreed with his or her therapist's at-times-pornographic interpretations, then psychological equilibrium would be restored. Even infants, Freud said, had significant sexual drives, quite contrary to common perception and common sense. Freudian psychology does not tell us much about humanity, but a great deal about Sigmund Freud. He often based his research on his own interests. After he realized that he had dreamed about his son's death in the First World War before it actually happened, he started investigating paranormal communication. Freud never gained much prominence until after he came to the United States. He repeatedly lost followers over his relentless emphasis on sex. His gift for stubbornness, such as smoking his way through thirty operations to treat cancer in the mouth, explains the consistency in his psychological findings. He died by assisted suicide in 1939, remarking that life "is nothing but torture and makes no sense any more."

From Nietzsche and Freud, taken at face value, one might readily conclude that God is nothing. Christianity, or any faith in God, is something between a farce and a lie, and should be scrapped wholesale in the interest of progress, *i.e.*, human improvement and the advancement of society, scientific knowledge, industrial production, and trade. Religious faith came from the past and belongs in it, having nothing to do with modern, monied, elite, educated society. God is only there to console the poor, the ignorant, and those who have taken leave of their senses for whatever reason. Over the nineteenth century, intellectuals who were set against God's existence and his participation in human life increased in number, ingenuity, passion, and apparent sophistication. The trend continues across the twentieth century into the twenty-first. The fundamentals of this secularist ideology, however, are not modern but millennia old, essentially unchanged since Biblical times. The Book of Wisdom anticipates the nineteenth-century West, its materialism, consumerism, and growing atheism among the highly educated. Recall the quotation from this book's second chapter, reflecting the mentality of the ungodly.

For they reasoned unsoundly, saying to themselves, Short and sorrowful is our life, and there is no remedy when a man comes to his end, and no one has been known to return from Hades.

Because we were born by mere chance, and hereafter we shall be as though we had never been; because the breath in our nostrils is smoke, and reason is a spark kindled by the beating of our hearts. When it is extinguished, the body will turn to ashes, and the spirit will dissolve like empty air.

Our name will be forgotten in time, and no one will remember our works; our life will pass away like the traces of a cloud, and be scattered like mist that is chased by the rays of the sun and overcome by its heat.

For our allotted time is the passing of a shadow, and there is no return from our death, because it is sealed up and no one turns back.

Come, therefore, let us enjoy the good things that exist, and make use of the creation to the full as in youth.

Let us take our fill of costly wine and perfumes, and let no flower of spring pass by us. Let us crown ourselves with rosebuds before they wither.

Let none of us fail to share in our revelry, everywhere let us leave signs of enjoyment, because this is our portion, and this our lot.

Let us oppress the righteous poor man; let us not spare the widow nor regard the gray hairs of the aged.

But let our might be our law of right, for what is weak proves itself to be useless.

(Wisdom 2:1–11)

To attribute nineteenth-century thought to socio-economic structures, to literacy rates and industrial-imperial profits ignores the greatest of human weaknesses: pride, vanity, and sensuality (this last a much broader term than sexuality). Given the opportunity and the resources, people can readily fall into the trap of thinking that we may use God's creation, all aspects of it, according to our tastes, delights, and will, with nothing holding us back. While there is no evil in comfort per se, we can become addicted to it, lose sight of the origin and meaning of creation, and fall into apathy, making everyone around us suffer for our boredom. When we persuade ourselves that life is for physical pleasure and really nothing else, we are admitting that death wins in the end, and often grant ourselves allowance to live life according to our pleasure, with no higher guide or standard. The presence of disposable wealth makes the temptation almost unavoidable.

Still the Christian West

Despite the eloquent voices railing against Christianity and its intellectual heritage, the fact of the matter is that the nineteenth century was a strongly religious age in the West as a whole, at least as much as in the eighteenth century if not more so. Well over half of the population still worked the land and lived and worshiped in their country parishes according to the traditions they had maintained for many centuries. By contrast, in the city of London, 1902–3, only 19 percent of the population attended church, and this number includes Irish immigrant workers, whose rates were considerably higher than the norm. But growing cities still hosted civic religious practices and almost all of the great cathedrals of the eleventh to the sixteenth centuries. Missionaries preached and ministered to the urban poor at home as they did to foreign, colonial people abroad. No worthy church, whether Catholic, Lutheran, Anglican, or other, saw a serious decline or crisis in vocations. The West was still overwhelmingly Christian, granting freedoms to Jews in many areas (though, unfortunately, not all).

Education of the young was still mainly in the hands of the churches, and yet, the state in the nineteenth century West, under the influence of its urban elite, actively sought to expand its control of basic education at the expense of the churches that traditionally supplied the teachers. Britain, France, and Germany led the way with government initiatives to provide primary education for all children. In these countries, the state, in setting standards for satisfactory performance, moved in and took over part of the churches' former purview, and, in places, undermined their educational mission. France saw a long, protracted struggle between its two, rival school systems, the one Catholic, the other secular, mutually mistrusting and exclusive. In Germany, the situation was worse. After the unification of that country in 1870, the chancellor, Otto von Bismarck, pursued a policy of pushing the Catholic Church out of education or subjecting it to state control. The administration of marriage and family law met the same fate.

Nonetheless, the nineteenth century also saw a genuine religious revival, probably in part a response to the anti-Christian excesses of the French Revolution and its aftershocks, the growth of massive, exploitive, dehumanizing cities, and God's reminding his people that he is, after all, still very much in the picture. The Holy Spirit gives rise to new movements in the universal Church, just as he moves hearts to love and forgiveness. Spontaneous devotional movements and centers of adoration sprung up after people experienced remarkable visions in Paris in 1830, at Lourdes in 1858, in Knock, Ireland in 1879, and, amidst the carnage of the First World War, in Fátima, Portugal, in 1917. New Catholic orders from the nineteenth century, such as the Salesians of Don Bosco, who ministered to homeless street boys, and the Oblates of St. Francis de Sales, an educative and missionary order of priests, look back to St. Francis, the great doctor of the Church from the late sixteenth and early seventeenth century, who taught that anyone can find holiness in life, no matter what their station, vocation, or career. Protestants were hardly to be left out, as new ecclesial movements such as Methodism, which stems from the eighteenth century, continued to prosper and spread to and throughout the United States, especially during the "Great Awakenings." Religious and political leaders of the United States in particular emphasized their own special American, divine vocation, as God's chosen people, to spread the gospel and prepare the world for Christ's return.

The nineteenth century also certainly did not lack in great intellectual lights who supported a Christian view of current affairs. In the first half of the nineteenth century, Thomas Carlyle, a Scottish writer who was raised in a devout Calvinist family but refused to follow his parents' wishes for him to become a Presbyterian minister, dedicated his life to writing works of social criticism and recent history. His essay of 1829, "Signs of the Times," attacked utilitarianism, a trendy new British philosophy that argued for using the "principle of utility," referring loosely to the greatest happiness for the greatest number, as the only rational standard for weighing government policy and legislation, all other moral considerations aside. Carlyle bemoaned the dehumanizing, mechanistic thinking of his age, which had taken over everything—politics, economics, society, and even the education of the young:

> Instruction, that mysterious communing of Wisdom with Ignorance, is no longer an indefinable tentative process, requiring a study of individual aptitudes, and a perpetual variation of means and methods, to attain the same end; but a secure, universal, straightforward business, to be conducted in the gross, by proper mechanism, with such intellect as comes to hand.

With inimitable style, Carlyle railed against his society's slavish adoration of earning and amassing money, and the deep-seated horror at "not succeeding," *i.e.,* not making mounds of it. Business owners' blithe attribution of starvation-level wages for their workers to market forces epitomized, for Carlyle, the cultural disease of the day. The belief that everything in life was a kind of mechanism and that every problem had a mechanical solution, Carlyle argued, removed God from the world, opened the door to atheism, and denied humanity its inherent dignity. While his approach to serious social problems, such as the horrific poverty of the industrial centers, was romantic at best, placing hope in heroic, dynamic political leadership, Carlyle remains a relevant Jeremiah for capitalist consumerists everywhere.

A diverse tradition of Christian intellectual and social critique thrived during the course of the nineteenth century. In Denmark, Søren Kierkegaard's philosophical works from the 1840s and '50s attacked established churches and the whole idea of Christendom as a political order, but also promoted faith lived as a personal decision. Later generations of existentialist thinkers look to him as a founding father. John Henry Newman, an Englishman whose life spans almost the whole nineteenth century, devoted much of his learning and brilliance to Christian theology and apologetics, first Anglican, then, after 1845, Catholic. He defended liberal education as proper training for the mind, but he fought against "liberalism," a blanket term for those attitudes and ideas, stemming from the Enlightenment and the French Revolution, which prize human freedom in all walks and aspects of life as the highest of all goals for the human being, denying that there is fixed truth in religion. Obviously this cannot be, if one believes that the greatest thing one can do in life is to serve God, literally *to be there* for him. While we cannot free ourselves from our own natural limitations, while we cannot recreate ourselves perfect and anew, the truth can set us free—free from . the temptations that so often bring us crashing to the ground.

Pope Leo XIII (r. 1878–1903) was an intellectual in his own right and made Newman a cardinal in 1879. Leo XIII took on the immense and difficult task of engaging nineteenth-century modern, liberal thought and politics, rather than condemning them, while yet upholding traditional Catholic teaching. While he urged Catholic theologians to revisit St. Thomas Aquinas as a prime example for reconciling faith and reason, he opened the Vatican archives to researchers, praised objectivity in Catholic historical writing, and supported research projects in the natural sciences. His encyclical *Rerum Novarum* (1891) is a major work of socio-economic thought, in which he recommends a living wage for all workers and their families, upholds the human right to private property, and articulates ways to mollify and even overcome the growing barrier between social classes. Leo XIII commenced a tradition of papal teachings about social justice that has thrived ever since, and his writings are still of distinct relevance in the twenty-first century globalized economy.

The nineteenth century was as fraught with problems, considerations, arguments, ideas, and issues as any other. We cannot forget the Protestant Reformation in the sixteenth and seventeenth centuries or the great debates over heresies in the centuries before. The historical drama rarely enjoys a short intermission, and if it does, it is merely getting ready for the next act. Standard narratives of Western Civilization pay extra attention to the nineteenth century, because most of the current, mainstream ideologies of our day stem from its thinkers, and many of the industries for our technologically enabled standard of comfort have their roots firmly planted in that period. Furthermore, in the wake of the French Revolution, the nineteenth century saw the continuing political contest between left and right, progressive and conservative, parliamentary democracy and aristocracy, republicanism and monarchy, yet another phase in the eternal human search for freedom.

The Struggle for Freedom

All people everywhere want to be free of their pains, worries, and burdens. This is a timeless, universal human truth. No one rises in the morning in the hope that their child, spouse, neighbor, employer, or local and state authorities will trounce them and annihilate their dignity. The problem is that people cannot agree among themselves about how to arrange affairs of state so that such abuse of power will not occur. In previous centuries, when almost all rulers acknowledged God as sovereign, they squandered money and spilled blood, invoking his name for justice. Lip service is not an effective prophylactic against error. During the nineteenth century, however, political movements had more to do with recent history than with humanity and our creator. As they grew in fervor and extremism, they laid the groundwork for the twentieth century's obscene massacres, the worst in human history. Nationalism, liberalism, conservatism, and socialism would not be bad in themselves if people did not love them so completely, to the exclusion of God.

Nationalism is a political ideology with specific implications, as opposed to patriotism, which is a general love of country. The thinking behind nationalism is perhaps as old as humanity. All people have tribal impulses, wanting to stick together in groups according to forms of common identity, such as ethnicity, race, culture, language, and history. We see it at work all across the world and throughout recorded time. These groups want autonomy for themselves and their members. Nineteenth-century nationalism acknowledged these urges but linked them to the modern state apparatus, constructing and empowering relatively new identities over masses of people who would never get to know each other. Nationalist groups in Europe believed that the French, or the Germans, Polish, Irish, or whoever, existed as a biological race distinct from its neighbors, if not immediately noticeable in facial features, then certainly through language and cultural heritage. Nationalists wanted the state and its borders to reflect that supposed reality. The people itself would be sovereign, managing their own affairs free from any other state or imperial, dynastic claim.

While the idea applied more easily to the nation-states of France and Spain, it was very problematic for Germany, Italy, Poland, Hungary, and the rest of Eastern Europe, where four empires, the German (after 1870), the Austrian, the Russian, and the Ottoman lorded it over more ethnicities than one, and usually several. Where the German Empire entailed minorities of Jews and Poles, the Austrian had, in addition to German speakers, Hungarians, Czechs, Slovaks, Slovenes, Croats, Italians, Poles, Romanians, Ukrainians, and others. The Russian and Ottoman Empires were even more ethnically diverse. Nationalism became the justification for anti-imperial, revolutionary groups who wanted to establish an independent state for people such as themselves. Nationalism, which united elsewhere, could detonate in these empires.

Liberalism tended to sympathize with nationalism, but not invariably. Liberals generally viewed the French Revolution as a necessary and good event, despite its excesses. Nineteenth-century liberals preferred constitutional governments over princely dynasties; they wanted to be citizens of a state and not subjects of a king. Sovereignty, for them, lay in the state's meritocratic bureaucracy, not in a person or

God. The university-educated, the professionals, the lawyers, doctors, professors, business elite, and merchants, the members of the upper-middle class tended to have strong liberal leanings. They were usually anti-democratic, distrusting villagers with their seemingly foolish piety and childish allegiance to aristocrats, whom they distrusted even more. Nineteenth-century liberals agreed with Adam Smith, and generally wanted the government out of their business interests. They espoused free trade and unregulated labor wages and conditions, and would have preferred a world without labor unions. The poor, they thought, should make out as best they can on their own devices.

Conservatives, on the other hand, regarded the French Revolution as a real tragedy, although only serious reactionaries argued for trying to turn back the clock and pretend as if it never happened. Conservatives favored monarchy in general and saw little benefit in constitutional republics or democracies. Nineteenth-century conservatives wanted political authority to remain in the hands of the landed nobility, religious authority to remain in the established church of the land, and sovereignty to stay with the ruling dynasty of monarchs, as God, they believed, had appointed them for it. Conservatives preferred an integrated, hierarchical society of varying orders rather than an amorphous society of urbanites differentiated chiefly by monetary income and net worth. They generally tended to support government interventions on behalf of the poor and had nothing against labor unions as long as they behaved in an orderly fashion. In central and eastern Europe, nineteenth-century conservatives regarded nationalism as destabilizing, if not outright destructive.

In 1815, the Congress of Vienna had done the right thing; it had picked up the pieces of Napoleon's shattered Europe and tried to contain France rather than punish her. Prince Metternich, the Austrian chancellor who played a leadership role during the congress, wanted to avoid further bloodshed at all costs. But the revolutionary cat was long out of the bag. Almost everywhere in Europe, Napoleon had had his supporters, and the nationalist, liberal call for equality, liberty, and fraternity still resounded in the ears of the disgruntled. In the early nineteenth century, the immediate aftermath of the French Revolution, numerous aftershocks of violent, revolutionary upheaval disturbed the peace of Europe, with mixed results. Spanish liberals rose up against their king, demanding a constitutional government, but the French and the Austrians helped Spanish conservatives to put it down. In the

1820s, Greek liberals tried to free themselves of Ottoman rule, assisted by Britain, France, and Russia, each for the sake of their own imperial ambitions in the Mediterranean. The Serbs followed the Greeks in 1830, only to fall under the shadow of the Austrians and the Russians, each claiming to be the rightful "protector" of the Balkans' Slavic peoples.

Across the wider West, in Latin America, the 1810s and 1820s saw numerous uprisings against Spanish imperial authority, which Napoleon had so successfully undermined. But these revolutionary movements were actually more conservative than liberal. Simon Bolívar and others like him declared that authority in the newly formed Latin American republics should lie in the hands of the Spanish descendants who made up the local elite. Latin American revolutionary movements threw off the yoke of the Spanish monarchy but left a legacy of instability. In the early 1830s, a reactionary French king, Charles X, finally had to learn that the liberal revolution could not be undone, and he fled the country in disgrace. Britain, however, facing major discontent in England and Ireland, basically muddled through. The government, with its unwritten constitution for parliamentary monarchy, made enough concessions to prevent the outbreak of violent revolution.

The later nineteenth century saw new political movements take more extreme tacks, especially in terms of denying God's existence and attacking his Church as a source of falsehood, corruption, and oppression. Socialism, which in the early nineteenth century had begun as tiny utopian communal experiments, such as Robert Owen's in New Lanark, Scotland, was not necessary anti-Christian but for the tendency among socialist thinkers, such as the Count of Saint-Simon and Charles Fourier, to favor free expression of sexuality at the expense of the nuclear family. By the mid-nineteenth century, Karl Marx's communist revolutionary ideology gave socialism a set of fangs. Other little revolutionary groups popped up during the later nineteenth century, groupings of anarchists who hated capitalism, the state, major industries, all churches, and almost all forms of organization. Some protested peacefully, while others perpetrated murder for no stated purpose apart from chaos. One young Italian anarchist stabbed Empress Elisabeth of Austria in 1898, who had had little to do with politics throughout her sixty years. The only reason he gave is that he wanted to kill a royal. The presence of groups condoning such behavior gives us an indicator of the level of nihilist degeneration in the West.

If all these and other political movements called for liberation, and none were content with the spiritual freedom that comes from faith in Christ, what did they mean by the term? In the nineteenth century, the term "liberty" took on another meaning in addition to the legal one, about the freedom from suppression of basic rights, such as the right to move, infringed by arbitrary seizure and imprisonment. The sometimes enigmatic Abraham Lincoln summed it up when he articulated two rival conceptions of liberty: for some, "liberty" means each can "do as he pleases with himself and the product of his labor"; for others, it means "for some men to do as they please with other men and the product of other men's labor." In the latter Lincoln was obviously referring first to slavery, but the broader point is that he uses "liberty" to refer to use of products, implying material livelihood more than rights and privileges.

One could argue that the American Civil War, the costliest war in the history of United States, both in terms of people killed in raw numbers and in proportion to the general population, would never have happened if the political leaders had agreed on a process of emancipation for the slaves, such as occurred in Russia in 1861. There, Tsar Alexander II, in spite of opposition from aristocrats and many landowners, issued the Russian serfs a blanket grant of freedom and rights to the lands they lived on, at the price of a heavy bond, to be paid back over many years. Through it, the landowners received an indemnity for the loss of their unpaid labor force. The arrangement was fraught with difficulty, but it did not lead to a million military casualties, 620,000 of them deaths (most due to disease), to say nothing of devastated cities and a ravaged countryside, especially in the South. If the Russian Empire could manage to emancipate its many millions of serfs without resorting to civil war, then the United States should have been able to find a way, too.

Domestic wars and revolutions are noisy, bloody, wasteful, destructive affairs, usually with few improvements in law and the state to recommend them. Many come from excessive love of ideology. In the face of miserable harvests, food shortages and high prices in the cities, which already suffered from rising unemployment, too little social welfare, and horrific living conditions, the year 1848 saw violent revolutions surge across the face of Europe. All combined various revolutionary, ideological impulses, and all foundered in their extremism. Middle-class liberals wanted the usual list of political reforms – written constitutions, less economic regulation, and greater liberties and suffrage for themselves – but they pulled back when the poorer proletarians and young students took to the streets.

In France, the bourgeoisie wanted the French Revolution's reforms but without another Terror. France's king fled the uprising, and the rebels set up another republic, which its first president toppled in a coup three years later. In the German states, princes gave up their monopoly on power and accepted liberal constitutions. In 1848–9 a parliament in Frankfurt tried to set up a constitution to unite all the German states except for Austria, but when they offered the crown to the king of Prussia, he rejected it, saying in effect that the crowns were only worth the trouble if they came from God. The project failed, and German unity had to wait for another day. The Austrian Empire and the states of Italy saw similar revolutions but with a stronger, more pronounced nationalist element. In all cases, the middle classes, scared by the street violence, threw in their lot with established authority. Military forces cracked down and restored order using regrettable means.

The next major political events showed the growing power of state governments, nationalist ideals, and the perennial willingness to use war to achieve political ends. From 1859 to 1870, the Italian states managed to form a single nation-state, following the leadership of a liberal constitutionalist, Camillo Cavour, the prime minister of the kingdom of Piedmont. France sided with Piedmont in a war against the Austrian Empire to force it to relinquish Italy's northeast, at the price of Piedmont's territory in the northwest. As in the French Revolution, the nationalists divested the Church of its lands, and the popes hunkered down in the Vatican, objecting to their losses but unable or unwilling to do much about them until 1929.

Germany unified as well, under the leadership of a conservative statesman, and the process was even bloodier. In the 1860s, Chancellor Otto von Bismarck, a Prussian nobleman mentioned earlier, orchestrated a series of crises and wars in order to bring all German states into union with Prussia and to drive Austria out of their affairs once and for all. The strategy culminated with the Franco-Prussian War of 1870, set off by Bismarck, mainly through lies and deceit. The French fell for his trap and declared war, and the southern German states threw their lot in with Prussia, fearing yet another French invasion of their lands. The war ended in 1871 with the French soundly defeated. The French emperor fled the country, and the German Empire declared its existence. France sank into a brief civil war, the Paris Commune, between left-wing urban rebels and the authority of the French central government. In the midst of the violence and chaos, Marxists thought their day had come, but it was over in a matter of weeks. 20,000 died before the fighting stopped. The Commune made the French political left and right even more mutually suspicious and loathing than ever.

Wars in the nineteenth century were about as gruesome, costly, wasteful, and unnecessary as those that came before. Republics and constitutional monarchies are no freer of the addiction to armed violence than absolute monarchies or petty principalities. A political system in itself, a mere form of organization, is no guarantee against human fallibility. Nor is religious orientation! Enlightened polities in the nineteenth century were every bit as warlike as the old-fashioned, ostensibly Christian, multinational empires, whose emperors claimed to rule by the grace of God. Humanity struggles on in the eternal present, its greatest capacity the ability to make peace and go on with life after fits of senseless hatred and gratuitous violence.

By the end of the nineteenth century and the dawn of the twentieth, the lands of the West were more populous, productive, and prosperous than ever. Its farms produced more and more food, and its businesses churned out more and more products at lower and lower prices. Their interests spanned the globe. The overwhelming majority of the world's people lived under the dominance of some Western state, with one quarter under the British. London was the world financial center, and British ships carried most of the world's trade. Throughout the West, however, at least half of the population still lived on farms and in villages, worshipping and meeting in their old churches. They felt little of the new wealth and had limited exposure to the revolutionary ideas of the urban elite. Literacy rose on all sides, but the realities of life kept it simple. Only a few perspicacious individuals predicted the nightmare that would beset the West in 1914–8, and no one could really do anything to prepare for it, despite the fact that people, in their freedom, had dug their own, ample graves.

10

Slaughter and Surfeit

When you hear of wars and insurrections, do not be terrified;
for such things must happen first, but it will not immediately be
the end.

(Luke 21: 10)

For most people, the twentieth century is synonymous with modern times, with *modernity*. Modernism, a set of ideas and attitudes stemming from the Scientific Revolution, Enlightenment, French Revolution, and the nineteenth century, gained strength, sophistication, and wide popularity in the twentieth century. But these terms—modernism, modernity, or modern times—should not denote a new stage in humanity's evolution, in the sense that modern men and women are fundamentally, essentially different from what they were in other centuries and eras. The twentieth century shows, in no uncertain terms, that the Renaissance periodization of ancient, medieval, and modern history really fails to do justice to the fact that humanity has not fundamentally changed. The history of the West shows us the same kinds of struggles, triumphs, and failures, on a human level. God's creature stands, and stumbles, as ever.

The twentieth-century West is a case study for the timeless temptations of wealth, and for humanity's unchanged, flawed nature, as observed in the behavior of states and individuals. The twentieth century ushered in airplanes, nuclear bombs, computers, space flight, and other technological achievements, and the greatest growth in population,

235

industrial and agricultural production, and wealth creation, especially in the West, in the whole of its history. Technology and consumption patterns altered lifestyles faster than ever before, but nothing changed people's souls fundamentally. The twentieth century owes most of its basic ideas and behaviors to those found in past. There is nothing new under the sun.

While the next chapter will explore the basic attitudes, values, and beliefs in modernism, this one shows what Western humanity did with its newfound power and riches. Casting off God's revealed injunctions, people great and small, powerful and weak, took moral matters into their own hands and used God's creation for their own purposes. They had done so in the past, but with poorer tools. The result was as expected: living hell for other people, and themselves.

A Century of War:
World War I and its Offspring

Barbarism is a universal human failing, the sign of a perverted heart, which employs machetes, bludgeons, handguns, surgical tools, or high-tech weaponry to express its love of destructive power. The extent to which a culture, society, or regime embraces evil, especially in the form of hatred and violence, is a measure of its barbarity. No grouping of humanity, civilized or otherwise, is totally free of it, because we have the freedom and the weakness to choose it over the better course of action. War is a barbarous plague on humanity, one that is of our own making. The temptation of war has proven unavoidable in every period of history, but people can end wars, too, when they come to their senses and decide that enough madness is enough, that it is time to reconcile, rebuild, and let life regain the upper hand. There is probably not a single year in all of human history in which one group of people somewhere did not savage another. No state system or international political order will effectively guard against it, just as no religion will, either. War is an aspect of the unchanging human condition.

Modern progress, whatever ideas, systems, institutions, and gadgetry are associated with the term, provides no prophylactic against war. Military technology, from the hurled rock to the neutron bomb, enhances war's savagery rather than reducing it, chiefly because it increases the distance between combatants, between the killers and the killed, so that lethal fighting becomes increasingly faceless, to the point of invisibility and anonymity. One who merely loads shells or presses a button probably suffers fewer qualms than those who commit face-to-face butchery (sadists and psychopaths aside). Modern twentieth-century politics, whatever its supposed advantages over what came before, plunged the West into war on a scale as yet unseen. In the First World War, republics, parliamentary monarchies, and old-fashioned empires slaughtered millions over nothing, because their leaders thought it a viable option for their interests. With its new and marvelously terrifying devices, the twentieth-century West, so proud of its real progress and achievements, tore itself to shreds.

The fall into war in 1914 was so unlikely and uncoordinated that it appears almost as a spontaneous reflex for murder-suicide. In late June, a young Serbian nationalist assassinated an Austrian archduke and his wife in Sarajevo, while most European leaders were either on vacation or planning one. Germany's emperor sent his Austrian counterpart a brief telegram promising his support, then got in his yacht and sailed to Norway. About a month went by before the Austrian Empire issued an ultimatum to Serbia, an independent, Slavic, Balkan state, holding it responsible for the assassination and dictating the terms for uprooting the alleged conspiracy. Almost every power in Europe threatened the others not to get involved, saying that if they did, there would be war. Within about a week, however, the Austrian Empire, the Russian Empire, the French Republic, the German Empire, and the British Empire had either sent their soldiers to the front or made an official declaration of war. Little Belgium proclaimed its neutrality in vain, and Italy bided its time before taking sides. Spain's king and parliament did the right thing and did not get involved.

The folly of 1914 belongs as much to the preceding centuries as to the twentieth. Mobs of young men volunteered for service, singing and dancing in the streets. The war, so many thought, would be over by Christmas; it would clear out the dross, show the neighbor who's boss, and make everything better. Sigmund Freud, on hearing the news, noted that he finally felt proud to be an Austrian citizen. Putting national politics in place of morality, churches and clergymen invoked God's blessings on their troops, and hell-fire on their opponents in the field.

Generals, many of whom had last seen military combat in the nineteenth century, lined up their artillery and infantry with the goal of punching a hole in the enemy's lines for the cavalry, which, they were certain, would wrap it all up. Some voiced doubts whether machine guns could stop a charging horse. An alarmingly small number of military and political professionals feared that recent developments in weapons technology would lead to stalemate, prolonging the conflict, and unprecedented slaughter.

In July 1914, after Austria had made its ultimatum to Serbia, Pope Pius X offered to act as mediator for negotiations in order to avoid war. Rebuffed, he issued a plea to all Catholics of the world. Just as the warring states lined up for slaughter, on August 2, 1914, the pope, himself just days away from his own death, prophetically warned that "nearly all Europe is being dragged into the whirlpool of a most deadly war, of whose dangers, bloodshed and consequences no one can think...." Proclaiming his profound anxiety and bitter grief, he exhorted all Catholic laity and clergy to join him in special prayers "that God may be moved to pity and may remove as soon as possible the disastrous torch of war and inspire the supreme rulers of the nations with thoughts of peace and not of affliction." But their hearts were hardened.

The first year of battle in 1914 should have made it obvious to all that no single power could win a clear victory over its enemies. The Germans could not handily defeat the French if the British backed them, but they could hold back the Russians, something that the Austrians could not. Because German soldiers and officers had to bolster the Austrian army against the Russians, they could not throw their whole military might against the French and their reluctant British ally, whose great navy had imposed a total blockade against all German sea trade. The Italians, who had been allied to Germany and Austria, threw in their lot against Austria in 1915, but they accomplished little. Later, Balkan countries attacked each other and the Ottoman Empire, and the British diversion against the Turks came to nothing. British colonists in Africa and Asia dutifully invaded their German counterparts where geography allowed. Throughout the West, the circus had a truly global appeal.

The years wore on, and the meat-grinders of war massacred young men by the millions, turning large areas of Europe into a morbid wasteland. Why should European leaders call off the horror as long as they had young blood to spill and money to spend in pursuit of imperial ambitions that few dared to question? "War has nothing to do with chivalry anymore," a German general wrote to his wife after the first "successful" chlorine gas attack against the British in Flanders in 1915. "The higher civilization rises, the more vile man becomes." Political leaders hardened their resolve and would not relinquish belief in the possibility of a knockout blow. In the history of the world, World War I was the greatest annihilation of Christians by Christians, although certainly not every fighter was Christian. From 1914, Pope Benedict XV tirelessly called for peace, for reason, for momentary cease-fires, and negotiations, but warring parties either dismissed him as irrelevant or condemned him for partisanship. Only Charles I, the young, new Emperor of Austria who ascended the throne in 1916, strove to negotiate an end to the war, but all his efforts likewise came to nothing.

American involvement in the final year of the war boosted the massive, developing country into Great Power status. American deaths from German submarine attacks, as well as German scheming with Mexico, made it possible for the American president, Woodrow Wilson, to align his generally isolationist people with the French and the British. This became even easier after the Russian monarchy collapsed and withdrew in 1917. Then Wilson could argue three falsehoods: that this was the war to end all wars; that monarchy as such, the political system itself, was responsible for it; and that the war would make the world safe for democracy. Needless to say, it didn't. Wilson was very much a man of the nineteenth century. He was profoundly racist against blacks, and his peace plan, the famous Fourteen Points, was utopian. It was meant to appeal to his domestic political front, and none of the main combatants held much stock in it anyway. During the war, Wilson ruthlessly repressed the German minority in the United States, although they had done nothing to form a fifth column on the home front.

On his own time, not ours, according to his will, not ours, God heard the cry of the poor, the suffering, the wails of children, and took pity. The end came suddenly, almost surprisingly, in 1918. The most efficient and effective killing machine in the war, the German army, having achieved victory against the Russians in the east, surrendered, after yet another attempted knockout blow against its enemies in the west. Germany's western front had not broken, and two and a half million troops kept the defensive system intact. The Germans had fought entirely on enemy territory, not their own, for four years. Nonetheless, her supreme military commanders reckoned that they could not stop the combined forces of Britain, France, and the United States; with jarring suddenness they threw in the cards and told the emperor to share power with the Social Democrats in the German parliament. Reformers, not military leaders, sued for peace and accepted the terms. Before the fighting actually stopped, the military leaders instigated the legend that socialists, liberals, Catholics, and Jews had stabbed mighty Germany in the back. The lie then took on a vicious life of its own.

No one won the First World War, which had butchered ten million men for nothing, not to mention the wounded and traumatized. "Missing in action" usually meant blown to bits or buried alive during bombardments. To add to the punishment, a flu pandemic, which began in 1918 and raged over the world for the next two years, killed twenty million in the first seventeen weeks, and many more afterwards. Like the war, the death toll was highest among young adults. It killed more American soldiers training at the camps than German guns did at the front in France. To make matters worse, the peace settlement, the infamous, iniquitous Treaty of Versailles, made no attempt at much-needed reconciliation, and all but guaranteed the next war that was to come.

The way the Americans, French, and British behaved at the proceedings shows the hollowness and hypocrisy of the Fourteen Points, which had been the express basis for Germany's surrender. Neither German nor Russian delegations were allowed to participate in drafting the settlement. The allied negotiators dismantled the German, Austrian, and Ottoman Empires and redrew the map of eastern Europe and the Middle East with only the dimmest idea of which ethic groups lived where. They laid total responsibility for the conflict on Germany, which is historically preposterous, and tried to render her a pliant, client state for her neighbors, an unarmed, open market, principally for British and French trade. Germany was not even left in charge of her own ports, rivers, and rail lines. Through massive, crippling reparations payments, her industrial economy was to support her former enemies for at least a generation.

The arbiters of victors' justice totally truncated Austria and Hungary back to their thirteenth- and eleventh-century dimensions, respectively. Romania ballooned, as a reward for her suicidal declaration of war against the Austrians and Germans, and Czechoslovakia and Yugoslavia, two new states, were cobbled together, lacking any interior coherence but for the fact that the people of these regions had formerly lived under Austrian rule. None of the Allies, however, wanted to enforce the humiliation of their vanquished enemies with manned garrisons, and the Americans withdrew their two-million-man army with alacrity. The victors somehow thought the establishment of parliamentary democracies throughout central and eastern Europe would make for future peace. All of them fell apart in less than twenty years.

What had the war been for? What had it accomplished? The only honest answer is "nothing," but political ideology afforded other, empty replies. For the Americans, the world had been made safe for their democracy, and to this day, people argue that monarchy is conducive to war, whereas democracies further peace in general and do not go to war against other democracies. The British and the French achieved their imperial ambitions and confirmed their self-righteousness, but they mortgaged their empires' futures in doing so. Russian Communists, successful revolutionaries in 1917 and victors in the horrific, ensuing civil war until 1921, which killed millions, said the war was part of the inevitable self-destruction of capitalism and the end of its universal oppression of working people. For nationalists in the former Austrian Empire, the war proved the lie that the nation-state is the only feasible system of government regardless of culture, history, and circumstances. Unfortunately, in the years that followed, the new eastern European countries went to war with each other, and one by one decayed into fascist dictatorships. The Germans bemoaned their fate, and apparently learned nothing but to distrust their new republican constitution, their European neighbors, and themselves.

So the greatest war in Western history had been in vain. The march of progress was over, and in truth, to some extent, it had never been more than the blind leading the blind, or just a confused thrashing of oars on the ship of fools. What then was to be done with "modern" Western man, who had just demonstrated his greater, barbaric aptitude for destroying than building? Instead of turning back to God for love, hope, and inspiration, far too many succumbed to the temptation of abandoning truth, goodness, and beauty altogether as empty lies. Where the French Revolution had attempted to drive God out of politics, constitutions, and matters of state, and place man on his throne, the communist and fascist revolutions of the twentieth century aimed to annihilate God and create a new and improved version of humanity, to serve a deified state in God's place. Everyone suffered for it, especially those who loved God.

Russian communists, also called Bolsheviks and Marxist-Leninists, ruthlessly terrorized the Orthodox Church, its defenseless priests and adherents, as supporters of the toppled monarchy and potential counter-revolutionaries. Nationalized land and factories, a gutted middle-class, and total control by the state were supposed to replace marriage, family, and Christian culture with one devoid of inequality, abuse, and oppression. The leaders of the new order, however, were demons, not angels. Lenin exhorted his Bolsheviks to kill without remorse, but, to prove he was not a barbarian, he subsidized the Bolshoi ballet. Stalin, who assumed the summit of power in the late 1920s, murdered and starved perhaps as many as ten million, and he drove tens of millions more into state slavery, in the interest of speedy, forced industrialization. His demonic cult of work procured a 400 percent increase in industrial output from 1928 to 1940, with no thought of the horrific cost. Stalin's great ambition was to be the most terrible of all Russia's tsars, and he succeeded handily.

"Tear the very idea of God from the hearts of men," Pope Pius XI wrote, "and they are necessarily urged by their passions to the most atrocious barbarity." Compared to Stalin, even Hitler and Mussolini were lesser devils, in a manner of speaking, though of a similar nature. Acknowledging nothing greater than themselves, their fascist ideology embraced violence and war for the greater good of their chosen people. Fascist parties across the world did the same, setting themselves against communism, democracy, the rule of law, rationalism, and pacifism. Turning Nietzsche's worst ideas into political platforms and propaganda campaigns, fascists in eastern, central, western Europe, and even in the Americas exhibited that the First World War had taught them nothing. They picked their scapegoats and, where they managed to seize political power, armed themselves for the coming conflict.

It is actually incorrect to call Adolf Hitler a devil, a demon, or even a monster, because in truth he was just a human being, and a trite little narcissist at that. For most of his life he did nothing monstrous and actually lived a banal existence until he entered into politics. His indisputably hideous deeds stem from many years of misplaced love of himself and his delusions. As a child, he was unexceptional, terribly spoiled by his mother and harshly treated by his father, and exhibited both good and bad behaviors found in most youngsters. He aspired to urban sophistication, but his family lacked the money. He thought himself a born genius, a great, and unappreciated, artist, architect, and composer, although his total musical training comprised a few lackluster months of piano lessons. For him, rejection or apparent failure only revealed others' inability to appreciate his immense, innate talent. Basically lazy, he only worked on sketches and plans for his artistic projects, none of which came to anything. He lived in a world of his own, in which he believed he knew the worth of all things and people. While Catholicism struck him as the foolish nonsense of lesser mortals, Hitler's virulent anti-Semitism developed only later.

After his mother died in 1907 – Hitler showed profound, heartfelt thanks to the Jewish doctor who tended to her – he seems to have been able to love only himself, best expressed in his verbose cultural and political musings. He found life's greatest moments in his emotional reactions to the operas of Richard Wagner, performed in Vienna under the direction of Gustav Mahler, a famous Jewish composer, conductor, and Catholic convert. One companion remembers Hitler saying, "Opera is the best kind of religious service." He readily accepted and shared Wagner's titanic pride, especially his self-proclaimed artistic, revolutionary vision of nationalist, German cultural supremacy. Correspondingly, Hitler derided Czech, Hungarian, Jewish, and all modernist, cosmopolitan artistic activities.

Hitler had two exceptional abilities that came forward in early adulthood. The first was his memory: large and excellent, he could draw on it for hours of blather. After failing out of school, he moved to a subsidized poorhouse in Vienna, made a few coins selling his postcards and paintings, and taught himself about the political concerns of the early twentieth century. The cacophony of complaints, paralyzing quarrels, and brawls in the parliament of the multi-national, multi-ethnic Austro-Hungarian Empire taught him to hate institutions of democratic government and distrust all non-German people. He borrowed books from the local library about politics, social Darwinism, eugenics, anti-Semitism, and mythology, and he devoured cheap brochures and trashy newspapers published by marginal, paranoid political parties. His thought, reliably unoriginal, stems from these. Nothing disciplined his learning, neither school nor mentor; the selection of material was haphazard and his understanding largely emotional. He loathed schools, universities, and professors of all kinds. The fruits of Hitler's self-guided education were such things as the swastika, the mock-Roman "Heil" greeting, and the deep-seated, perniciously false belief that some people, namely the so-called Aryans, are more worthy of life and liberty than others.

Hitler had a second uncanny ability that came out in the 1920s: he knew how to read and exploit in speeches the emotions of a crowd, particularly its anger or enthusiasm. He had left Austria to enlist in the German army in World War I, and he thoroughly enjoyed the experience, receiving minor injuries instead of death. After the war, his oratorical talent propelled him into the leadership of a small, fascist, nationalist, anti-Communist, anti-Semitic protest party, which later became the National Socialist (Nazi) party. In his fulminating speeches and his long, turgid, boring, incoherent book, *Mein Kampf* – too lazy to write it, he dictated it to a supporter – he said his goal was to "save" the German race by purging it of its Jewish and other minorities. He also wanted to push Germany's border farther east. The great enemy, he said, was Marxist-Leninist Russia, the Soviet Union, the existence of which he blamed on Jews, liberals, and others. Hitler developed a following of fiercely loyal people, such as Heinrich Himmler, who later led the SS (Hitler's paramilitary) and oversaw the Holocaust.

Greed gave him and his thugs their chance. The German economy had already collapsed once, in 1923 when hyperinflation rendered the currency worthless and the French invaded the Rhineland to collect their reparations payments-in-kind by force. In the years that followed, the German economy recovered, benefitting from investment from the US, but boundless lust for effortless profit finally sent the American stock market, and much of the world economy, off a cliff. Desperate economic conditions in Germany in the early 1930s turned many an ear toward Hitler's angry rants against his long list of supposed enemies of the German race. Pointing toward the great Russian communist beast in the east, Hitler successfully scared enough Germans into tolerating his political coup. Popular fears soared after the burning of the Reichstag, the seat of the German parliament, in 1933, allowing for the passage of the notorious Enabling Act that empowered him to protect Germany from domestic revolutionaries. Where the specter of communism failed to persuade, his Nazi thugs in the streets and the party's concentration camps, built in the 1930s, soon brought the rest of the country to heel. The camps were but preludes to far greater horrors, all in the name of a purified human race and society.

Adolf Hitler of all people, prim, duplicitous, and murderous without remorse, shows better than anyone that civilization is no protection against the temptation of barbarism. Though Germany's cities, industries, universities, and hospitals were held as models around the world, and roughly half of all Nobel Prizes went to German scientists, Hitler screamed that German society was corrupt and decadent. To people young and old, he preached the need to create a new kind of human being. Anyone in history who does such a thing shows intolerance for humanity as it is, and usually resentment against the creator. "Humanity needs an idol," Hitler said in 1942, and the idol he proffered in Germany was the deluded vision of a pure, unified, powerful Aryan race. That vile, seductive cult demanded more blood than had ever been shed in human history—even more than in World War I and Stalin's reign of terror combined.

The German Nazi and the Russian Soviet regimes mirrored each other in atheist, inhuman horror, their hatred of God and his beloved creation. Both governments used and abused their people as means for indefensible ends. Their crimes dispel the illusion that one end of the political spectrum, either the Nazi right or the Stalinist left, is somehow better or worse than its opposite. Both show what obscene lengths humanity can go to when it feels entitled to do anything to anybody for any reason. Hitler had his sterilization, euthanasia, wars, and extermination systems, and Stalin had his purges, the Gulag, orchestrated famines, and mass expulsions into the vast Siberian wilderness. Many Roman emperors would have felt right at home with those nightmarish bastions of raw power.

Number Two, and Then Some

The Second World War and its aftermath prove that there is no such thing as a war to end all wars. Everyone knows the story, so there is no need to tell it blow by blow. In a nutshell, Hitler started it for ideological reasons, and Mussolini was fool enough to join him. Stalin, also a prisoner of his own ideology, supplied Germany with food and fuel in the beginning; he really seemed to have thought that the main Western capitalist powers (Britain, France, and Germany) would destroy each other. The German attack on Russia in 1941 took Stalin totally by surprise. An unlikely alliance of Soviets, British, and (thanks to Japanese imperial hubris) Americans pursued the conflict until their enemies lay abject and ruined before them. The three allies were committed first and foremost to keeping the others in the contest; the only thing that kept them together was the mutual desire to use the other to smite the German enemy they held in common. Italy was an afterthought, and Japan, the US scorched basically on its own. When the madness came to an end, the war and its attendant horrors, above all the Holocaust, had claimed some 50 million human lives. Levels of death were unprecedented. In a mere four years, the war butchered one fifth of the entire Polish population, one half of them Jewish, and one quarter of the entire Serbian population, but fighting spread the evil all across the world. The winners took pride in their triumph, and the innocent dead could not raise their voices in solemn protest.

But this does not mean that World War II was not *necessary*. A demonic Nazi regime, armed with the most lethally effective military the world has ever seen, unleashed a plague of obscene and wanton violence across Europe and the Mediterranean. Japan followed suit in Asian and the Pacific. To stop this wave of evil, might met might as it usually does. It was truly necessary to fight back, but the war *in its conduct* was still as barbaric as any other, if not more so. All participants behaved deplorably, committing horrific crimes against innocent non-combatants. All contributed to the terror, whether rained down from the sky or perpetrated on land or at sea. Allied bombers reduced a thousand German cities, towns, and villages to ashes, and Japan's pain was of the same order, with dubious distinction in Hiroshima and Nagasaki. Only the slaughtered innocent came away clean—the millions of children, their mothers, the sick and the elderly, hapless non-belligerents whose indiscriminate murder no one can justify. The war showed that the modern state is as flawed as its predecessors. Humanity's undeniable progress in science and technology has had no corresponding improvement in ethics, morals, and manners. When the situation tries us, we are as beastly as we have always been throughout recorded time.

Despite the inherent evils committed during the Second World War, the aftermath shows us the vital importance of reconciliation, no matter how imperfect. The Western victors, this time, did not repeat the Versailles Treaty debacle by enshrining punishment of Germany in a document, even though this war was entirely of her own making. The

Soviets, however, plundered the eastern areas under her control and raped two million women, although the French were not much kinder in their sector of Germany. But the British and especially the Americans, after a cursory process of "denazification," encouraged Germany to get her industrial economy rolling again and to sustain and protect her revived democracy. In Germany the British and the Americans wanted a strong, committed ally against the Soviet bloc in central and eastern Europe. American occupation of Japan was similarly light, and the US also wanted a reliable ally in Asia against the Soviet Union and the newly revolutionized communist China.

A genuinely enlightened gesture, in the immediate aftermath, the victors established a world discussion forum meant to include the defeated, when the time was right, and to prevent such conflicts from happening in the future. In 1948 the United Nations stated its purpose as an institution with its Universal Declaration of Human Rights, a very Western concept with deep Christian roots, that confirms the inherent rights of every human being against monstrous renditions of the state that seek to usurp or remove them. While hardly perfect, the UN reflects the hope that unity can be found in diversity, and its core documents insist on the human freedom to embrace God in the form of religion.

That being said, the evil of war did not end in 1945. The violence that spread over the world makes any century in the so-called Dark and Middle Ages look peaceful, stable, and well-organized by comparison. Across eastern and central Europe, twelve million Germans fled or were expelled from their ancestral homes by the Red Army and angry local authorities. They headed west, in the largest act of ethnic cleansing in history; two million died en route. Stalin's brutal, paranoid tyranny over the poor peoples in his thrall wore on into the 1950s. The French and the British, deeply resistant to the fact that they had neither the rights nor the means for world empire, handled the inevitable retraction usually quite badly.

Dying empires spawned war in the Indian subcontinent, Vietnam, and Algeria, killing millions more. The newly independent Middle East, long under the yoke of the British, French, Ottoman, and earlier empires, used their freedom for war. Where the French and the British relinquished control, the state of Israel and her inimical Arab neighbors fought repeatedly; ethnic cleansing perfected in Europe was applied to parts of the Holy Land. All over Africa and Asia, through the 1960s and

70s, where empires retreated, violence often characterized the new order. Latin American countries in particular, although long free from European control, suffered terrible internal civil wars between adherents of far left and right ideologies. Treating money as the most unholy of idols, they killed in its name, whether to perpetuate their own greed or to sanctify with blood their own version of state authority or "social justice."

Just as terrifying was the very real possibility of world destruction through the use and misuse of nuclear weaponry. The so-called Cold War between the United States and her NATO allies on the one hand and the Soviet Union, her Warsaw Pact, China, and other communist countries on the other, threatened to explode into a war of mutually assured destruction, with an ensuing nuclear winter that would have rendered much or all of the planet unfit for human life. The obscene production and proliferation of tactically useless nuclear bombs seemed to make error all the more likely. The divided, occupied city of Berlin, the former capital of a partitioned and occupied Germany, was a constant, potential flash point, but Cuba was another. The Cuban Missile Crisis of 1962 brought the world to the very brink of nuclear war. Decision-makers of the time, looking back later on those tense days and weeks, attest to the dire severity of that situation. But there were more trouble spots that threatened to plunge the world into self-destruction, namely Korea, the Holy Land, and Vietnam. American leadership justified intense military involvement, leading to multiple millions of deaths, as necessary for stopping the spread of communism. Robert McNamara, Secretary of Defense under two presidents, later explained war in Vietnam with the words, "We were fighting the Cold War." For the mightiest of industrial, capitalist democracies, agrarian communist states appeared to threaten its very existence.

Thanks to God's grace, no nuclear war broke out. Even as God permitted world wars and genocides, he granted the world a few imperfect individuals who would not take the final step into global death. Above all, Mikhail Gorbachev, leader of the Soviet Union in the 1980s, induced a miracle from his blindness. Under intense international pressure, and facing defeat in an arms race with the US, Gorbachev really believed that the Soviet Union would persist and even prosper if it ended its repression and admitted some of its errors. Under his rule, the communist party in Russia stood by while the Warsaw Pact dissolved and many Soviet republics and Eastern European countries wrested liberty from Moscow. Perhaps never before in Western history did such a massive, awful empire retract so completely, without being forced to do so at the cost of a vast outpouring of blood and misery.

In addition to Gorbachev's blindness, Pope John Paul II's clear vision deserves a great deal of credit for emboldening the Poles to retake their God-given right to worship and live freely. The pope tirelessly repeated to them the gospel message, "Do not be afraid!" After the fall of the Soviet Union, Gorbachev himself stated, "One can say that everything that has happened in eastern Europe in recent years would have been impossible without the Pope's efforts and the enormous role, including the political role, he has played in the world arena." Lech Walesa, leader of Poland's Solidarity movement, and General Jaruzelski, head of the Polish communist regime, said as much as well. And other political leaders at the time, from the US and Western Germany, had the good sense to allow subject peoples to reclaim their natural human rights without using the moment to indulge too many of their own special interests.

In the later twentieth century, the mightiest militaries in the world, the American and the Soviet, did not engage in direct confrontation, which could have ended world history as we know it, even if the peripheral conflicts inflicted suffering and slaughter upon millions. Now, in the early twenty-first century, western Europe has enjoyed the longest period of peace and prosperity in her history, despite the ever-present threat of nuclear annihilation. The same goes for Japan. War now among France, Germany, Britain, Spain, and Italy is all but unthinkable. But the threat remains, as evidenced by the savage conflicts between Serbia and her neighbors, Russia's wars in Chechnya and against Georgia, the United States' in Iraq and Afghanistan, the existence of paranoid, bellicose states such as North Korea and Iran, and the ubiquity of murderous, terrorist groups. The West now enjoys unparalleled peace and material prosperity, but worldly wealth is a two-edged sword. If used for good, it can be a blessing. Abused, or squandered, it can become a curse: this is a truth throughout all of human history.

Twentieth-Century Surfeit

In the same century as the worst wars in history, the West's vast and growing wealth started to look more like a curse than a blessing. The universal power of money transcends all eras of civilization and entails the same temptations, the same afflictions of the rich: gluttony, pride, vanity, and a sensuality that feeds on violence. This statement is not moralizing—it is a simple description of actual behavior. Westerners also succumb to a variety of lethal diseases of the body that stem directly from their luxurious lifestyle. In addition to these, they suffer the spiritual malady that comes from the selfish refusal to accept any suffering for any reason: fear, loneliness, depression, neurosis, and despair. When pain is meaningless, then anything but perfect comfort is intolerable. Western souls are no better today than those of people three millennia ago, except for the fact that in lifestyle, contemporary Westerners are definitely better off. The truth may well be that the opulent West, in its desperate, futile search for salvation through material circumstances, may even be perverting the earth's climate.

From the early to the mid-twentieth century, industrialization and urbanization, the relocation of country dwellers to the cities, continued despite periodic economic and political turmoil. Mechanization of farm work coincided with rising demand for labor in industries and services. Educational opportunities for men and women, boys and girls, increased, as did wages, relative to basic commodity prices. And population grew with them. Despite the losses of the First World War, the number of Westerners had never been higher by the coming of the Second.

Western Europe, after terrible years in the 1940s, repaired the damage of war with astonishing rapidity, finishing mostly by the later 1950s, and continued to enjoy the rising trajectory of wealth creation in the 1960s. Regions under communist rule, however, weighed down by inefficient bureaucracy and hefty payments for Soviet "protection," rebuilt at a much slower pace and matched pre-war industrial output later than in the West. Most European states set up welfare programs to cover the basic needs of every person, including universally free education and healthcare, and generous provisions for the unemployed, disabled, and retired. The western side of Germany set a high standard with its Economic Miracle, bringing urban organization and comfort to a new level in human history. Without declaring "war" on it, as President Lyndon Johnson would do in the US, the Western Germans basically rid their society of the most abject manifestations of material poverty.

The United States reveled in its new status as the greatest of all world powers in terms of raw material wealth and military might. The New Deal, meant to roll back the Great Depression, had spared the country from major social and civil unrest in the 1930s. Real recovery had only come in the first years of the Second World War, when the British Empire poured its entire disposable wealth into the American military economy for weapons and supplies, and millions of young men entered the armed forces. For years after the war, the United States became richer than ever, having sustained no damage to its domestic infrastructure. Half of the world's manufacturing and two-thirds of the gold reserves resided in the US. The dollar displaced the British pound as the world reserve currency, and American exports flooded foreign markets. Young people went to college in droves, readily landed jobs in white-collar service industries, and purchased homes and properties of ever-increasing size. One can say that a genuinely enlightened attitude grew up with them. During the Civil Rights Movement of the 1950s and 60s, many people up and down the socio-economic scale examined their consciences and their prejudices, and ended legal discrimination against racial minorities and women. But as history shows us, phases of enlightenment do not usually last, or add up to what they promised.

The generations coming to adulthood in the late 1960s and 70s had never known war, depression, or serious dearth. Many generally assumed that national and personal prosperity was set on a permanently upward trajectory. Younger people rested secure in the assumption that they would have more than their parents. Consumption of products and energy soared, with few qualms about pollution getting in the way of people's pursuit of individual comfort or chosen lifestyle. In the late 60s and throughout the 1970s, younger Americans pursued a society of sensual pleasure with abandon. Whether at rock concerts or discos, such music gatherings became the communal, cultic events to celebrate free access to mind-altering drugs and sexual contact of any kind without a trace of accountability. For such people, this was true freedom, and so, inevitably, the contraceptive attitude toward sexuality grew even stronger than it had been. The Supreme Court complied, granting women the right to expel growing babies from their bodies at any time during pregnancy, in the name of the supposedly constitutional and universal right to personal privacy. President Johnson corroborated, declaring the creation of a Great Society and a "War on Poverty," even as he used horrific military force to stop the spread of communism in poor, rural Indochina.

In the twentieth century, a growing appetite for war and kindred behaviors accompanied consumption patterns. At the outbreak of

World War I, the American army had been the size of Belgium's. After the war, American political leaders quite reasonably disarmed. World War II, however, offered a temptation that the American elite could not resist—a world empire of sorts, characterized by financial and military dominance wherever it could go at reasonable cost, relative to the American economy, according to American interests. On the whole, it was not an empire of conquest, but of invitation, but with notable exceptions such as Korea, Vietnam, Panama, Iraq, and others. Foreign policy coincided perfectly with national business interests. Oil needed to flow cheaply and reliably from the Persian Gulf after American appetites began to exceed domestic production. The United Fruit Company contributed to a high-handed, violent policy toward Central American states wanting better conditions for their workers. Other international corporations lobbied for similar foreign policies in regions where they operated.

In many ways, the 1970s mark a tipping point in American and Western history. The student revolts of 1968–69 in Europe reverberated in 1970 in the US, at Kent State University, where students were shot and killed, and across the country. The sex, drugs, and rock 'n roll youth culture found millions of willing consumers on both sides of the Atlantic, and rising oil imports and costs, commodity prices, and unemployment rates noticeably cooled rampant economic growth. Fear of nuclear conflagration spread everywhere, but in Europe many people vociferously rejected the idea of serving as a battleground for a US-Soviet showdown. Since the 1970s, American consumption patterns, whether of individuals, families, or the federal government, reflect spending run amok, relying on readily available credit and the perverse faith that stocks, bonds, and property market values would never retreat. The scene was only marginally better in Europe.

During the 1980s, the US changed from creditor nation to debtor, and personal savings rates plummeted. Apart from a few boom years in the 1990s, the federal government has run spectacular annual deficits and shown itself incapable of reforming itself or reducing its size in any way. In the first years of the twenty-first century, the percentage of the American government's debt in foreign hands soared to more than 40 percent. Western European governments show the same addiction to debt and remarkable resistance to the truth that their cushy social systems, erected during the years of soaring growth, are unsustainable, particularly given the demographic reality of ever-greater numbers of elderly and fewer and fewer children, workers, and taxpayers.

With the explosion in consumer and government spending in the later twentieth-century West came an implosion of traditional, commonly held, Judeo-Christian values and standards of morality, which should not surprise us. Well-paid professional psychologists, their fees often covered by insurance companies, help their clients to let go of guilt-related, negative feelings, regardless of whether the cause of the guilt is behavior that would once have been seen as immoral. Unfortunately, this attitude is not limited to the counseling setting. A recent national survey of American mothers showed that the most important virtue they wanted their children to learn was "tolerance," not in the sense of enduring undesirable or bad things for the sake of a higher goal, but in the sense of not being judgmental. Discrimination has become a very bad word, losing any of its positive attributes, such as discriminating between right and wrong behavior. Nouns such as meekness, modesty, and humility are no longer considered positive attributes. "Wisdom," people frequently regard as old-hat and useless, compared to technical know-how. Tolerance, which past generations never even considered a virtue, is an idol of the current age.

The results are devastating. Divorce rates have risen to pandemic levels, roughly 50 percent for first marriages, and higher for seconds and thirds before lowering again. Pop stars and enormously wealthy media enterprises turn personal, private wishes and feelings into a fetish, prostituted before millions via TV. Entitled to indulge in whatever behavior pleases them, wealthy Westerners spend untold hours watching obscenely violent films, playing obscenely violent video games, and coveting the actual bodies of women, men, and young people, whose naked images and sexual deeds are readily available and virtually anonymous, courtesy of affordable technology, in the privacy of one's abode. Sexual exploitation and abuse, within marriage and without, even targeting children, has reached epidemic levels. Western elites, agreeing on little more than base relativism, are either unwilling or unable to do much about it. More than a few live quite contentedly with such behavior.

An unrestricted consumerist mentality also harms public and personal health in the West. Diets of industrially processed foods have sent rates of obesity, diabetes, heart disease, cancer, and auto-immune disorders

soaring. In terms of the numbers of deaths from these diseases, AIDS
pales in comparison. Despite the benefits of modern medicine, American
life expectancy does not even rank in the top forty of about 190
countries in the world, yet Americans spend more on health care per
capita than anyone else in the world, and more than double that of most
western European countries. Far too many people seek health through
pharmaceuticals and surgical procedures, trying to counteract the
diseases of wealth: atrocious diet and lethargic lifestyle. Some researchers
argue that the diet found in lifestyles sometimes dismissed as outmoded
and pre-modern are actually much richer in nutrition: a "peasant" diet
of a plant-based, whole foods, with low amounts of dairy and meat, high
physical activity, and low stress.

Perhaps the greatest woes in the West are spiritual, deriving from
unsustainably high levels of stress, loneliness, and apathy. Westerners
inure themselves to traveling at death-defying speeds every day, working
at a feverish pace, preparing and consuming three complicated meals per
day, bearing unbelievable levels of noise and other stimuli, filling their
closets, basements, and garages with possessions, and scheduling their
lives with endless activities. Real intimacy often bears the brunt of these
habits; lovers, couples, and family members have little time beyond their
own concerns, and the television automatically kills communication. The
irony of living in a Western world supposedly united by various satellite
and streaming technologies is that people are contenting themselves with
passing "relationships" and fleeting hook-ups rather than with real,
loving intimacy and firm commitment.

Love has become, perhaps for most people, merely a feeling, only one
aspect of the "relationship" rather than the life-giving bond itself. The
sheer numbers of people living alone in Western countries is alarming, as
marriages fail one after another and contraception and abortion provide
easy ways out of assuming the great responsibility of parenthood. Backed
up by social services and retirement pensions, people really do not need
to rely on any other person, as long as they have the bureaucratic state
to take care of them. Individuals are able to live only for themselves, but
they inevitably suffer for it, in the creeping sense of meaninglessness that
so frequently comes with selfishness.

The richest countries of the West, the US, Germany, France, Britain,
and Canada, among others, suffer from surfeit. Taking the US as
an example, about 3 percent of the world's population unabashedly

consumes 25 percent of the resources and seems to expect other countries either to support or imitate them in that project, as long as it does not impinge on American spending habits. Commercial advertising runs rampant in American popular culture, making today's new gadgets tomorrow's necessities. Energy consumption more often than not registers with people only according to the dollars they spend on it. Recycling is used as a way to obviate the need to consume less in the first place. Houses and many cars continue to grow in size and energy requirements. The enormous, amorphous middle class tries to live like royalty would have done in the past. The bathroom size of the average house built in the twenty-first century exceeds that of the Emperor of Austria's before the First World War. Most Americans buy products with little thought about questions such as where they come from, the conditions endured by the workers who produced them, and the pollution generated, as long as the price is right and credit is available. Americans invest their money similarly: wherever the return is highest in the short term. Most people view their houses as mere investments, intending to maximize profit in the future. "Resale value" is a realtor's marketing mechanism for potential buyers. Many people live as if the only real principle in life were money.

Another affliction of the rich is self-adoration, a form of pride and vanity, which is inevitably associated with hypocrisy. At the close of the twentieth century and the dawn of the twenty-first, no people in the world gives in to self-congratulation like the Americans. If one spends time in other countries and learns the local language and customs, American self-adulation becomes obvious. Indeed it seems to have become the prerequisite for patriotism. A limited, critical love for one's country, wishing it to become better than it currently is, is fine. Yet virtually all American politicians and public figures routinely refer to "this great nation," "our great people," "the greatest nation on earth," "the most powerful country in the world," and "the beacon of freedom." The American worker, according to our politicians, is said to be the best in the world, along with many other aspects of the country. Regardless of political party, when the American president gives his State of the Union speech before Congress, dozens of standing ovations interrupt him, sometimes over seventy, putting that assembly on par with the former, petty communist dictatorships of eastern Europe. American self-confidence now runs at highs comparable to the British in the latter decades of her vast empire; the self-flattering rhetoric often rings depressingly similar to that of fascist dictators, now thankfully dead and gone.

But praise of self rings hollow in the vast halls of truth. American high school students with soaring levels of self-esteem do not score as well, on the whole, compared to other wealthy countries east and west, especially in math, science, and reading comprehension. Endless praise of American business know-how tempered rather suddenly at the world credit crisis of 2008–9, perpetrated in part by the investment banking institutions that claimed to be engines of real economic growth. The medical service industry in the US is often purported to be the best in the world, but in relation to public health statistics, it falls woefully short. Medicine itself increasingly serves vain, cosmetic ends, shifting away from the treatment of disease and injury and increasingly toward elective enhancements, for no particular reason other than the patient's personal desire for the perceived benefit, provided they have the cash or the appropriate insurance coverage to pay for it. People routinely seek wildly expensive medical treatments to allow their consumerist lifestyle to persist unabated or to engage in the ultimate folly of trying to stop the natural aging process. In the vast majority of cases, plastic surgery and cosmetic medicine do nothing apart from serving the vanity of the client. And then there is sports medicine, a new field, not merely for treating sports-related injuries, but to keep athletes playing in spite of them. Sports medicine also seeks to enhance athletic performance through drugs and surgery. Whatever the situation, the primary consideration for all involved in the system is maximum monetary profit. Medicine has become part of the narcissist service industry.

Pride and vanity bestow a sense of entitlement. Feeling authorized to inflict violence on others, to excuse excesses readily, and to take pleasure in the effects, is an extreme form of narcissism and hubris. This was apparent in Britain, France, and Germany during the height of their empires. The United States in the twenty-first century now faces a similar, pernicious temptation. Snares of war lie everywhere, in bellicose "rogue" states, in the perpetually unstable Middle East, in the insatiable thirst of America's oil-based economy, and in the technological marvels of its mighty defense industry. For decades, America's preferred mode of war has been from the air, to rain down explosives in the vicinity of the stated enemy, while making real, honest efforts to minimize deaths of non-combatants, called "collateral damage." Many Americans honestly believe that high technology renders such warfare justifiable, in terms of means and ends. The main consideration is how many Americans must die in the campaign. The problem, however, is that ultimately, the only way to secure land is to put armed soldiers on it. And for that, some must die.

Humanity, throughout recorded time, ensures that the world will never be free of the scourge of war, which powerful people wage for gain, glory, or the fear of losing both. In the early twentieth century, Henry Ford's utterance, "History is bunk," has been frequently repeated by his ardent admirers and others in general agreement, but recent events say otherwise. In the 1990s, the United States military fought in Panama and Haiti, the Balkans, Somalia, Sudan, Afghanistan, and the Persian Gulf. During the same decade, an American political scientist, Francis Fukuyama, theorized about "the end of history," arguing that the great story of Western and world political and economic development was coming to an end, reaching a veritable zenith, in democratic capitalism. In Fukuyama's work, national self-love mingles perfectly with academic blindness to produce one of the most short-sighted interpretations of history imaginable. As with the ideas of Karl Marx, Fukuyama's thought is a direct product and reflection of his day, the giddy, self-congratulatory 1990s. In the early years of the twenty-first century, however, Henry Ford is long dead, and rich civilizations swagger and stomp their way through time as they always have. Western democratic capitalism still has many scenes and costume changes to endure.

Twenty-First Century Civilized Barbarism

The twenty-first century still suffers from barbarism, albeit in a civilized form. American inner cities, suburbs, and rural areas continue to see tens of thousands of tragic deaths from firearms abuse. The annual death rate in Allentown, Pennsylvania, is running comparable to fifteenth-century Paris, the former replete with burnings, stabbings, and even beheadings. Violence in European cities is far less than in the US, but still too high. Medical technology of affluent societies has even turned the womb into a place of violence. Abortion in the Western world kills about two million human beings per year, mostly between the tenth and twelfth weeks of growth, after the sexual organs have differentiated and the ovaries of little girls are stocked with eggs for the next generation. By the thirteenth week, a baby's body is complete and only needs to grow and mature to help ensure survival outside the sanctum of the mother's womb. Indeed, horrifically, the US even allows babies who have reached the full term of gestation to be murdered, as long as their mothers grant permission.

Meanwhile, fertility is falling all across the West. Germany, Italy, Spain, the Czech Republic, Russia, and other countries lose population every year, as deaths exceed births—by the hundreds of thousands in some cases. In the US, a fifth of women in their forties are childless. Also, conception has become more difficult for women and men, due to various factors: to poorer nutrition and health, and, some studies suggest, to residues of oral contraceptives in water supplies. In order to conceive, more couples resort to in-vitro fertilization, an expensive, invasive medical process that involves the conception of numerous human embryos that are never implanted in their natural mothers. Wealthier women, if they have children at all, are waiting longer to bear them, and very few are allowed to be handicapped. Genetic screening and analysis of embryos and a host of pregnancy tests help parents to identify potential handicaps and, backed by abortion, to avoid suffering the burden of raising children who do not meet societal or personal expectations.

Twentieth and twenty-first century civilized barbarism also victimizes the earth itself. Over a century of rampant industrial growth has perhaps generated enough pollution to poison life as we know it, but for nature's marvelous self-cleaning properties. Masses of data gathered from around the globe indicate that the earth is warming up, as it has in the past. It may indeed be the case that so-called man-made "greenhouse gases" are responsible, but at the same time, we must not forget that, independent of human activity, the earth's climate has changed over time, sometimes warmer, sometimes colder, and even in Ice Ages for long stretches, and no expert really knows why. Theories abound as to how, but none commands general agreement. Data is generally lacking for past climate changes, and statistical estimates based on them hold limited value. If the greenhouse metaphor correctly applies to the Earth, the burgeoning numbers of the world's poor are scarcely responsible, in contrast to the opulent West, where perhaps seven or eight per cent of the world's people consume about half its resources and generate as much pollution.

Only future generations will see if humanity pulls together and devotes its God-given brilliance to harnessing the perfectly clean, non-polluting energies God bestows upon the earth: the sun's rays, the driving winds, the pounding waves, the earth's inner temperatures, and others. But with the devil always lurking in the wings, the chief evil has already reared its ugly head. Institutional pressure is building, especially in the wealthy West, to push and pay for culling extraneous population in high-growth areas of the world, especially in the poorer countries. Experts go to the squalid cities of Asia and announce that the first things these people need, even before jobs, housing, and clean water, are contraception and abortion. The great temptation for the rich is to regard the rest of humanity as a competitor, a threat to their lavish lifestyle, if not a servant to do their bidding for the sake of their comfort and luxury. The more people believe that the earth is suffering under the weight of excessive human bodies, the greater the tendency is to share nothing but the instruments of infanticide and euthanasia. The problem with the world population, however, is not that it is too large or that the vast majority lack the American way of life. The challenge is for rich people to withstand the temptation to eat and shop themselves to death, and for them to help the poorer and weaker to make their modest way with dignity.

Of course, throughout all of history, no one suffers more from barbarism of all kinds than children. War is hardest on them. It destroys their families, the source of their love and the center of their world. Its terrors and appalling violence scar them for the rest of their lives. Crime destroys their trust. Drugs reduce their parents to incompetent fools and deny children the basics: food, shelter, clothing, and loving discipline. Wealth distorts their sense of justice, fairness, and entitlement in the world. Divorces, divided, broken marriages, weigh heaviest on children (except in cases of gross abuse), while their parents pursue their own self-fulfillment in other ways. Sexual perverts often abuse them as objects of pleasure, haunting their memories. Children are those with almost no voice in history. This book fares little better in that regard. But if we lack the sources to recall those of the past, we can lovingly attend to the needs of those of the present, knowing that in doing so, we do work pleasing to God, and make a positive contribution to the future.

11

The Third Millennium A.D.

"[B]ut [the Lord] said to me, 'My grace is sufficient for you: power is made perfect in weakness.' I will rather boast most gladly of my weaknesses, in order that the power of Christ may dwell with me. Therefore I am content with weaknesses, insults, hardships, persecutions, and constraints, for the sake of Christ; for when I am weak, then I am strong." (2 Corinthians 12: 9–10)

"For I am convinced that neither death, nor life, nor angels, nor principalities, nor present things, nor future things, nor powers, nor height, nor depth, nor any other creature will be able to separate us from the love of God in Christ Jesus our Lord." (Romans 8: 38)

Post-Modernity

Many historians claim that the modern era has come to an end. The close of the Cold War and the collapse of communism, the advent and acceleration of the information revolution based on computer technology, the globalization of capital and commercial markets, the enormous strides in bio-technology, and the general secularization of the West have ushered in a new era, dubbed "post-modernity." Perhaps the proclamation of a new era is in fact justified. A detailed list of changes from 1910 to 2010, whether political, social, economic, technological, scientific, military, diplomatic, medical, literary, philosophical, musical, artistic, cultural, or meteorological, easily fills multiple books about the period. Indeed it seems that history is accelerating, that the pace of change, especially in the West, is going from fast to immediate or instantaneous. Are human beings in fact getting smarter? Does recent history and the present show that humanity is evolving away from its more primitive, pre-industrial form into something higher and more technologically advanced? Is the Church, the universal prayer community, following Christ, devoted to God, a diminishing phenomenon of a bygone, backward age? Post-modern enthusiasts would generally say Yes.

This history says No. God's word is eternal, in every day of human existence. There is no denying that Christianity makes a poorer showing in the twenty-first century West than in prior centuries: Jesus' parables do not include electronics; Christian liturgies seem dull compared to the high-decibel, pyrotechnic, and garish light shows of popular culture; and many Christian charitable, educational, and missionary activities appear more remedial than progressive. Her moral code annoys lavish, permissive societies that entitle themselves to just about every form of self-gratification. In the context of a breathlessly fast-paced, globalized, celebrified, post-modern world, the Church can seem parochial, ossified, grouchy, defensive, and, worst of all, intolerant. But all these considerations are superficial, reflecting post-modern prejudices more than the Church as she is.

Christianity's strength lies in its quiet weakness. It remains as it was, the free choice of the human heart, mind, and soul in seeking answers to life's greatest questions.

Post-modernism and post-modernity may have some claims to novelty, but they do not grant people meaning, peace, and divine love. They, like all other cultural fads, do not satisfy humanity's greatest yearnings, and will not stand the test of time. They rely too heavily on money, power, and self-satisfaction in the here and now. But once one says Yes to Christ, once one says to God, "I love you, with my whole being, spirit and body," the world becomes a different place, and everything else going on in one's given time is backdrop—definitely real, but ultimately unessential.

Post-modernism is a nihilistic set of ideas, tired, old, unoriginal, but revived and rearticulated recently by professional theorists such as Michel Foucault and Jacques Derrida. Whatever the specific intentions of leading post-modern writers, there is no mistaking the way their views have taken root in the West, from schools to movie studios. Post-modernism prizes opposition and subversion for their own sake. It dismisses metaphysics as nonsensical, and shuns morality, reason, and divinity. It opposes differentiating thoughts and values from feelings, separating intelligence from the will. Truth, according to post-modernists, is something that can only be individual; it is what you want it to be. The only supposed virtue (actually attitude) they support is toleration and its sibling multiculturalism, both of which demand uncritical acceptance and even celebration of all values and beliefs except for those they detest. The only opinions that are *a priori* unassailable are their own. The only things of real value are money and power. In the name of empowerment, they subvert the Christian faith in any way they can.

Hannah Arendt saw it coming in the mid-twentieth century, although she did not call it post-modern: "To our modern way of thinking, nothing is meaningful in and by itself, not history nor nature taken as a whole, and certainly not particular occurrences in the physical order or specific historical events." In post-modernity, people regard everything historical as the result of some pernicious, oppressive dynamic of power, which deserves termination. They regard every material thing as the result of deterministic, mechanical processes, processes that ought to be altered or subverted according to one's desire. They refuse to acknowledge uniqueness. In the post-modern view, for example, a baby is not a unique miracle of God's creation, a new, inimitable union of spirit and body, but the result of cell multiplication according to a specific genetic code, which can and should be manipulated and disposed of by human professionals according to desire. Nothing can be sacred, except the idol one builds of one's own tastes.

Where Nietzsche tried to kill off God, post-modernists aim to do away with man. Post-modern writings, even children's books and stories, emphasize that anyone can be anything they feel like. People can change sex and sexuality – both amorphously subsumed under "gender" – as they see fit, and families are constituted however anyone wants them to be. Identity and reality are things we make for ourselves. Nothing can really be bad as long as one feels good about it. Beauty neither exists nor transcends, because it is solely subjective, superficial, and cosmetic. Ugliness is just a matter of pejorative opinion. There is no difference between natural and artificial. Nature has no inherent meaning, order, or significance; it is mere raw material, to do with as we please. Man is just a pleasure-seeking animal. Pleasure, the new god, entitles people to do anything with anybody, as long as it is pleasurable to at least one of the doers.

People in a post-modern society are entitled to be extremely sensitive, for truth itself is subject to one's feelings. One's "comfort" determines levels of freedom of speech, what one may say or ask. If someone feels a comment or question is racist, sexist, homophobic, judgmental, opinionated, or value-laden, then it is and must be oppressive, and therefore invalid, regardless of the content of what was said. Post-modernism on the social and political front finds its voice in the demand for unrestricted freedom in the name of perfect equality, an attitude that cannot abide any perceived restraint. Of course this is a self-delusion that actually leads to infractions against freedom of thought, speech, and expression. No one is allowed to say No to the demands of "political correctness." Western post-modernity exalts a banal, hedonist cult of personal consumption in the name of self-fulfillment, esteem, or realization. The temptation is as ancient as humanity itself, but the requisite degree of wealth has been lacking, for the general population, until the twentieth century.

We can detect post-modernism and its beloved idols in all walks of life today, all throughout the lands of the West, in legal regulations, bureaucracies, businesses, medical and educational systems and institutions, and throughout all media. When we love in this way, however, we easily come to regard God as an imposition, an affront, a psychological delusion, a restriction of privacy and freedom, and therefore much less rewarding than the material things of this world. If death is nothing but the end of the fun, then the last things, the end of life, the afterlife, the last judgment, and the true end of history are nobody's business, and not worth the trouble. If nothing can be authentically holy, then nothing can be mysterious, in the sense of having unfathomable or inexhaustible depth. If the sacred is a mere construct of profane practices, then it is nothing. And if nothing can really be sacred, holy, and mysterious, then nothing can be truly transcendent. If people have figured out everything in life and existence on their own, or if they will someday, then the only thing we can believe in is the universe we arrange to suit our pleasure.

The post-modern era purports to be new, but it is really just a variation on an old theme. In the West, things are now as they were in St. Augustine's day. People show their love for monetary riches in oversized houses crammed with all kinds of objects of at best marginal use. They care intensely about their feelings and relationships, less so about their promises, and still less about the state of their souls, which they deny they have. States, cities, school districts, and businesses build massive theaters and arenas for sports and shows – they are supposed to bring in more money than they cost – but they rarely do anything to encourage virtue, moral excellence, among the young and old. Media and local chit-chat concern scandal, greed, and violence much more often than they celebrate acts of graciousness and mercy, great and small. In the richest societies the world has ever seen, in material terms, shocking sums of money conglomerate around relatively few people whose activities are questionable at best: actors, ballplayers, financial speculators. And even if the poor comprise a minority within the borders of these rich states, the wider world offers myriad opportunities to rescue and care for the needy. While European countries bemoan their graying, shrinking populations, they do little to stop the slaughter of babes in the womb. The US, content with its immigration rates, legal and otherwise, massacres the unborn in the name of freedom. All Western states behave like bankrupts, seemingly secure in the vain hope that their financial and material resources are inexhaustible, at least within the lifetime of the voter.

So, one might reasonably ask, what are we left with? Is nihilism really driving us into a new Dark Ages? For many, the answer is No—because we have science! Does not the West, wherever it may be found, love science? The adjective "scientific" is synonymous with *reliable* and *accurate*. We believe that the scientific method, pioneered, in our historical memory, by Aristotle and modernized, so to speak, by Francis Bacon and the gentlemen of the Scientific Revolution, can be applied to solve any problem, to make anything human better. The scientific approach has been applied to every aspect of human inquiry in the West, from applied physics to biblical exegesis, from radiology to human relationships, and the results amaze us month after month. With innovations emerging rapidly so that many of the newest consumer electronics become obsolete not long after they arrive on the market, no one knows where or how far the current revolution in computer and information technology is going to go.

Science is the mature god of the third millennium, to all appearances. Born somewhere in the irrelevant past and grown up in the distant nineteenth and twentieth centuries, science commands our total obeisance. We shape our lives around it. We indoctrinate our children to its dictates as soon as they can comprehend them. We hurl money endlessly at its golden feet, with or without any hint of possible usefulness, as long as the work confirms man's mechanical nature. Neuroscientists, such as Mario Beauregard at the University of Montreal, have taken MRIs of praying nuns to see if they share a common "God spot" in the brain. Still others use MRI and single-photon-emission computed tomography (SPECT) on Buddhist monks, to observe how brain activity surged here and fell here. While the brain certainly partakes in human mental and spiritual experience, many in science assume that the brain *is* mind.

Sweeping theories answering the greatest of all human questions dizzy us, without diminishing faith in science. While the Big Bang theory of the universe's origins still holds sway, some have observed that the distances between galaxies are expanding, and at an increasing rate of speed. Astronomers theorize about dark energy, a kind of anti-gravitational energy or force occupying the great vacuum of space, which works to keep the universe from contracting and collapsing in on itself from the force of gravity. Some now even speak of the multiverse instead of the universe. Since the mid-twentieth century, a few cosmologists have championed a theory called "eternal chaotic inflation" that accounts for "a self-reproducing, eternally existing multiverse where all possibilities can be realized." Whatever the impracticality and even absurdity of such a conclusion, there is no doubting that cosmologies are inviting people to see the world in a mind-boggling way that only tends to increase people's faith in science.

On a darker note, a few path-breaking scientists in Britain are making substantial progress in the deconstruction of the human being and the natural family. One team claims to have produced a viable human embryo with DNA from a man and two women, giving new meaning to the term "designer baby." The team killed the embryo after it had grown, apparently normally, for six days. What is to stop three people from "conceiving" a child if technology allows for it? What is to stop a woman from cloning herself, from replicating her DNA in a child completely her own, without any male participation?

Standing next to the golden idol of science is one of freedom and liberty. Freedom and liberty, in the West, now refers more to lifestyle than to release from oppression. Freedom / liberty are now words invoked to condone almost every kind of sexual behavior, and absolutely every kind of virtual and sometimes real violence. Worship of this idol has also turned the womb into a place of violence, and children into threats and burdens rather than blessings to be celebrated. One of the most popular, prize-winning television commercials in Europe in 2007 showed a handsome young man dealing ineffectually with an angry, unrestrained child during a meal; the ad was selling condoms. In *Planned Parenthood v. Casey*, the majority of the United States Supreme Court ruled, "At the heart of liberty is the right to define one's own concept of existence, of meaning, of the universe and the mystery of human life." The implications of this claim are extreme. It could mean that nothing is simply given us, that nothing means anything, unless we want it to. In this kind of freedom, however, everyone is totally alone, trapped in his or her little cosmos, one's own subjectivity. Sigmund Freud would agree.

The media establishments in the West actively further the agenda of individual freedom against anything that feels as if it stands in the way. Movies preach this message by depicting beautiful people engaged in ludicrous amounts of simulated violence and farcical sex, intensified all the more by computerized visual effects and backed up by loud, pulsating music. People, especially teens and twenty-somethings, watch these films in droves, in theaters, on rented DVDs, and streamed into the house over airwaves and through cable and Internet. And behavior follows. A study published by the American Academy of Pediatrics put into numbers what should have been obvious: young people aged 12–17 who watched the most risqué and sexually charged TV shows, such as *Sex in the City* and *Friends*, were about twice as likely to become or make someone pregnant, almost certainly without any mention of commitment.

But not all are pleased. The Anti-Defamation League, a group hardly inimical to media companies, conducted a poll that found that about 60 percent of adults, not youngsters, think that the decisions of TV and movie moguls do not reflect the religious and moral values of the American majority. The same proportion said people were actively undermining those values, and 43 percent said the media companies were engaged in an actual, coordinated campaign to weaken these values. A poll of 1,000 adults tells little about hundreds of millions of others, but it does remind us that the two-dimensional, on-screen world reflects only a tiny measure of reality. The West still has many, many families who believe firmly in lifelong, loyal marriage, based on self-giving love, the blessing of children, the innocence of childhood, and the value of modesty and humility in all their manifestations.

The West's flashy, filthy-rich world of garish lights, high speed, and overstuffed closets leads to nothing enduring or worthwhile. While it certainly fascinates, it does not fulfill. There is no divine love in it—or true, pure human love either. It is no wonder that stress, at once emotional and physical (it is a term adapted from engineering and metallurgy), has reached epidemic proportions. And right on its heels come apathy, boredom, and loneliness. People lose their natural ability to pray, which makes life beautiful and meaningful. They no longer celebrate, fast, or feast for any particular reason except to please themselves, which they never quite can. All hours of the day and night become the same. The seasons are meaningless except for the inconvenient sensations they impose when the human being, perpetually accustomed to conditioned air, moves from building to car. The energy bill sums up one's relationship to the seasons of earth. Life plods, with no end in sight or goal in mind but banal death.

All this, however, sounds worse than it is. Nothing is new in nihilism. Denial of the spiritual realm is as old as man's rejection of God, where he prefers instead a solely material existence according to the five senses. All adults are liable to forget the innocence of their childhood, and make the error of reducing love to sex. We can ignore God if we wish to live as the animals, or we can lift our minds, souls, and bodies to him, and love him, if we wish to emulate the saints, the angels, the humble and pure of heart.

The West in the Third Millennium A.D.

What are we left with, given the current nihilist reign of scientific fundamentalism?

God! Salvation! Eternal life! God's love and resurrection show us the greatest of all gifts to humanity, the chance to love him forever in return. The gift has not changed! Death, judgment, heaven and hell are all real, practical considerations for people, because in choosing them we can live for something lasting and worthwhile, not just for our passing desires for things made apparently appealing by professional marketers. Those who say that this sounds appealing, but they need proof, should just look at history. Look at nature! Look at the wonders God works every day. If you choose to love God, you choose truth over appearances, you treasure nature over its perversions and devastation. In loving God first, you embrace the simple things in life, the basics, the gifts that come from him either directly or through human ingenuity, like children and family, pure water, simple food, clothing, and shelter. Loving God nurtures peace in the soul and the family, develops virtues, and gives support for suffering.

We are also left with humanity—God's unique, mysterious creation, a spiritual being, a body in a soul, not a machine assembled by random occurrence. Take the brain, for example. The human brain is a wonder in itself. Researchers estimate that the average brain has more than one hundred billion neurons, interconnected in hundreds of trillions of synapses, and that it performs somewhere between ten trillion and ten quadrillion operations every second. A human brain puts the world's supercomputers to shame. Another scientist theorized that the total number of possible brain states is probably greater than the number of particles in the universe. All of these dramatic numerations, if they mean anything at all, point to the infinite. The point is that the brain functions not according to our codes, rules, and constructs, but according to those of its creator. Attempts to liken the brain to a computer will lead to nothing, because the brain lives, like all human organs, with and within the soul of each human being. Human beings, for all their stupendous ingenuity, will never get to the bottom of the mind, or the brain for that matter, whether it belongs to Einstein or a baby born with Down's Syndrome.

So what will God let happen in the West in the third millennium A.D.? What will humanity be and do in its ongoing history? Because no one can predict God or develop a calculus for human behavior, the past is the best indicator of the present and the future, and we should not be afraid of the answers.

Western democratic cultures and political organizations will not last, because no worldly system can withstand human weakness. In the fourth century B.C., Plato anticipated the West's twenty-first century A.D. with uncanny accuracy; he opined that excessive love of liberty, at the expense of everything else, ruins democracy and leads to despotism. As self-restraint declines, people elect flatterers and panderers instead of leaders who will tell their people the truth about their choices. Libertinism, Plato warned, infects the family, turning parents into children and nullifying education. The apostle Paul saw it coming just as well:

> People will be self-centered and lovers of money, proud, haughty, abusive, disobedient to their parents, ungrateful, irreligious, callous, implacable, slanderous, licentious, brutal, hating what is good, traitors, reckless, conceited, lovers of pleasure rather than lovers of God, as they make a pretense of religion but deny its power. ... For the time will come, when people will not tolerate sound doctrine but, following their own desires and insatiable curiosity, will accumulate teachers and will stop listening to the truth and will be diverted to myths. (2 Timothy, 3: 1–5, 4:3–4)

As self-restraint and self-reliance, the fundamental maturity vital for adulthood and family life, decline in the West, masses of people will turn to impersonal institutions to take care of them. These legalistic bureaucracies, even with the best intentions, will be unable to prevent the vices that brought them into existence. Democracies cannot flourish in such a situation, and other forms of government will take their place. And so it goes.

The West itself may cease to exist, according to the wishes of many post-modernists. For those who conceive of history as the tale of money and violence, shifting power bases will continue to tip toward east and south. The United Nations, a world forum established just before the collapse of the British and French empires, reflects an international order now dead and buried. Germany, Brazil, India, Pakistan, and Turkey make the current membership of the UN Security Council look increasingly out of date. One sees the products of industrialization and the proliferation of technology in many parts of the world. The division of the planet into first, second, and third worlds, according to politics and economic development, really no longer applies. If the mainstream culture of the West successfully expunges its Christian heritage, what will be distinctive about it? Its liberal tradition, now decayed into nihilism, will lead to nothing but a bureaucratic system.

So what if the West diversifies itself into something new, multi-cultural, and different? Something like it happened before, and the process of cultural change always goes on whether one likes it or not. God lives and reigns, with or without the West, now and forever. The universal Church, the body of Christ living in those who love him, will never fail, and it is present in all parts of the world. In her whole history, the Church was never confined to Western Europe alone; she never died in the Middle East and Ethiopia, for example, and today she thrives in many parts of Africa and Asia. If the richest countries of Europe and the western hemisphere drive the Church underground, she will shrink in terms of numbers, but not in terms of commitment. When persecuted, she purifies herself. Her members have no choice but to live their faith, and in some cases, to die in testimony of it.

Predicting doom and gloom for the third millennium, and then devising technical ways to avoid it, is nonsensical. God will not let the West expire, let alone the entire world. There are too many there who love him, if they constitute even a minority, and God loves his creation. The earth will not expire due to overpopulation; there is plenty of space in our one world for everyone. God created the world to provide for us, if we just take care of it. Humanity is not a blight but the greatest asset the world has, if we make the right decisions to minister to the needs of all, including all forms of life and landscape. Global warming is undeniable, but also unpredictable and inexplicable, even if it is true that humanity causes it to some extent. It happened in the past, and no one can explain the dynamic. The earth is not a greenhouse, or anything constructed by mankind. The planet is a stage for wonders, the seat of myriad mysteries. It is true that in the nuclear age we have the technology to bring hell on earth to everybody, and this is a terrible error we must constantly work to avoid.

Another is the belief that we can bring heaven to earth by means of technology as well. Technological change will continue, but, judging from the past couple of centuries, probably no one will discover a cure for the common cold, cancer, or any number of highly complex diseases. No one will find the elixir of eternal youth. Even as rich states try to extend life at all costs and under all circumstances, they bankrupt themselves in the process. Death will remain an unavoidable, essential aspect of being human. Despite the tremendous advances in biotechnology, people will someday come to realize that the 25,000 or so human genes, about 97 percent of which are identical to a chimpanzee's, do not account for all individual human traits, actions, and thoughts. The search for the so-called gay gene or those that supposedly make for success in sports will most likely come to nothing. The human being is a miracle, a living spirit, not a mere device that works according to genetic software, so to speak. Computer technology will allow for greater, faster transfers of numbers, words, sounds, and images, but whether these have anything to do with reality is another question.

God's plan for the world is the gradual, mystical unfolding of unity in diversity, not according to our will and our planning, but according to his, in his justice and mercy. He created humanity to be one, and through history, humanity, in its manifold diversity, shows its oneness in ever-changing ways. In the third millennium, the Church is called to make for peaceful co-existence with Islam, with those Muslims who love God over the weak self or the madness of war and indiscriminate slaughter.

The much ballyhooed process of globalization will continue in commerce and finance, but the outcomes will always be unpredictable and irregular. People will never properly share the wealth and minimize exploitation during economic booms, nor will they be able to avoid and learn from the bursts, bubbles, and other nasty meltdowns. Those who capitalize on bad debts, credit collapses, and shady dealings will usually run away with the ill-gotten gains, because people have a desperately hard time aligning real, moral value to money. Money will forever remain a dangerously attractive object for misguided love. The world economic crisis of 2008–9 shows that people have a hard time controlling their spending; debt is at once a necessity in economic activity and a temptation.

The wealthy excel at these things, and for their delights they make the poor suffer most. In 2009, higher food prices, falling real wages, and rising unemployment hit poor families the hardest. While grain and food commodity speculators profited in the US, in poorer countries, where families spend 70–80 percent of their income on food, another 64 million people fell into extreme poverty. At least half are children. All they need is simple food, clean water, a few basic medicines to fight disease, and some basic schooling, all available at a steep discount, but the rich usually say they never have enough money for that.

Addressing world poverty seriously is possible, affordable, and a good investment; only sin prevents it. According to published financial statistics, less than half of the amount of money spent developing and producing weapons would suffice to bring the world's billions of poor out of dire poverty. The moral imperative is obvious, but apart from that, think of the economic growth that could come from such a good, worthy venture! But the super-rich and hyper-powerful often have other matters to occupy their time and attention, such as maximizing their personal profit regardless of the circumstances. By way of example, in 2008 the CEO of American International Group, Inc., one of the worst offenders in the creation and sale of worthless financial instruments, resigned after three disastrous years and received a $47 million severance package for his bad decisions. The head of the division in charge of most boondoggles was kept on as a consultant after he was fired, receiving $1 million per month in compensation. Sadly, many corporate heads and boards across the West show the same revolting attitude toward money. Such greed and abuse lead a few people to exalt themselves monetarily; they do not help the cause of human solidarity.

God's love, however, points toward oneness, the central core of Christian history. According to St. Irenaeus in the second century A.D., Christian history is unique in its unity of the worldly and the divine: "that there is one Father, the creator of Man, and one Son, who fulfils the Father's will, and one human race in which the mysteries of God are worked out, so that the creature conformed and incorporated with his son is brought to perfection." Jesus told his followers, *You, therefore, must be perfect, as your heavenly Father is perfect* (Mt 5:48). The command seems outlandish, impossible; indeed, it reveals to us the desperate state and extent of human imperfection. But the command fits the gift. God's grace, freely given to those who will love him for all eternity, is every bit as dramatic, almost outrageous, in its wondrous, ineffable goodness.

Jesus Christ shows us that history is powerless over the lives of those who live in love with God. Their afterlife extends immeasurably further than a human being's brief sojourn on this miraculous planet. Human history, in that context, is really nothing; it is by definition all gone. The past no longer exists; it is not present in any way but human memory. All that is real is this present moment. Life is a free gift to each human being from God, and we all struggle with our freedom to love, in the ever-changing present. To grant history the power to make new, improved, or other versions of mankind is to turn history into a false idol, one with a terrible death toll. We ought to have seen enough of it in the past to avoid making the same mistake in the future, but, based on the record of the last few thousand years, those in power will not learn. The Church will always be there to point out the error. She must never fail to speak for the individual soul, for the natural family, for the Christian community of prayer, and for the whole of humanity, all God's creation.

While embracing the diversity of humanity, Christianity looks for truth, realism, goodness, and beauty in mystery. The religion does not claim to have figured everything out, because no human being can. God is the source of never-ending complexity and surprise. Jesus Christ proclaimed and the Church witnesses a path, a way, not an ideology or a science. Happiness and liberation come from encountering the living God who is love. God is good, and so is the whole cosmos, which he created out of nothing, as well as each human being. Evil, too, exists, we must admit, but merely as the free choice of self-love, not as an equal and opposite force to good. And the story goes on, right before our eyes, of our making, unfolding along the crooked lines stemming from past millennia.

Christ's salvation makes all things new and redeems those who have faith in him, but this is no recipe for utopia. The angel tells the seer in no uncertain terms, *Let the evildoers still do evil, and the filthy still be filthy, and the righteous still do right, and the holy still be holy.* (Revelation 22:11) The world is and shall be as it always was, but the new world is that of the Holy Spirit, open to those who embrace it on this side of eternity. In the vision of John, who wrote the book of Revelation, Jesus says through his angels:

> *Behold, I make all things new .... It is done! I am the Alpha and the Omega, the beginning and the end. To the thirsty I will give water without price from the fountain of the water of life. He who conquers shall have this heritage, and I will be his God and he shall be my son.* (Revelation 21:5–7)

A new age is coming. It is here now.

Afterword

Christ is that morning star
Who when the night
Of this age is past,
Promises unto his saints
The light of life
And opens everlasting day. (St. Bede, 673–735 A.D.)

May the study of history lessen the darkness and help to prepare us for that blessed morning.

Select Bibliography

Biblical quotations derive from *The Holy Bible, Revised Standard Version* (San Francisco: Ignatius Press, 1966) and *The Catholic Study Bible (New American Bible)* (New York: Oxford University Press, 1990).

Western Civilization textbooks consulted: Donald Kagan, Steven Ozment, Frank M. Turner, *The Western Heritage* (9th ed., Prentice Hall, 2006); John P. McKay, et al., *A History of Western Society* (9th ed., Houghton Mifflin, 2008); Mark Kishlansky, Patrick Geary, Patricia O'Brien, *Civilization in the West* (7th ed., Longman, 2007); Lynn Hunt, et al., *The Making of the West* (3rd ed., Bedford/ St. Martin's, 2009); Jackson J. Spielvogel, *Western Civilization* (7th ed., Thomson Wadsworth, 2009); Judith G. Coffin and Robert C. Stacey, *Western Civilizations* (16th ed., W.W. Norton, 2008).

For philosophers and major intellectuals, the preferred source was Frederick Copleston, S.J., *A History of Philosophy*, 9 vols. (New York: Doubleday, 1962–77, 1993).

The following books and articles provided information and quotations throughout the text, and they also serve as recommendations for further reading.

Introduction to Chapter 2

Kyle S. Brown, *et al.*, "Fire as an Engineering Tool of Early Modern Humans," *Science*, vol. 325, no. 5942, pp. 859–862.

Leonardo Bruni, *History of the Florentine People*, vol. 1, edited and translated by James Hankins (Cambridge, MA: Harvard University Press, 2001).

E. H. Carr, *What is History?* (2nd ed., New York: Penguin, 1987).

Cicero, *De Officiis,* trans. W. Miller (Cambridge, MA: Harvard University Press, 1913).

Christopher Dawson, *Enquiries into Religion and Culture* (New York: Sheed and Ward, 1933); *The Dynamics of World History* (New York: Sheed and Ward, 1956); *The Making of Europe: An Introduction to the History of European Unity* (New York: Meridian Books, 1956); *Progress and Religion* (New York: Doubleday, 1960); *The Formation of Christendom* (New York: Sheed and Ward, 1967).

Donald J. D'Elia, Patrick Foley, eds, *The Catholic as Historian* (Naples, FL: Sapientia Press, 2006).

David Hackett Fischer, *Historians' Fallacies: Toward a Logic of Historical Thought* (New York: Harper Perennial, 1970).

Harald Fritzsch, *Vom Urknall zum Zerfall: die Welt zwischen Anfang und Ende* (München: Piper Verlag, 1999).

Keith Lemna, "Mythopoetic Thinking and the Truth of Christianity," *Communio*, vol. xxxvii, no. 1 (Spring 2010), pp. 69–98.

Birgit Mampe, Angela D. Friederici, Anne Christophe, Kathleen Wermke, "Newborns' Cry Melody Is Shaped by Their Native Language," *Current Biology*, vol. 19, no. 23 (December 2009), pp. 1994–1997.

Stephen Mitchell, *Gilgamesh: A New English Version* (New York: Free Press, 2004).

Joseph Ratzinger, *God and the World* (San Francisco: Ignatius Press, 2002).

Iegor Reznikoff, "On Primitive Elements of Musical Meaning," *The Journal of Music and Meaning*, 3, Fall 2004/Winter 2005, Section 2.

James J. Sheehan, "The Problem of Sovereignty in European History," *American Historical Review* (2006), pp. 1–15.

Robert Sokolowski, *Christian Faith & Human Understanding: Studies on the Eucharist, Trinity, and the Human Person* (Washington D.C.: Catholic University of America Press).

Chapters 3–4

John Boardman, Jasper Griffin, Oswyn Murray, eds., *The Oxford History of the Roman World* (Oxford: Oxford University Press, 1986).

J. K. Davies, *Democracy and Classical Greece* (Stanford: Stanford University Press, 1983).

M. I. Finley, *Early Greece: The Bronze and Archaic Ages* (New York: Norton, 1981).

Edward Gibbon, *The Decline and Fall of the Roman Empire* (6 vols., 1776–88).

Marcel Le Glay, Jean-Louis Voisin, Yann Le Bohec, *A History of Rome* (2nd ed., Oxford: Blackwell Publishers, 1996).

Walter Emil Kaegi, Jr., and Peter White, eds., *Rome: Late Republic and Principate* (Chicago: University of Chicago Press, 1986).

Lucretius, *On the Nature of Things,* in *The Portable Roman Reader,* Basil Davenport, ed., (New York: Penguin Books, 1951).

Thomas Martin, *Ancient Greece: From Prehistoric to Hellenistic Times* (New Haven: Yale University Press, 1996).

Karl F. Morrison, ed., *The Church in the Roman Empire* (Chicago: University of Chicago Press, 1986).

Oswyn Murray, *Early Greece* (Stanford: Stanford University Press, 1983).

Martin Robertson, *A Shorter History of Greek Art* (Cambridge: Cambridge University Press, 1981).

H. H. Scullard, *From the Gracchi to Nero: A History of Rome from 133 B.C. to A.D. 68* (5th ed., New York: Routledge, 1982).

Chapters 5–6

Thomas Bokenkotter, *A Concise History of the Catholic Church* (New York: Doubleday, 1979).

Thomas Cahill, *How the Irish Saved Civilization* (New York: Anchor Books, 1995).

R. H. C. Davis, *A History of Medieval Europe: From Constantine to Saint Louis* (2nd ed., London: Longman Group, 1970).

Christopher Dawson, *The Formation of Christendom* (New York: Sheed and Ward, 1967), *The Making of Europe* (New York: Meridian Books, 1956), *Medieval Essays* (New York: Sheed and Ward, 1954).

Stephen Jaeger, "Pessimism in the Twelfth-Century 'Renaissance,'" *Speculum* 78 (2003), pp. 1151–83.

J. N. D. Kelly, *The Oxford Dictionary of Popes* (Oxford: Oxford University Press, 1986).

Julius Kirshner and Karl F. Morrison, eds., *Medieval Europe* (Chicago: University of Chicago Press, 1986).

Robert E. Lerner, "Fleas: Some Scratchy Issues Concerning the Black Death," *The Journal of the Historical Society*, viii: 2, June 2008, pp. 205–228.

Régine Pernoud, *Those Terrible Middle Ages: Debunking the Myths*, trans. Anne Englund Nash (San Francisco: Ignatius Press, 2000).

Julia M. H. Smith, *Europe after Rome: A New Cultural History, 500–1000* (Oxford: Oxford University Press, 2005).

Bruno Steimer, ed., *Lexikon der Heiligen und der Heiligenverehrung*, 3 vols. (Freiburg im Breisgau: Herder, 2003).

Brian Tierney, *Western Europe in the Middle Ages: 300–1475* (6th ed., Boston: McGraw-Hill, 1999).

N.T. Wright, "Jesus' Resurrection and Christian Origins," *Gregorianum*, 83/4 (2002), pp. 615–635.

The Qur'an, trans. by Abdullah Yusuf Ali, (10th ed., New York: Tahrike Tarsile Qur'an, 2003).

Chapter 7

Euan Cameron, *The European Reformation* (Oxford: Oxford University Press, 1991).

Eamon Duffy, *The Stripping of the Altars* (New Haven: Yale University Press, 1992).

Brad Gregory, *Salvation at Stake: Christian Martyrdom in Early Modern Europe* (Cambridge, MA: Harvard University Press, 2001).

Hans J. Hillerbrand, ed., *The Protestant Reformation* (New York: Harper, 1968).

Mack P. Holt, *The French Wars of Religion, 1562–1629* (Cambridge: Cambridge University Press, 1995).

Benjamin J. Kaplan, *Divided by Faith: Religious Conflict and the Practice of Toleration in Early Modern Europe* (Cambridge, MA: Harvard University Press, 2007).

Heiko A. Oberman, *Luther: Man between God and the Devil* (New York: Doubleday, 1990).

Steven Ozment, *Protestants: The Birth of a Revolution* (New York: Doubleday, 1992).

R. Po-Chia Hsia, *The World of Catholic Renewal, 1540–1770* (Cambridge: Cambridge UP, 1998).

Brennan Pursell, *The Winter King: Frederick V and the Coming of the Thirty Years' War* (Aldershot: Ashgate, 2003).

J. J. Scarisbrick, *The Reformation and the English People* (Oxford: Wiley-Blackwell, 1991).

Chapter 8

Jacques Barzun, *From Dawn to Decadence: 500 Years of Western Cultural Life; 1500 to the Present* (New York: HarperCollins, 2000).

John Carroll, *The Wreck of Western Culture: Humanism Revisited* (Wilmington: ISI Books, 2008).

François Furet, *The French Revolution 1770–1814* (Oxford: Blackwell, 1996).

Steven Ozment, *A Mighty Fortress: a New History of the German People* (New York: HarperCollins, 2004).

Mona Ozouf, *Festivals and the French Revolution* (Cambridge, MA: Harvard University Press, 1991).

Paul A. Rahe, "The Enlightenment Indicted: Rousseau's Response to Montesquieu," *The Journal of the Historical Society,* viii:2, June 2008, pp. 273–302.

Shirley Elson Roessler & Reny Miklos, *Europe, 1715–1919: From Enlightenment to World War* (Lanham: Rowman & Littlefield, 2003).

Steven Shapin, *The Scientific Revolution* (Chicago: University of Chicago Press, 1996).

Wolfram Siemann, *Metternich. Staatsmann zwischen Restauration und Moderne* (München: C. H. Beck Wissen, 2010).

Alexis de Tocqueville, *The Old Regime and the Revolution*, trans. Alan Kahan (Chicago: University of Chicago Press, 1998).

Chapter 9

M. S. Anderson, *The Ascendency of Europe, 1815–1914* (3rd ed., Harlow, UK: Pearson, 2003).

David Blackbourn, *The Long Nineteenth Century: A History of Germany, 1780–1918* (2nd ed., Oxford: Blackwell, 2002).

Gregory Claeys, "The 'Survival of the Fittest' and the Origins of Social Darwinism," *Journal of the History of Ideas* (2000), pp. 223–40.

Michael Blumer, "The Theory of Natural Selection of Alfred Russel Wallace," *Notes & Records of the Royal Society*, 59 (2005), pp. 125–136.

Eric Hobsbawm, *The Age of Revolution, 1789–1848; The Age of Capital, 1848–1875; The Age of Empire, 1875–1914* (New York: Vintage, 1996).

J. M. Roberts, *Twentieth Century: The History of the World, 1901 to 2000* (New York: Penguin Books, 1999).

James J. Sheehan, *German History, 1770–1866* (New York: Oxford University Press, 1993).

F. M. L. Thompson, *The Rise of Respectable Society: A Social History of Victorian Britain, 1830–1900* (Cambridge, MA: Harvard University Press, 1990).

Chapters 10–11

Johan Åhr, "On Primo Levi, Richard Serra, and the Concept of History," *The Journal of the Historical Society*, vol. ix, no. 2 (June, 2009), pp. 161–189.

Carl Bernstein and Marco Politi, *His Holiness: John Paul II and the Hidden History of Our Time* (New York: Doubleday, 1996).

T. Colin Campbell, *The China Study* (Dallas: Benbella Books, 2006).

Matthew Connelly, *Fatal Misconception: The Struggle to Control World Population* (Belknap/Harvard University Press, 2010).

Jörg Friedrich, *Der Brand: Deutschland im Bombenkrieg, 1940–1945* (Berlin: Ullstein Buchverlage, 2002).

John Lewis Gaddis, *We Now Know: Rethinking Cold War History* (Oxford: Oxford University Press, 1997).

Brigitte Hamann, *Hitlers Wien: Lehrjahre eines Diktators* (München: Piper Verlag, 1996).

Holger Herwig, *The First World War: Germany and Austria-Hungary, 1914–1918* (New York: Oxford University Press, 1997).

John Keegan, *The Second World War* (New York: Penguin, 1989).

Paul Kennedy, *Preparing for the Twenty-First Century* (New York: Random House, 1993).

Peter Longerich, *"Davon haben wir nichts gewusst!" Die Deutschen und die Judenverfolgung, 1933–1945* (München:Siedler Verlag, 2006).

Reinhold Niebuhr, *The Irony of American History* (Chicago: University of Chicago Press, 1952, 2008).

R. A. C. Parker, *The Second World War: A Short History* (Oxford: Oxford University Press, 1989).

Keith Robbins, *The First World War: The Outbreak, Events, and Aftermath* (Oxford: Oxford University Press, 1984).

J. M. Roberts, *Twentieth Century: The History of the World, 1910 to 2000* (New York: Penguin, 1999).

Stuart Robson, *The First World War* (2nd ed, Harlow: Pearson Education, 2007).

Jeffrey Sachs, *The End of Poverty: Economic Possibilities for Our Time* (New York: Penguin, 2005).

"Unequal America," *Harvard Magazine*, July-August (2008), pp. 22–3.

Keith Windschuttle, *The Killing of History* (Paddington, Australia: Macleay Press, 1996).

About the Author

Originally from California, Brennan Pursell went to college at Stanford University and obtained his AB in History in 1990. After graduation, he devoted two years to work and travel in the Middle East and Asia, until he went to Harvard for graduate training in European history, where he received his MA in 1994 and his Ph.D. in 2000. For his dissertation he worked in archives in Germany, Austria, Spain, England, and several other European countries.

His scholarly articles and book reviews have appeared in *History*, *The Historical Journal*, *The Sixteenth Century Journal*, *The Court Historian*, *German Studies Review*, the *Royal Historical Society's Camden Fifth Series*, the *American Historical Review*, *LOGOS: a Journal of Catholic Thought and Culture*, *Catholic Social Science Review*, and other publications.

His first book, *The Winter King: Frederick V of the Palatinate and the Coming of the Thirty Years' War*, appeared in 2003. In 2008, he published *Benedict of Bavaria: an Intimate Portrait of the Pope and His Homeland*. Promoting this work has led to appearances on CNN, EWTN, and other television stations, in addition to 80 radio outlets, and interviews with over a dozen major American newspapers.

A member of the DeSales University faculty since 2001, he teaches courses on European history ancient to modern, as well as the history of India and the Middle East. He also leads travel-study hybrid courses to Germany and Austria for DeSales students. He lives with his wife, a Bavarian pianist, and three children in Allentown.

Of Related Interest

Thomas D. Williams
The World as It Could Be
Catholic Social Thought for a New Generation

"This is an important book—a richly sourced, intelligent, and engaging overview of the roots and current state of Catholic social thought." —Charles J. Chaput, Archbishop of Denver

Providing insight and into the world's most pressing concerns—those of human rights, human dignity, and world peace—bestselling author and priest Thomas D. Williams adds his reassuring voice to the panoply of issues that call to question the meaning of faith. One of the most trusted and dynamic voices from the Catholic community and the official Vatican analyst for CBS News, Father Williams helps parishioners step back from today's controversies and understand Catholic teachings in a deeper way.

Addressing the most heated debates ripped from national headlines and fervently discussed between Catholics—from abortion and capital punishment to the economy—Father Williams draws upon his years of teaching in this detailed yet accessible analysis of the moral dilemmas and political challenges that Catholics face every day. Examining these moral conflicts, and the often opposing forces of individual rights versus those of the community, Father Williams speaks to orthodox Catholics and non-Catholic observers alike in this examination of the Catholic faith, its influence around the world, and what it teaches millions of followers about human rights and a better world.

Check your local bookstore for availability.
To order directly from the publisher,
please call 1-800-888-4741 for Customer Service
or visit our website at *www.CrossroadPublishing.com*.